Where Have All the Guernseys Gone?

by Duane E. Young

Table of Contents

WISCONSIN GUERNSEY PICNIC

State Wide
Judging
Contest

West Salem
Band

Talks by
J. C. Penney
and others

Come and Bring
the Family

-WEST SALEM-
[La Crosse County]
JUNE 21, 1928

The Annual Gathering of all Wisconsin Guernsey Breeders

Chapter One:

Remembering

Seeing a beautiful fawn and white Guernsey makes my heart skip a beat. This is all the more true after years of absence, and I remember so many experiences with Guernsey cattle on my parents' western Wisconsin dairy farm. I broke down in tears when I knew it was time to quit dairying after the interstate highway bisected our farm. I would not miss the long hours, fresh air, or especially the machinery; I was twenty-nine, unmarried, my parents were not well, and I longed to study and read. The Guernsey was the only compelling reason not to quit. Watching a benevolent cow or calf chewing her cud brings to me a special peace of mind. After tossing a thousand hay bales in the hot summer and being totally exhausted, feeding the animals and especially milking the cows were always relaxing and enjoyable. Some may argue this is not the reason to be a dairy farmer. I disagree.

My first summer after high school graduation, my parents and aunt and uncle went to the Dakotas on holiday. I was alone to handle the dairying. In the field used for strip grazing behind the barn a calf was born whose mother immediately developed milk fever, a calcium and phosphorus imbalance. Dr. Johnston provided glucose and other medicines. He instructed me on everything I could do to save the cow by making sure she stood as soon as possible. Pulling on a halter and physically kicking her rump were to no avail. I even tied the strap end of the halter to a tiny tractor and gently tried pulling with this increased force. She tried, but it was no use and she died shortly thereafter. I convinced myself at that moment that I would be a failure at dairying. However, by the time I "retired" eleven years later, productivity per cow had increased fifty percent. My self worth had improved.

The miracle of birth unquestionably remains one of my most rewarding memories as a dairy farmer. In the winter calving pen, typically cement covered by a small manure base and much dry straw for warmth, a wet slimy head slowly emerges from the straining cow. After much effort a sudden convulsive heave forces the remaining three-quarters of the calf to plop unceremoniously onto the straw mattress. A clean warm sack cloth is used to open the nostrils and wipe off the little newborn, and within moments the calf is standing and being licked by her mother. I remain watchful for the emergence of the placenta onto the bedding. This afterbirth must be removed as soon as it is expelled to prevent the mother from eating and possibly choking on it – an evolutionary response to destroy evidence of birth and protect the young. If the placenta did not detach within three days, a veterinarian was needed to clean the uterus and place medications. Without this diligent attention and care, infection could set in and the reproductive cycle interrupted or destroyed.

Until recent times, farmers by their very nature believed that profit margins were more assured by cutting costs rather than by enhancing proceeds. Observing my father saving veterinary costs by cleaning the cow himself was enlightening: the cow never had another calf. This experience as well as a lifetime of observations has caused me to believe that those who could not get themselves to loosen up on the almighty dollar or those who considered themselves to be shrewd financial players usually lost. Not always, but eventually.

Guernsey calves are susceptible to dysentery and pneumonia more so than other dairy breeds. Our dairy herd was no exception. I can remember in my youth my father traveling to Iowa State University for some special serum to vaccinate newborn calves. I don't remember it helping very much. Dr. Kenneth Johnston, my veterinary hero, provided a pink powder that he said was a vitamin and energy mix which would help. Immediately after birth, I would take an oral plastic tube with a big rubber bulb on end, fill it with warm water and the pink powder, open the calves' mouth, and squeeze the bulb, sending the mixture into the stomach. From that time on, we seldom lost a calf to this malady.

In the 1950s we began moving from using medicine and veterinary services only when required to preventive procedures. I remember, in particular, treating dry cows between lactations with medication in each teat to assure the cleaning up of a possible bacterial infection. This was to prevent mastitis from occurring in a healthy animal and to clear up any lingering mastitis in a cow that had prior infection or an udder injury. Done at least a month before calving, medication had time to work and did not present any problem in producing quality milk. There was the California Mastitis Test with four shallow cups wherein a couple of squirts of milk from each teat would be mixed with a purple liquid that would show abnormalities and the start of an infection. Bacteria and other single-cell life forms, as well as physical injury to the udder, can cause mastitis.

There is no more painful experience for the cow and a disaster for the milker than a stepped-on teat. Machine milking on three of the four quarters and then hand milking to relieve the pressure without further aggravating or causing pain to the injured teat can be a trial. Sutures are often needed as well as continual application of healing salve. I also remember other prevention methods used by Dr. Johnston that helped us.

A particularly heart-breaking situation for us occurred when, after deciding we wanted uniformity in dairy character and productivity, we chose to use bulls from McDonald Farms of Cortland, New York, exclusively in the future. The bull chosen for the first and only year proved disastrous: heifers sired by this bull developed acute arthritis immediately after their first calf was born. A few were able to stand on their own, but found getting to their feet difficult. However, the unlucky majority needed to be hand-cranked up by the hips in order to be milked, eat or drink. Within a few weeks all these were disposed of, including one taken to market on a raw winter day. This ended our dream of herd uniformity.

Decades later, I walked behind the only Guernsey left in the dairy barn on the University of Wisconsin-Madison campus. A nostalgic feeling of love emanated from me to this cow. Much to my surprise, she turned her head fully around and looked me straight in the eye. I could feel her love returned to me. This was a few years back and the last time I visited not even a single Guernsey remained. During my last visit to the barn, I noticed that all the cows' tails were docked. The world is changing and waits for no one.

I was to be the third generation in our family to raise registered Guernsey cattle. Alas, it was not to be. My father, Vilas Young, was the owner of our dairy farm called Justemere Farm. Vilas and his father, Edward Young, started their registered herd after moving to the thriving Guernsey environment of West Salem, Wisconsin, from Burr Oak, Wisconsin, in the first decade of the twentieth century. The move was prompted by my grandparents' desire for their children to have a high school education.

•   •   •

The fertile broad valleys, or coulees, situated between the bluffs of western Wisconsin included the area which would become West Salem. In the mid nineteenth century this coulee region attracted many newcomers. These newcomers tended to inhabit lands which most resembled their former homes, thus the Norwegian immigrants settled the steep hillsides while the Germans settled in the valleys. The Mississippi River and the booming river town of La Crosse lay just fifteen miles away, center for the shipment of grains, lumber and other commodities. More importantly was the Chicago and Northwestern railroad that ran between Chicago and the Twin Cities and passed directly through West Salem. This abundance of fertile land and ready transportation put West Salem on the map. So vital was this railroad that the nearby village of Neshonoc abandoned its settlement and moved to be near the railroad tracks at West Salem.

When Wisconsin went from a soil-depleting wheat state to a dairy state, the hills of the coulee region too steep for row crops were ideal for pasture. Serendipity, more than anything else explains the environment and pioneers conducive to creating a world class Guernsey industry. Before there was a La Crosse County Guernsey Breeders Association there was a West Salem Guernsey Breeders. The settlers and their descendents have contributed to a bountiful history beyond the dairy industry. West Salem demands a closer look into the accomplishments of its community and citizens.

Errol Kindschy, a West Salem history teacher, asked a class in the 1960s if the community had anyone of renown or an event that was deemed noteworthy. After a long silence, someone hesitatingly suggested that perhaps a famous author had lived there. That author was Hamlin Garland, 1922 Pulitzer Prize winner for his book *Daughter of the Middle Border,* a story about his mother and the trials and tribulations she goes through, with poignant descriptions of their life in West Salem.

The worlds' largest privately owned candy company can partially be traced to West Salem. Ethel G. Kissack, a school teacher, was raised on St. Joseph Ridge, just south of West Salem. In 1902 she married Franklin Charles Mars from Minnesota. Frank C. Mars was a polio victim as a youth. His mother Alma, hoping to entertain her son, taught him the art of hand dipping chocolate candy. In 1901, at the age of nineteen, he sold his creation of molasses chips. According to West Salem legend, Ethel Kissack Mars' special Christmas candy later became the foundation for Mars, Incorporated after being test marketed in West Salem and Bangor. Frank and Ethel's son Forrest Mars, Sr. was born in 1904 in Wadena, Minnesota. The parents divorced and Franklin married Ethel V. Healy in 1910. In 1923 Franklin introduced Forrest's candy creation known as the "Milky Way" which became the first commercially distributed filled chocolate bar and the company's top selling bar. Today Ethel Kissack Mars along with other family members, lies in a large, dignified plot in the rural Hamilton Cemetery, located between old West Salem and the original Henry D. Griswold farm. In her memory her sons opened the exclusive candy shops named Ethel M.

West Salem was a small, close-knit rural community, and the 1910 census listed 840 citizens. My father Vilas Young was born in 1902 and claimed as a young man to know everyone in town. His high school graduating class of sixteen included Edna Gardner (Whyte). She became a famous aviatrix, friend of Amelia Earhart, and competed in 356 major airplane races and events winning 128 trophies. My father proudly introduced her to me when she visited us on our farm in the late 1950s. Ms. Whyte had logged over 34,000 hours of flying time during her career in sailplanes, Aero Commander 200, Comanche, helicopters, open cockpits, and jets. She told me she always felt safer in a plane than in a car. In 1938 Look Magazine named her the top woman flyer in the United States. Dubbed as "The Flying Nurse" during World War II, she was not allowed to fly combat missions. This did not stop the feisty combat nurse from being the instructor for those who did. After the war she traded pilot lessons for help in digging runways for her own airport near Dallas, Texas.

She flew freight as a pilot throughout Central and South America. She is in the following Halls of Fame: Aviation, OX-5 Pioneer Pilots Association, World Women (in London, England), Oklahoma Air Space Museum, and Texas Womens. The Pioneer Pilots Association is quoted as saying in 1967 that she was "the woman who contributed the most to aviation". Doris L. Rich in her book, *Amelia Earhart*, published by The Smithsonian in 1989, said Whyte was "probably the best and certainly the most competitive woman pilot in closed-circuit racing."

When she was in her 80s a special fete to honor her was held in West Salem. She intended to fly, but better wisdom prevailed and she took a commercial flight. Paul Harvey on his national newscast promoted her visit. Her visit revealed her deep feelings about the unnecessary obstacles she needed to overcome in a male-obsessed society.

•   •   •

Father was on the Board of Directors of the La Crosse County Guernsey Breeders for forty-one years, Secretary-Treasurer for thirty-two years, and for two decades ran the Guernsey sales at the world's largest Guernsey sale barn called the "Pavilion." He always pointed out to me that there were more Guernsey cattle going out of West Salem in the 1920s and 1930s than any place in the nation. He proudly showed me a letter received from Alfredo Volio of San José Costa Rica dated February 1, 1932, inquiring about Guernsey open heifers available for sale. The stationery prominently displayed the heads of both a mature Guernsey bull and a Guernsey cow. The semi-annual Guernsey sales were a family ritual. I walked to the sale barn after school to imbibe the excitement. After writing an article about the sale barn for the West Salem Historical Society and receiving favorable comments, I became motivated to tell this history before it was lost forever.

Haciendas "Retes" y "Felipe Diaz"

ALFREDO VOLIO SUCS.

GANADO "GUERNSEY"
CERDOS "POLAND-CHINA"

MANTEQUILLA
"CABEZA DE VACA"

San José,   *Feb.* 1   19 32

Mr. Vilas E. Young,
Sec. La Crosse County G. Breeders Inc.
West Salem, Wis.

Dear Sir:

I would greatly appreciate some information (prices, pedigrees u about a good lot of heavy producing, high grade Guernsey open heifers.

Yours very truly,

Alfredo Volio
Apt. 767,
San José, Costa Rica, C.a.

Richard Schomberg unearthed a box of La Crosse County Guernsey Breeders' secretary records and memorabilia to get me started. Arne Marking told me about the Griswold Guernsey legacy of keeping forty cows on forty acres. Harry Griswold, a friend and West Salem attorney, provided valuable insight into this legacy and also several financial daybooks spanning his great grandfather's entire career as a farmer. Corey Geiger of Hoard's Dairyman loaned me several books on W. D. Hoard and accompanied me to the library of the National Dairy Shrine in Fort Atkinson, Wisconsin. As Corey was showing me around my research area of interest, he excitedly exclaimed that I should look at a book he happened to pull off the shelf which was written

8

in the first decade of the twentieth century by a West Salem, Wisconsin, Guernsey farmer by the name of A. J. Phillips. This book entitled *Queen Vashti* purported to tell from the cow's viewpoint her life and that of Mr. Phillips, a renowned propagator of apples. Mr. Phillips brought the first pure-bred Guernsey to West Salem, and he was a founding member of both the La Crosse County Guernsey Breeders and the Wisconsin Guernsey Breeders. Not only was Mr. Phillips one of the pioneers of the Guernsey breed in the United States, but he also set milk and butter production records that were competitive nationally. In spite of all my background in West Salem and with Guernsey cattle, I had never heard of him. My wife Kathy gave me a copy of his book for Christmas which was inscribed: "Compliments of author. You sent me the first dollar I recd. A. J. Phillips." It had originally been given to Samuel B. Green, first head of the University of Minnesota Horticulture and Forestry Department, established in 1888. The discovery of this West Salem dairy and apple farmer was the crowning inspiration for my writing an American Guernsey history before it was too late.

Prominently displayed on the inner farm shop doors after my father's retirement where he spent many an hour were two large posters of the June 21, 1928, Wisconsin Guernsey Picnic held in West Salem. The guest speaker was J. C. Penney, retail magnate known throughout the land. Even given his innovative marketing skills, why have a man with this retail background speak to a group of Guernsey breeders? My father was twenty-six at the time and serving his second year as La Crosse County Guernsey Breeders' Secretary-Treasurer. He probably met Mr. Penney at this picnic and certainly did in 1934 when Penney visited the home farm. This time in his life and the memories were obviously extremely important to him, but always a quiet man, my father kept these memories to himself. This poster is now framed and hangs in my office near my father's desk. My wife and I often wondered at the possible connection J. C. Penney had with dairy farming. The reason behind the department store leader coming to West Salem remained an elusive curiosity of idle speculation, until we began our search to find the text of the speech he gave to those gathered at the Guernsey picnic in 1928. We never found the text, but the amazing life of J. C. Penney, Guernsey farmer and agricultural entrepreneur, began to emerge. After studying the man, I cannot help but believe the entire agricultural segment of his life to be more significant than all his other achievements, as vital as they were. Truly, whatever is most momentous about James Cash Penney's accomplishments has somehow been lost to history even in his hometown of Hamilton, Missouri. He created the prominent Foremost Guernsey herd, one of the best in the world, which he later bequeathed to the University of Missouri.

My love for the beautiful fawn and white Guernsey and my family legacy provided the backbone for an exciting discovery process which led to this text. While there were many Guernsey pioneers throughout the United States, this book will focus on the lives of four men who, with their extraordinary courage and vision, helped make the Guernsey breed of dairy cattle prominent in the twentieth century.

Our registered Guernseys by Bacon's Pond on our farm

Chapter Two:

Origins

The registered Guernsey dairy animal is credited with coming from the Island of Guernsey, although many came from England and Alderney Island. The Channel Islands of Guernsey, Jersey and Alderney are British Crown dependencies located in the English Channel near the French coast of Normandy. Guernsey Island is only 24 square miles in size. Bill Luff, Secretary of the World Guernsey Cattle Federation and a lifelong resident of Guernsey Island, says he experiences extremely strong bitter winds on a regular basis. High tides, swirling currents, and dangerous rocks on the Island all contributed to keeping it isolated from the changing world. During the age of religious persecution, Victor Hugo fled France to Guernsey Island in 1851 and wrote his best literary works while exiled there.

According to the "official" version on the origin of the registered Guernsey breed as published in 1950 by the American Guernsey Cattle Club, a colony of monks was sent by the Catholic Church in 960 A. D. to colonize Guernsey Island. Their mission was to protect the native inhabitants from pirates using the island for nefarious purposes. They sent back to Brittany for Fromont du Leon cattle. Fromont du Leon are noted for their fawn and white color, a refined quality, and production of golden-yellow milk. In 1060 A. D. monks from Cherbourg, Normandy brought Brindle dairy cattle with them to the Isle of Guernsey. The large and rugged Brindle dairy animals produced milk known for its tasty butter. Their fine-flavored milk of a rich primrose color as well as their exterior skin and interior fat carried the yellow pigment characteristic of the future Guernsey breed. Furthermore, their horns curved forward and inward similar to those of the future Guernsey breed.

According to Bill Luff, there may be some truth that these cattle are part of the foundation of the Guernsey breed. He feels there is not enough proof to the legend that for centuries the monks carried on a very careful breeding program for high productive dairy qualities. Even assuming that Catholic monks brought cattle to the Island of Guernsey, the years 960 A.D. and 1060 A.D. must remain open to doubt. The English Common Law statute of 1276 established that time prior to the reign of King Richard the First in 1189 "was a time before legal history and beyond legal memory." This law of well-established understanding as well as the environment on the Island of Guernsey prior to the middle nineteenth century dismisses any argument for systemic breeding of dairy traits by those early Catholic monks. It was not until the American Guernsey Cattle Club established rules for importing Guernsey cattle that any orderly breeding program became established.

Admittedly, while the two crosses may have created the Guernsey, there is more of an influence by the Brindle on the Guernsey. There was much interchange of cattle between the neighboring islands of Guernsey and Jersey, and Jersey Island cattle were more influenced by the Fremont du Leon. The Guernsey has been called the royal breed, producing copious amounts of golden-colored milk high in solids and butterfat.

Western Europe is rich in culture and history. A book published in 1940 entitled *The History of Channel Island Cattle Guernseys and Jerseys* illuminates economic life in western Europe up to the end of the eighteenth century as not being much different than before the birth of Christ. Man's everyday environment had not significantly changed over the many centuries. Guernsey Island was truly cut off from ideas and agricultural practices elsewhere. The instruments for production and husbandry remained unchanged from prior centuries. Narrow understanding assumed improvements to be impossible. Intensive hand-labor cropping utilizing seaweed as fertilizer provided only the most meager subsistence. Guernsey cattle were staked by the horns with a twelve foot line to a peg and moved four or five times a day to conserve grass. Women cared for the cattle, usually no more than twelve head per family unit.

Thomas Dicey described the Island of Guernsey in 1751 as "abominably infested with common beggars and thieves" providing a rich environment of superstition, magic, and witchcraft. William Barry in 1815 described the ignorant, credulous superstitions of the island to be rampant.

In 1800 Dr. James Anderson described the Guernsey animals as the smallest breed of animals of European descent he had ever seen. From the latter part of the eighteenth century to the middle of the nineteenth, the practical value of these cattle deteriorated badly. Beef demand in Europe was so intense that there was essentially no demand for small animals. Around 1800 some larger animals were introduced to the island for beef production. Statutes were created by the Island of Jersey in 1789 and the Island of Guernsey in 1819 to prevent the French from using their islands as intermediary cattle shipping points for export to England. The Guernsey statute emphasized keeping the island free of foreign mixture. The large lucrative demand for beef during the first half of the nineteenth century had by 1818 "completely drained the Islands." A law prohibiting the import of cattle from Britain and continental Europe except for immediate slaughter was passed in 1862. This was done for reasons of disease control.

There was not, nor had there ever been, any attempt to breed for dairy qualities anywhere in the world until the latter half of the nineteenth century. In fact, no "breeds" of dairy cattle were known to exist before the late nineteenth century. There was no dairy industry on the Island of Guernsey because no one was engaged in the development of dairy cattle. There was no attempt for breeding for any standard or particular trait. Butterfat tests were unavailable before 1890. Production records and reliable pedigrees for the development of dairy traits would have been extremely difficult before then.

No records on island breeding were kept until a herd book was started in 1878. The American Guernsey Cattle Club which began in 1877 created the following rule in 1881: "No animal, hereafter imported, shall be entered in Herd Register of the American Guernsey Cattle Club, unless not only it, but its sire and dam have been previously registered in a herd book in the Island of Guernsey."

The first official milk and butterfat tests on the Island of Guernsey were in 1907. Advanced registry tests began in 1912. These tests did not allow bulls to be registered until they were at least fifteen months old and whose female ancestors met minimum production standards. The privately held herd book of 1878 was later put under the administration of the Royal Guernsey Agricultural Society. A competitive herd book started in 1881 was called *The General Herd Book of the Island of Guernsey*. This book was established for American importers who insisted that all cattle be registered before leaving the Island. However, it included all the animals on the Island, and in 1902 the American Guernsey Cattle Club refused to recognize the *General Herd Book*.

What is special about a purebred Guernsey dairy cow? She is a producer of milk with a golden yellow color which comes from its carotene. Cheese and butter produced from this milk have a natural golden appearance. Guernsey milk is high in protein, solids and butterfat. Of the major dairy breeds, Jersey milk has the most nutrition: 9.6 ounces of Holstein skim milk equals the nutritional levels in just 8 ounces of Jersey skim milk.

Most significant has been the recent classification of milk based on the molecular makeup of the casein protein. There are two types of milk which are designated A1 and A2. Milk containing the A1 beta-casein protein is commonly known as A1 milk, while milk not containing this is known as A2. This resulted from a genetic mutation estimated to have occurred almost 8000 years ago. The mutation has subsequently spread throughout herds in the western world. Iceland, the Island of Guernsey, and France have the most A2 milk of any place in the world, presumably because their herds were more isolated. The French and the Masai, both having high dairy diets containing A2 milk, have lower levels of heart disease compared to the Finns whose diets include predominantly A1 milk.

The difference between A1 and A2 milk is change in a single amino acid in the 209 amino acid chain making up the casein molecule. A protein molecule such as casein exists in a complex folded pattern determined by the atomic forces that act between the various amino acids along its length. In the case of A2 vs A1, in position 67 the amino acid proline in A2 is replaced by histidine in A1. This might not seem like such a great change, but the forces between histidine and its neighboring amino acids are weak enough to cause breakage. When during digestion this weak bond in the A1 beta-casein breaks, a small peptide fragment of seven amino acids results. This fragment is known as beta casomorphin (BCM7). BCM7 is resistant to further breakage during digestion because the bonds between the seven remaining amino acids are strong. This fragment is a biochemical oxidant particularly responsible for damaging the low density lipoproteins which transport cholesterol from the liver to body tissues, causing arterial linings to become inflamed. This allows the formation of arterial plaque, increasing the risk of heart disease. BCM7 is also a strong opioid that can cross the blood-brain barrier and bind to opioid receptors to cause symptoms of autism and schizophrenia.

It is also suggested to have a role in Type 1 diabetes. *Devil in the Milk* by Keith Woodford (2010) provides an excellent discussion of this most intriguing hypothesis of the beneficial aspects of A2 milk over A1 milk. Offsetting this is scientific opinion by Food Standards authorities of Europe, Australia and New Zealand refuting Woodford's hypothesis based on failure to replicate results.

The Guernsey breed has 10% of their beta-casein as A1, the Jersey breed has about 35%, while the Ayrshire, Holstein and Freisian breeds tend to produce 50% or more. Goat milk has no A1 beta-casein.

Beta carotene found in green vegetable matter cannot be digested by the Guernsey. Therefore the carotene passes through to the Guernsey cow's milk, producing the rich golden color. This milk has many of the health-enhancing effects that the green forage provides, including cancer, heart disease, and diabetes prevention. The Guernsey is the only dairy animal to produce such healthy milk. It is reason to be alarmed about the almost negligible level of Guernsey animals in the United States today and the need to enhance their ability to survive and grow.

The Guernsey cow is easy to work with and of a quiet and gentle nature. The fine hair is soft to the touch and shiny when brushed, bringing out its natural oils. Its color is always white and brindle to pale red and brown fawn. The underlying yellow flesh can best be seen at the base of the horn (if not dehorned), on the inside of the ear, and around the eye, as well as at the end of the bone on the tail.

When, and why, did the first Guernsey cattle come to the United States? Without the march of progress, the twentieth-century story of the Guernsey in America could not have happened.

Chapter Three:

American Guernseys

In 1831, the American sailor Captain Prince, while returning home from France, landed his vessel on Guernsey Island. He was enchanted with the rocky coast, rolling countryside, and streams. The superb quality of the milk and other dairy products served to him by the Islanders so astonished him that he took a Guernsey bull and two cows with him as he sailed home to the United States. These were the first known Guernsey cattle to have reached the American shore. His brother had a farm on an island in the middle of Lake Winnipesaukee, New Hampshire. One of the cows died, but the remaining cow and bull were mated. They became the foundation for America's first Guernsey herd. Complete records were kept. The animals were transferred to the General Moody A. Pillsbury Farm also in New Hampshire. These original immigrants became known as the Pillsbury cow and bull. The American Guernsey Cattle Club (established 46 years later) eventually officially registered the pair and many of their descendants. The island where the cow and bull settled was soon dubbed "Cow Island." The New Hampshire State Legislature officially named the island Guernsey Island.

Three pregnant cows were the next imports to America by Nicholas Biddle of Bucks County, Pennsylvania in 1840. The earliest imports to the west coast were by J. N. Knowles via the steamship *Glory of the Seas* as recorded in the record of November 4, 1872. In March 1883 eighty head were imported for auction by S. C. Kent to the Port of Baltimore, thirty-seven of which went to Henry Palmer, including Lady Emily Foley 1700 for which Mr. Palmer paid $1900. For years this remained the record price of a single Guernsey cow. As way of comparison, in 1967 at the sale of my father's registered Guernsey herd the top price was $1200. Toward the end of the nineteenth century imports increased steadily reaching a peak in 1914. After 1930 imports were minimal. The growth of the Guernsey breed in the 1920s and 1930s was the most outstanding event in dairy breed history in America. A total of 13,000 head had been imported by 1950.

In 1876, a group of twelve men interested in Guernsey cattle met at the home of Augustus Ward in Farmington, Connecticut. Mr. Mason C. Weld of Pennsylvania, an importer of Guernsey cattle, motivated the individuals present to pledge money for the purchase and importation of fourteen Guernsey cows and a bull. These importers agreed that the Guernsey should never be crossed with any other breed. On February 7, 1877, eleven men from Massachusetts, Connecticut, New York, New Jersey, and Pennsylvania met at the Astor Hotel in New York and formally organized the American Guernsey Cattle Club. This new organization held its first formal meeting in New York ten months later. The American Guernsey Cattle Club at that moment had forty members and 193 animals in the club herd book. The American Guernsey Cattle Club took sixty-four years to register its first million animals. Two million were in registry by 1950.

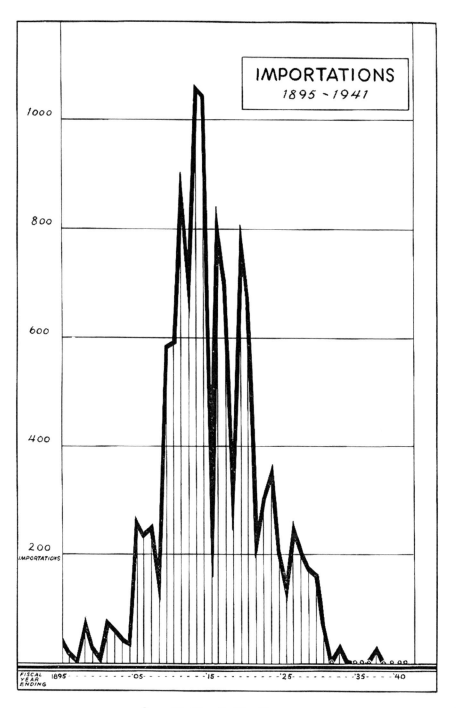

IMPORTATIONS
1895 ~ 1941

from Caldwell, *The Guernsey,*
American Guernsey Cattle Club, Peterborough, N.H., 1941

19

In the early decades of the twentieth century the Guernsey dairy breed was the most prominent among all the dairy breeds in America. The rich golden color and good taste of the milk were self evident, and no enhancement of color was needed to produce cheese and butter from Guernsey milk. Advertisements stressed its quality by local bottlers. Claims that so and so was really using a small percentage of Holstein or other inferior milk were met with written newspaper denials or advertisements by entrepreneurial Guernsey milk bottlers.

Guernsey promotion had its golden days during those times. The American Guernsey Cattle Club had its own public relations director. An audacious stunt for its time occurred at the 1929 National Dairy Show in St. Louis, Missouri. A Guernsey cow named Elm Farm Holly owned by Sunnymead Farms of Bismarck, Missouri, was flown at 135 miles per hour 5000 feet above the city while being milked. Too many spectators at the arena airfield in Forest Park made it impossible to land. While the plane flew low, twenty-five one-half pints of the cow's milk in Sealright paper bottles was parachuted down to the waiting crowd.

This stunt was soon eclipsed as the crowning glory of Guernsey promotion when arrangements were made to send three Guernsey cows with Admiral Richard Evelyn Byrd on his second expedition to Antarctica in 1933. Admiral Byrd had requested three cows to accompany him so that he might have fresh milk. The request made October 7, 1933, was for a loan of three cows to spend a year on the ice barrier of the Antarctic. Guernsey cows from Deerfoot Farm of Southboro, Massachusetts, Emmadine Farms of Hopewell Junction, New York, and Klondike Farm of Ellan, North Carolina were loaded on the ship *Jacob Ruppert*. Sand and straw for bedding, twenty tons of hay, twelve tons of beet pulp, and two tons of bran accompanied the animals.

Milk bottle caps especially designed for the expedition read "Byrd Antarctic Expedition, Golden Guernsey Milk produced on board the *Jacob Ruppert.*"

The 22,000 miles of sea travel, the terrific heat while crossing the equator and the terrible cold on the ice did not deter the continuous production of golden Guernsey milk the entire time. As if this wasn't enough excitement for the three Guernseys, on December 19th, after two months at sea, Klondike Gay Nira gave birth to a bull calf unanimously christened Iceberg, as at the time the ship was just entering the Great Antarctic Ice Pack, 275 miles north of the Antarctic Circle. There is a discrepancy over which cow had the bull calf named Iceberg. According to William H. Caldwell in his book *The Guernsey,* the mother was Klondike, while the American Guernsey Cattle Club commemoration designated the mother as Emmadine. However, in the October 1935 National Geographic article *Exploring the Ice Age in Antarctica,* Admiral Byrd definitively writes: "Klondike had declined to wait for destiny. ... The frosty breath of icebergs informed her that her journey was about run, and not caring about a few degrees of latitude, she quietly achieved the everlasting duty of her sex.... It was a bull calf, and by unanimous consent he was called 'Iceberg'."

At the Bay of Whales supplies were put ashore for transport to Little America, the Antarctic Exploration Base previously established by Admiral Byrd in 1929. Rapid breaking up of ice forced a speedy two and three-quarter mile hike for the three cows and the month old bull calf until lack of visibility necessitated an overnight stop. For a long miserable month at Little America they were stabled in a tent until the barn was made ready for them. Melting enough snow for water for the animals was a constant serious problem. Frequently they ate snow. As cow body heat penetrated the straw, they sank and needed to be helped to their feet. The cattle weathered the hardships except for Klondike who developed frostbite and eventually died in Little America. The world's farthest south dairy barn measured fifteen by thirty-one by eight feet and was complete with electricity and a milking machine. A coal stove was kept burning continually. The crew named the animals after the farm from which they had come. Klondike's registered name was Klondike Gay Nira. She was owned by Thurmond Chatham of Klondike Farm, Elkin, North Carolina. Deerfoot's registered name was Deerfoot Guernsey Maid. She was owned by J. E. O'Leary of Deerfoot Farms, Southboro, Massachusetts. Emmadine's registered name was Foremost Southern Girl. She was owned by J. C. Penney of Emmadine Farms, Hopewell Junction, New York.

Beginning on March 25 to late August 1934 Byrd lived alone deep inland making weather and auroral observations. His coal stove had been converted to burn kerosene and it was improperly vented, causing a buildup of carbon monoxide fumes in his shack. Byrd's personal diary revealed the bewildering nature of his illness, and he didn't think he had a chance at survival. He tried minimizing the time the stove was used, but at night the temperature dropped to -30°F in his shack, freezing his food and causing metal to fracture. He was determined not to inform the Little America base camp as he did not want to risk the lives of his men in a midwinter rescue attempt. Byrd crawled with exhaustion to crank his hand generator, as a lapse in communication was the same as an SOS. His men became suspicious that something was wrong. After several aborted attempts, an overland expedition from Little America fought the cold and dark to reach him. Byrd returned to Little America in October 1934. The story of his ordeal with temperatures down to -82°F (-63 °C) is told in his 1938 book *Alone*.

**Commemorative Byrd Expedition Medallion given to Vilas Young
in appreciation for his work on behalf of the Guernsey breed.**

A rundown Admiral Byrd later commented, "The milk really pulled me out of my tailspin." He praised the hardiness of the Guernsey animals and the quality of the milk. No one on the expedition drank more milk more enthusiastically than did Admiral Byrd, as related in the book *The Guernsey* by William H. Caldwell, published by the American Guernsey Cattle Club in 1941. Mr. Caldwell was the Guernsey breed Secretary-Treasurer from 1894 to 1924 and Vice-President from 1923 to 1941. The American Guernsey Cattle Club, just an idea in 1877, became a thriving institution in the twentieth century.

Chapter Four:

American Guernsey Association

On August 29, 2009, we visited the American Guernsey Association in Reynoldsburg, Ohio. In the entrance to the office hung a monstrous portrait of Yeksa Sunbeam, the first registered dairy animal of any breed to produce one thousand pounds of butter in a single year. Yeksa Sunbeam was the daughter of Yeksa's Prince, the full brother of Queen Vashti owned by A. J. Phillips of West Salem, Wisconsin, as we shall soon learn more.

There are three primary sources of information at the American Guernsey Association: the record summary books listing all registrations and transfers; binders of all the publications by quarter year; and a very limited shelf of books and publications.

The most intriguing book was Volume One Reports of Annual Meetings 1877 – 1893 by Secretary-Treasurer Edward M. Norton. The preface note is as follows: "There were no formal Secretary's records, office notes, published proceedings, and the co-operation of *The Country Gentleman* provided the essence." *The Country Gentleman* was a glossy monthly national farm publication during my youth and undoubtedly the voice of record in early American agriculture.

The following is a summation of the early formative years of the American Guernsey Cattle Club as gleaned from the pages of this Volume One Reports.

The first meeting was held December 19, 1877, and the report was confined to one short page. There were eleven members, each having paid a life-time membership fee of $20. In this as well as in all subsequent reports names of attendees and members were never included. The report included a total of 193 registered animals of which 114 had been imported, as well as the claim that there were additional 200 animals in the United States not yet registered.

Nothing was included for an 1878 annual meeting. Whether or not an annual meeting was held remains unknown.

Assuming there was a meeting in 1878, then the third annual meeting was held December 17, 1879, with a reported membership of forty-five. The minutes reported an increase of thirteen from the prior year. It was noted that Dr. W. B. Eager did not join. Dr. Eager represented a club "who did not favor it." The first financial statement was presented:

Membership fees	$260.00
Registrations & Transfers	249.75
Proceeds	$509.75

Herd Registry Printing	$220.00
Ed Norton	250.00
Advertising	9.00
Postage Stamps	4.65
Executive Committee	13.96
Total Cash Expense	$497.61
Gain	$12.14
Total cash on hand at the end of the year	$427.79

The one page report of the fourth annual meeting held December 15, 1880, noted that three years earlier there were eleven members and now there were fifty-six. During the prior year the Executive Committee met twice at Centennial Hall in Philadelphia. There was no financial statement, but the following was recorded: "The Guernsey is now accepted at any county or state fair in the country whenever presented. The supply of Guernsey cattle both on the Island and in the U. S. is too limited to meet the demand."

The fifth annual meeting was held at the Grand Hotel in New York City on December 21, 1881. It was decided to raise the life-time membership fee from $20 to $50. Apparently the Association was prosperous, but no financial report was given. This annual meeting established the rule that all animals imported after July 1, 1882, must be registered in one of the Island herd books. This Island, of course, meant the Island of Guernsey. All these animals must have a certificate with a description attested to by the breeder, the owner, and one witness. A copy of the said certificate must be mailed under the American consul's signature directly to the Secretary of the American Guernsey Cattle Club. Prior to 1878 there were no records kept on the Island of Guernsey. Whatever happened was simply stored only in the breeder's head. Bulls were mated to cows based on whoever was closest or cheapest. The beginnings of the recorded history literally came out of the thin air.

This Volume contains no record of a meeting in 1882. Assuming there was the sixth meeting in 1882, the seventh annual meeting was held December 20, 1883, at the Fifth Avenue Hotel in New York City with twenty-two members present out of a total membership of seventy-eight. In the year ended December 19, 1883, proceeds were $1629.22 and expenses were $1139.75 including $600 for the Secretary's salary. This report noted that it was discovered immediately after the last meeting that the entry fee increase violated the constitution and could not be enforced due to lack of sixty days notice. A new constitution and by-laws were passed. The new membership roll included a Canadian, 25 from Pennsylvania, 15 from Connecticut, 12 from Massachusetts, and 11 from New York, two each from Illinois, Ohio, Vermont and Wisconsin, with one member each from California, Delaware, Georgia, Maryland, and New Jersey. It was adopted at this meeting to register in the herd book all animals imported whose sires and dams were not registered in the Island Herd Books as long as this did not become a precedent for future registrations.

On the Island of Guernsey several new Parrish shows were created with the purpose of choosing animals for registration based on "type" according to the judge's particular ideas of the time. Since many animals were rejected and many owners refused to exhibit their cattle, the new herd book became controversial to say the least. Those whose animals were rejected and those who refused scrutiny started a rival herd book based on the premise that all animals on the Island must be thoroughbred and entitled to registration. They regarded this as acceptable as long as the animal and its sire and dam were born on and living on the Island at the time of registration. Both competing herd books refused to register a deceased animal or one previously exported. Some animals were entered in both registers with different names and different numbers. The real purpose of both herd books and the objective of registration were to create a pedigree for American Guernsey Cattle Club dairy animals that could be traced in full. Registration was supposedly denied to those that could not, but where was the beginning?

The eighth annual meeting was held once again at the Fifth Avenue Hotel in New York City on December 10, 1884. Twenty-five members out of a total of eighty-seven were present. In the prior fiscal year 575 cows and 263 bulls were registered and 72 animals were imported. An auction in Philadelphia yielded poor results because of the country's financial depression.

The ninth annual meeting was held at the Fifth Avenue Hotel in New York City on December 9, 1885, with nineteen members present. There were five new members. This was the start of a trend wherein as membership increased, devotees at the annual meetings decreased. A probable reason was the economic price depression from March 1882 through May 1885, including the economic panic of 1884. According to the National Bureau of Economic Research chronology of business cycles, only the Great Depression and the long depression of 1873 to 1879 were longer. Proceeds for the year were $2548.47 and expenses were $1320.32. It was noted that England had formed a Guernsey Cattle Club and a herd registry book.

The annual meeting reports from 1883 to 1885 were quite lengthy. They actually were enclosed as separate formally-typed books within the reports volume itself; the 1884 report alone was fifty pages including a new constitution and by-laws.

The report for the tenth annual meeting on December 8, 1886, at the Fifth Avenue Hotel in New York City reverted to the prior skimpy style with only one page and no financial records. Only fourteen members out of the total of ninety were present. It did mention that 3048 cows and 1443 bulls had been registered in the prior fiscal year.

The report of the annual meeting of December 14, 1887, was limited to one-half page. It stated that there were now ninety-five members, with 3521 females and 1664 bulls registered the prior year. As in prior annual reports, nothing was included about issues discussed.

The next annual meeting was held on December 14, 1888. There was no indication of membership, members present or registrations. It did report the fiscal year had proceeds of $1829.36 and cash expenses of $1560.70. It went back a further year stating proceeds of $1884.75 and expenses of $1468.75. While cumulative financial progress was non-existent it appears that the Club was doing very well.

The Fifth Avenue Hotel continued its monopoly for annual meetings when they next met December 11, 1889, with twelve members present. Three cows were purchased at $500 each for study at a New Jersey Experiment Station. Even though there was $2448.26 in proceeds and cash outflow of $3170.91, there was a positive cash position of $1415.67 on December 1, 1889. Forty-eight animals were imported during the prior fiscal year.

Only nine members attended the annual meeting of December 10, 1890, at the Fifth Avenue hotel in New York City. It was recorded that G. E. Gordon was expelled from the Club for acts derogatory to the Club. While we are not told how many members there were, it noted that there were three new members and three members had died. The barns and animals in the New Jersey experiment had burned, but the total loss was covered by insurance. Two herds were dispersed including that of I. J. Clapp of Wisconsin.

At the December 9, 1891, annual meeting again nine members were present. There were five new members including W. D. Hoard of Fort Atkinson, Wisconsin. The infamous G. E. Gordon was reported as having disappeared and his herd dispersed into Wisconsin and Minnesota, but without any registration or transfers. Net worth of the Guernsey cattle club was stated as $1710.95.

On December 14, 1892, ten members attended the annual meeting at the Fifth Avenue Hotel in New York City. The average lifespan during those early days is telling, as with such small membership each of the past few years saw three or more members pass away. During the year thirty-four animals were imported and 6439 females and 3169 bulls were registered. The ending year cash balance was $1753.23.

Nine members attended the annual meeting at the Fifth Avenue Hotel held December 13, 1893. There were now 103 members from sixteen states and Canada. The 1893 Columbian Exposition (the Chicago World's Fair) was the first international opportunity to show off the Guernsey breed of the United States. Thirty-five animals were sent to Chicago of which twenty-five were selected for show. The report indicated that the fairgrounds were "cold, windy, swampy, and malarias." Three of the best cows died calving. Food and drinking water were described as terrible. To sponsor the Guernsey exhibit the American Guernsey Cattle Club spent $6804, necessitating borrowing two thousand dollars in 1893. Cash on hand at the end of the year was $1232. Net worth was a negative $768.

This ends the text of a hard-bound book describing the formative years of the American Guernsey Cattle Club. William Dempster Hoard, the creator of Hoard's Dairyman, became the 115th member in 1891. He served on the executive committee from 1903 to 1911 and Vice-President from 1911 to 1919. As a hobby Hoard enjoyed scaling points on a dairy score card. He influenced the final result in the revision of the official Guernsey score card emphasizing one-third of points to the udder and one-third for "a good dairy cow," the last third presumably to the general conformity of the animal. His was the primary wording used for the scorecard. Hoard was on the Executive Committee when the Guernsey Breeders' Journal began. The historic character of the publication was due to his influence.

The American Guernsey Cattle Club stated: "His singleness of purpose and devotion to agriculture made him not only the father of modern dairying but a true servant of humanity. He gave his life for the betterment of dairying and dairy livestock and his services in this respect as well as those which he rendered to the American Guernsey Cattle Club assure a lasting memory of this truly self-made man." By 1913 Hoard's health deteriorated to the point where he could no longer communicate except by writing, but his skills in that regard continued undiminished.

The American Guernsey Cattle Club published its first volume of registration of cows, bulls, and sale transfer of animals in 1884. The registry number represents in numerical order the registration of cattle by the Club, and there is a separate numerical order for males and females. A transfer is a recorded sale of an animal from one party to another. Two items of note from that publication: there were a total of seventy-eight members with I. J. Clapp of Kenosha as the only Wisconsin member, and secondly, the average farm on the Island of Guernsey consisted of six to ten acres with four to six cows.

There are multiple entries of registrations and transfers in each volume prepared by the American Guernsey Cattle Club. As the numbers of animals increased so did the useful information. Taking Volume 28 at random encompassing the years of 1912 and 1913, we find 367 active members including one from Canada. Of these, fifty-one members or fourteen percent were from Wisconsin. Christian Christensen from La Crosse and Ray Lewis, Harry W. Griswold, and Alfred L. Stubbs all from West Salem were members as was W. Nichols from neighboring Trempealeau. By 1915 La Crosse County added two more Guernsey breeders to national membership, J. J. Bean and W. J. Dawson. H. W. Griswold imported thirteen cows from the Island of Guernsey on March 12, 1913. H.W. Griswold was the prominent son of Henry Daniel Griswold, an early West Salem, Wisconsin dairy pioneer whose financial records and accomplishments make up a major portion of our later story and whose family had a lasting impact on the community and farming practices.

Animals were not only accepted for registration from the Island of Guernsey, but also from Alderney and England. The total imports accepted by the American Guernsey Cattle Club for 1913 were as follows:

ORIGIN:	BULLS	COWS
ALDERNEY	3	80
GUERNSEY	17	355
ENGLAND	16	142

England had created its own herd book by this time. The animals recorded as registered in Volume 28 were born in 1912 or 1913 and included those owned and registered by such institutions as Stanford University in California, Iowa State College, Connecticut Agricultural College, University of Wisconsin, The Dairy Division of the Bureau of Animal Industry in Beltsville, Maryland, C. H. Mayo of Rochester, Minnesota, Franciscan Sisters of Saint Joseph, Wisconsin, and Massachusetts Agricultural College.

Registering qualified animals was not limited to members. Those from La Crosse County, Wisconsin, registering animals in 1912 and 1913, were Ray Lewis, Otto Wolf, D. F. Miller, H. D. Griswold, H. W. Griswold, C. D. Griswold, J. M. Halderson, M. J. Humphrey, H. M. Bonsack, W. J. Dawson; M. B. Lee and his wife of Hillsboro, Wisconsin separately registered animals. They later purchased a farm at West Salem owned by Henry Daniel Griswold's father-in-law.

In 1914 forty-nine bulls and 1101 cows were imported with 122 from Alderney, 922 from the Island of Guernsey and 106 from England. At that time there were 425 members including 76 members each from New York and Pennsylvania, and 69 members from Wisconsin. Those three states combined had over half the membership.

In 1915 thirty-five bulls and 532 cows were imported with seventeen bulls and 365 cows from the Island of Guernsey, nineteen cows from

Alderney, and eighteen bulls and 148 cows from England. From May of 1905 through May of 1915 there were a total of 361 bulls and 5366 cows imported. The American Guernsey Cattle Club had seen excellent growth. Their rounded estimate of registrations for 1915 was 4000 bulls and 7000 cows.

This has been a survey of the establishment and growth of the pioneering registered Guernsey phenomenon in the United States. There are many volumes of fine print in registrations and transfers. Written records were sent to the cattle club to be accepted and then they were coalesced into hard-covered volumes. By luck I came across a registration by my grandfather in one of the volumes. Edward Young registered bull number 66449 born January 13, 1920. The bull's name was Manette's Meteor of La Crosse Valley. His dam (mother) was born July 15, 1916. Her name was Manette of Lakeside, registry number 71458, with the owner and breeder being Edward Young. The bull's sire was Cora's Sequel, registry number 25168. This bull was bred and owned by the University of Wisconsin. Grandfather either bought the bull from the University or rented the bull from someone who did. The interesting story concerns the mother of the new born bull, Manette of Lakeside. Her sire was Jerry Valentine registration number 21461. Jerry Valentine was transferred from W. J. Dawson to William Moos of Onalaska, Wisconsin. This is just over the hill from Grandfather's. The dam of the mother of the new born bull was Hilo of Whitehall, registry number 19802. Her original owner and breeder was H. A. Bartholomew of Whitehall, New York who later sold and transferred her to Charles Foote of Burlington, Vermont. I doubt that the grandmother of the newborn ever made it to Wisconsin from Vermont to become the mother of Manette of Lakeside. Since Grandfather was the breeder and owner of that cow, he would have had to purchase her mother from Charles Foote or a later owner. Even though Hilo of Whitehall was listed as being born February 15, 1905, this is quite a stretch prior to 1916. One would need to pore through all the entries from the birth in 1905 to 1916, as there is no orderly progression of entry or an index in the volumes. According to the records, Edward Young sold this young bull to Willie A. Myhre of Caledonia, Maine. A few miles from Grandfather's farm across the Mississippi River lies the farming community of Caledonia, Minnesota!

Let us assume that Hilo of Whitehall stayed in Vermont or a least did not make it to the Edward Young farm. Let us also assume that Manette's Meteor of La Crosse Valley never went any further than Caledonia, Minnesota. Information originated from the applicant of registry and/or transfer. It was accepted by the American Guernsey Cattle Club and permanently recorded in its records. At the end of a fiscal period it was put into permanent record book form for reference and historical purposes. This was before computers! There was no systematic reference point for follow-through or correction.

Owners and breeders probably had no way of knowing if anything had been recorded incorrectly. If the information transferred to the permanent book was copied incorrectly for whatever reason, but was correct up to that point and was never used as a reference for future registrations, correct pedigree information may have been carried forward. The permanent summary book still makes for a suspect reference and is wholly unsatisfactory for most purposes.

There appear to be weaknesses in the recording. How extensive were these weaknesses, or am I not giving Grandfather enough credit for bringing a cow from Vermont and selling the cow's grandson to someone in the state of Maine? If there is an error in the registry, could it be that I came across the only one or two that ever happened? How vital is the possibility of numerous errors on the validity of the annual combined registry?

Prior to 1878 there were no records on the Island of Guernsey or in England or Alderney. Most knowledge of pedigree resided in the head, if that. Nothing had been said about the basis of registry for those registered animals coming from Alderney. In the United States pedigrees, milk and butterfat records were correlated to establish positive breeding programs to improve not only production but also the appearance and longevity of the animal.

The originators of the American Guernsey Cattle Club and its members would be horrified to learn that all of their best efforts may have succumbed to errors and sloppiness. However, one would speculate that they were more prevalent than acceptable. It is impossible to know what effect, if any, this had on the long-term future of the breed as a whole. There is no justification whatsoever to doubt the veracity and capabilities of those involved with the Guernsey breed from the farmer, to the breed executives, to those involved in the day-to-day operation of the cattle club. As education, technology, and experience were enhanced so was the accuracy of the record keeping. The American Guernsey Cattle Club and The American Guernsey Association of today have been leaders in the progressive dairy experience in the United States of America.

At the American Guernsey Association headquarters is a vast collection of semi-monthly Guernsey Breeders' Journals. During the mid-twentieth century they were a little larger than a sheet of typewriter paper and in many cases half an inch thick. Each is chock full of information that the centennial issue in 1977 did not match. I had an interest in the issues from 1952 as that was the year J. C. Penney bequeathed his Foremost Guernsey herd to the University of Missouri. This was also the seventy-fifth year after the creation of the American Guernsey Cattle Club. Each issue devoted substance to the history of dairying. The inside front cover of every issue displayed a full page advertisement of Foremost Farm Guernseys.

The first issue of 1952, dated January 1, includes the fascinating article "Seventy-Five Years in Breeding" by V. A. Rice of the University of Massachusetts. Rice began with the first scientific understanding of breeding, noting that the German botanist Rudolph Jacob Camerarius in 1694 recognized the sexual nature of plants. The English nurseryman Thomas Fairchild in 1717 produced the first artificial plant hybrid. The Englishman Robert Bakewell in 1750 demonstrated that animal forms were amenable to pre-conceived ideals when subjected to a proper system of breeding and selection. V. A. Rice maintained there were five fields in the science of breeding: reproduction, heredity, variation, breeding systems, and selection.

The Origin of Species by Charles Darwin published in 1859 ushered in the experimental approach to the many problems of biology, thus unshackling men's minds from ancient "authorities."

V. A. Rice said, "It can readily be seen that from 1875 to 1900 livestock breeders had little solid knowledge of reproduction, inheritance, or variation by which to guide their operations. In the light of the paucity of knowledge and the preponderance of misinformation, it is remarkable that any progress could ensue as it undeniably did."

"For instance, it was believed that the environment was genetically carried over to the next generation. Theories of how and when to breed and the result were all over the place. In 1876, all a dairyman had regarding the mechanism of reproduction, inheritance, and selection, (like begets like), was superstition and hocus pocus."

Gregor Mendel established the principles of inheritance through experimental pea plant breeding from 1858 to 1865 and published his paper, *Experiments on Plant Hybridization*, in 1866 in *Proceedings of the Natural History Society of Brünn*. His work was criticized and virtually ignored until rediscovered in 1900. His two generalizations, the Law of Segregation and the Law of Independent Assortment, collectively known as Mendel's Laws of Inheritance, gave birth to the field of genetics. Through this we know that inheritance is an orderly process controlled by genes. Inbreeding merely intensifies what we start with.

The Guernsey Breeders' Journal included many more scientific articles throughout the 75th anniversary year. Pages were numbered consecutively from issue to issue, and many issues were in excess of 200 pages. A biography on W. D. Hoard in the March 15, 1952, issue began on page 786.

Seventy-five years after its inauspicious beginning, the American Guernsey Cattle Club reported at the end of fiscal year 1951 that there were 42,500 Guernsey breeders using its registry compared to thirty-four in 1877. Actual membership was 4230 with 2930 participating in "Performance Registry." The Journals' circulation was 15,244. Total revenue was $1,168,429. Total expense was $1,114,639. Net income was $44,090.

In a brand new building on Main Street in Peterborough, New Hampshire, two hundred people handled the work and record performance. For fiscal 1951 there were 79,448 female and 14,181 male registrations. There were also 48,930 female transfers and 11,280 male transfers.

Arguably the most extraordinary effort to promote the future of the Guernsey breed of dairy cattle or, for that matter, the future of *any* dairy breed, was the gift of the Foremost Herd of registered Guernsey cattle to the University of Missouri in 1952. Foremost Guernseys was one of the world's highest producing, successful dairy herds of all time. The purpose behind this astounding gift was to continue J. C. Penney's legacy in perpetuity so that his herd would always be the foundation for a powerful registered Guernsey presence in the United States of America.

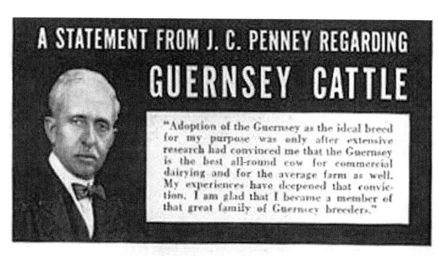
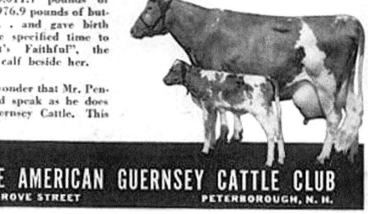
1937 advertisement

Where Have All The Guernseys Gone?

Foremost Guernseys to Have Permanent Home in Missouri was the title of an article in the June 15, 1952, *Guernsey Breeders' Journal* written by A. C. Ragsdale, Professor of Dairy Husbandry and Chairman of the Department of Dairy Husbandry at the University of Missouri. The article quoted in part:

> Foremost Guernseys will soon be given a permanent home in Missouri the native state of their founder and owner, J. C. Penney. The final step in assuring perpetuity to this dairy herd has been taken 44 years earlier than he originally planned. In 1936, when he formed the Foremost Guernsey Association in New York and had it incorporated, he provided that in the year 1996 this herd of some 250 head valued at approximately $200,000 was to be transferred to the University of Missouri. Now Mr. Penney is proceeding with the dissolution of that Association so that Foremost Guernseys can be the property of the University of Missouri during his lifetime.

> The story behind this generous gift is one of careful planning for the future so as to perpetuate the Guernsey Breeding Program begun at Emmadine Farms (now Foremost Guernsey Association) more than 30 years ago.

Professor Ragsdale then quotes the remarks of Karl K. Musser, Secretary of the American Guernsey Cattle Club, from the January 15, 1937, issue of the *Guernsey Breeders' Journal*:

> Mr. Penney, in founding this organization has built a living monument to a cause and not to himself. He has chosen to keep mobile his great interest in American Agriculture after he is gone, rather than have it fixed in granite, bronze, or marble statue which time will look upon with a query as to the meaning. His monument shall live in the warm bloodstream of man's greatest source of life's sustenance, the dairy cow.

Professor Ragsdale continues his own remarks:

> The University of Missouri plans to establish the J. C. PENNEY FOREMOST GUERNSEY FOUNDATION at

Columbia, Missouri. It is tentatively planned that the Board of the new foundation will consist of members of the staff of the University and representative Guernsey Breeders in Missouri to act in an advisory capacity. Supervision of the farm is delegated to the Department of Dairy Husbandry, College of Agriculture. The herd will be operated as a distinct breeding unit and the Missouri farm will be known as J. C. PENNEY GUERNSEY FARM.

The terms of the Foundation will make it possible for those in charge at the University of Missouri to procure the necessary land, erect buildings, and set up a program to continue the herd along its present lines. It is planned to use the herd as a breeding unit, utilizing all information obtained in a research program. No work will be undertaken which would inhibit growth and development. It is planned to test so that all animals may make the best possible records. The herd will be operated on a practical basis.

The Missouri farm layout and buildings will be simple, and relatively inexpensive but attractive.

Professor Ragsdale was on the Board of Directors of Foremost Guernsey Farms, Inc. at the time of the transfer. He was well acquainted with the herd and its accomplishments. The rest of the article provided a production and pedigree history of the herd of such depth as to only have come from someone who deeply cared about its history and its future.

The *Guernsey Breeders' Journal* continued the full page advertisement for the Foremost Guernsey Herd on the inside front cover after the June 15, 1952, issue announced the property transfer. The only change was that Columbia, Missouri was listed as the address.

If you are a Guernsey history buff it is possible to be immersed for a very long time in the collated issues of the *Guernsey Breeders' Journal*. Time marches on as do the fortunes of the cattle club. The tiny library at the headquarters of the American Guernsey Association does contain a gem or two, including *The Dairy Cow Today* by Sidney L. Spahr and George W. Opperman. The authors on pages 56 and 57 commented on Dutch Mill Telestar Fayette, the bull destined to revolutionize the future of the Guernsey breed even into the twenty-first century. "It became obvious that he combined outstanding type and genetic superiority for milk production as well as any bull the breed has produced. His descendants were particularly outstanding in body traits. He sired tall cattle with smooth shoulders, greater than average width, straight legs, and pleasing udders. His daughters were stylish in appearance, and were prominent in the show ring throughout the country during the late 1980's and early 1990's."

The American Guernsey Cattle Club moved to Columbus, Ohio in 1982 to economize, more efficiently serve its members and work jointly with the Jersey breed. The Guernsey breed was losing its competitive edge, and Russell J. Wirt, president from 1979 to 1984, was clearly concerned about its future. He felt the future of the Guernsey breed would be established by demand for Guernsey animals by the non-purebred commercial dairy farmers of the 1990s. The popularity of the Guernsey in commercial enterprises in the twenty-first century is almost non-existent.

This concern brought about registration changes to bolster numbers, a practice which would have outraged the original founders. In 1984 the American Guernsey Cattle Club decided to register in a separate fashion those animals having fifty percent or more purebred Guernsey genes. In 1987 the name of the organization was changed to the American Guernsey Association. In 1990 the Association recorded females that were twenty-five percent Guernsey and males that were fifty percent Guernsey. Due to strong opposition and lack of participation, in 1992 the membership and board of directors voted to discontinue the program. In 1994 another deviation in registration from the original constitution and by-laws of the American Guernsey Cattle Club was initiated. If the offspring from a cross between a purebred registered Guernsey and another dairy animal was bred back to a purebred registered Guernsey, this second generation offspring was allowed to be registered, even though it contained only seventy-five percent Guernsey genetic makeup.

Troubled times indeed! The American Guernsey Association is facing tough times as is the entire dairy industry. At the time of our visit, the home office in Reynoldsburg, Ohio consisted of just four people housed in a condo office which was part of a one floor strip of office units. Two magazine editors publish the *Guernsey Breeders' Journal, The Brown Swiss Bulletin*, the *Ayrshire Digest*, and *Milking Shorthorn Journal*. They are incorporated as "Purebred Publishing." This well-run corporation's goal is to help offset losses from the American Guernsey Association. This subsidiary, however, had a loss of $53,000 in 2009. In 2010 a profit of $50,000 was realized through the use of a lower cost printer and cuts in editorial time. The Records Department Director is Ida Albert, who actually is the entire records department responsible for registration, transfers, and looking up the historical record for anyone calling in. Mary Ann D'Ippolito is the contract accountant for the six corporations under the aegis of the American Guernsey Association. The General Manager, Executive Secretary-Treasurer Seth Johnson operates from his home in Vermont. In order to control costs the Board of Directors did not meet in Reynoldsburg, Ohio, in December, 2009, as was the usual practice, but met via telephone and internet. The drop in registrations in 2008 was offset by higher registration fees.

The first six months of 2009 saw a dramatic drop in purebred source income and publication ad sales as the dairy economy sank. To further economize, beginning in late 2010 the American Guernsey Association rented space from COBA/Select Sires in Columbus, Ohio. In 2011 AGA rented out their condo offices in Reynoldsburg. According to Seth Johnson, the combined moves bring $15,000 to the bottom line of the AGA. Both locations are in sharp contrast to the one-time new and splendid building in New Hampshire with accommodation for two hundred employees. The downsizing only emphasizes the losses throughout the years.

This is the story of the registered Guernsey breed of dairy cattle from its first introduction to the United States of America, to a position of dairy prominence in the early and mid twentieth century, and to its decline in the evolution of the dairy industry. There are many causes of this decline, in hindsight some of which may have made the decline less dramatic but could not have been prevented.

Let us continue on our journey with our first pioneer: America's Father of Dairy Farming, William Dempster Hoard.

Chapter Five:

The Legacy of William Dempster Hoard

"The cow is the foster mother of the human
race ~ From the day of the ancient Hindoo to
this time have the thoughts of men ~ turned to
this kindly and beneficent creature as one of
the chief sustaining forces of human life."

–W. D. Hoard

William Dempster Hoard was the beginning moving force in creating an entrepreneurial intelligence-focused dairy farm industry producing an abundance of healthy dairy products.

W. D. Hoard was born October 10, 1836, in the town of Munnsville, Madison County, New York. On October 1, 1857, Hoard left his family home for Wisconsin and traveled by train from Oneida, New York to Chicago, Illinois. He remembered the marshland quagmire on the edge of Lake Michigan next to Chicago. Hoard's destination was the home of his cousin G. G. White who owned 200 acres and lived on the edge of Crossing Prairie, Wisconsin.

Hoard had worked for a successful dairyman in New York and hoped to use those experiences in Wisconsin. Farming in Wisconsin at the time consisted of mostly raising wheat which by 1870 had depleted much of the state's soil. Nearly broke when he arrived, he became a member of the family of David Blissert, a former friend of his father's, near the village of Lowell. In order to survive Hoard became a traveling music teacher and sometime salesman. He was proficient enough in music to become one of the fifers of his company during the American Civil War.

Abraham Lincoln became the exemplary source for W. D. Hoard's character, ideals and purpose in life. In 1858 he borrowed a horse from a neighbor in Dodge County, Wisconsin, to travel one and a half days to Freeport, Illinois, for the Lincoln-Douglas debate. The inspiration perceived from Lincoln at that debate was so profound that the return trip of two and a half days was spent mulling over the wisdom of Lincoln.

In physical appearance Lincoln and Hoard were very much alike. They were both rugged individuals, tall and angular for their time, with unattractive, irregular features and deep-set eyes whose depths suggested a particular sadness. The National Dairy Shrine in Fort Atkinson, Wisconsin, attached to the former Hoard home, contains a powerful full-size diorama of an eerily life-like Lincoln complete with prominent veins. The very melancholy of his soul washes over anyone who stands gazing into his eyes.

Hoard's respect for Lincoln was total. He remarked: "I enlisted in the war because it seemed to me that I owed it to this good man to help him in his task of preserving the Union. As I look back upon these times, I do not recall that there were any heroics about enlistment. Men and women were so wrought up by the agitation upon slavery and 'states rights' that no other course was possible, and I went to the village to enlist, it seemed that about every other man was there to enlist."

Hoard's devotion to Lincoln was so profound that he became much like Lincoln in the later years of his life. The physical and mental similarities were so manifest that Hoard became known as "the Lincoln of Wisconsin."

Abraham Lincoln was part of a military encampment at Fort Koshkonog in Jefferson County, Wisconsin during the Blackhawk Indian War in 1832. During that time, Lincoln's horse was stolen from the Township of Cold Spring after he was released from active duty. This is the same county as the home of Hoard's Dairyman, The National Dairy Shrine, and the Hoard's Dairyman Farm. Just before Lincoln arrived at Fort Koshkonog, the future President of the Confederacy Jefferson Davis left Fort Koshkonog and moved to an encampment at Prairie du Chien, Wisconsin roughly 140 miles away.

At the age of 33 W. D. Hoard found his calling establishing a sixteen-column, four page weekly newspaper. The date was March 17, 1870. Hoard started in Lake Mills, Jefferson County, but moved to Fort Atkinson when businessmen persuaded him he could receive a larger circulation and more advertising by locating there. He finally had his own building and printing plant when he published his first edition on May 2, 1873. The name of Hoard's newspaper was the *Jefferson County Union*. He began to publish a page devoted to dairy farming to enhance both his knowledge and that of the local dairymen. Local farmers, naturally, considered W D. Hoard to be a book farmer and theorist.

William Dempster Hoard

Mr. Hoard purchased a 193-acre farm in 1899 to practice his theories and disseminate knowledge gleaned from his own practical experience. Hoard had a very positive attitude about the legume alfalfa that he obtained from California. He believed the high protein hay would help preserve Wisconsin soils as well as provide dairy cows with nutrition to enhance milk production. Dean Henry of the University of Wisconsin College of Agriculture sternly warned Hoard that Wisconsin soils would not tolerate alfalfa nor would it survive a Wisconsin winter. By experimenting on his own farm Hoard was able to disprove Dean Henry and all the other University naysayers in the upper Midwest. He proved that acid soils needed lime to bring the pH to 7.0 (neutral) so that alfalfa might grow abundantly. Alfalfa must not be harvested after the first frost, especially the first seeding, to provide adequate root growth and rest to survive the tough winter. As early as 1905 Mr. Hoard through his magazine, speeches, institutes, and associations was urging harvesting alfalfa in the early bloom stage. At this stage it is more palatable with more digestive nutrients than when cut later. The crimping of stems with a hay conditioner beginning in the 1950's enhanced drying, while saving more high protein leaves and allowing for earlier cutting. Hoard was decades ahead of accepted alfalfa farming practices. His practical research and promotion of alfalfa earned him the nickname "Father of Alfalfa Culture."

By the 1950s there were 18,000 acres of alfalfa growing in Wisconsin up from only 460 acres in 1889. In 1980 Wisconsin farmers were harvesting over three million acres of alfalfa each year averaging 3.5 tons per acre.

The University of Wisconsin provided meaningful practical research. A proper soil acidity test was developed to determine the amount of lime needed per acre. The University introduced bacterial inoculation of seed to allow for nitrogen fixation, as the live rhizobium bacteria (*Rhizobium meliloti*) needed for this was not native to Wisconsin soils. Without bacterial inoculation, alfalfa could not utilize ("fix") atmospheric nitrogen; the plants would survive but have a yellow appearance with low yields. Thirty years of research into nitrogen fixation by natural organisms, including breeding programs to synthesize agronomic traits of winter hardiness and wilt resistance, led to the creation of Vernal Alfalfa in 1954 by the University of Wisconsin. This superior variety dominated alfalfa production into the 1970s when higher yielding varieties developed from Vernal Alfalfa germ plasm became available.

Producing alfalfa seed is natural in the western states. The Midwest with its cold extended winter is where the properties of much of that seed are put into forage. After Justemere Farm near West Salem, Wisconsin, owned by my father, went out of the Guernsey business in 1967, part of the remaining farm was sold to Cal/West Seeds in 1972. Cal/West Seeds, headquartered in Woodland, California, is the largest U. S. farm co-operative devoted exclusively to the seed business with several hundred seed producers in the western United States. Its members produce 130 registered proprietary varieties currently in world-wide commerce in alfalfa, ladino clover, red clover, Sudan grass, safflower, teff grass, and dichondra seeds. According to its President/CEO Paul Frey, Cal/West Seeds has an unwavering dedication to develop new high value varieties that deliver leading edge technologies to the seed industry.

The West Salem facility is the first private alfalfa breeding program to develop its own forage biotech laboratory. This location's research and development focus is on dormant alfalfa, ladino clover, and red clover. Dr. David Johnson is the plant breeder in charge of the facility, and he was appointed by Secretary of Agriculture Tom Vilsack to serve on the USDA Advisory Committee on Biotechnology & 21st Century Agriculture. We spoke with him when we visited Cal/West in June of 2009. According to Dr. Johnson successful plant breeding is both science and an art. Production yield is the first priority and quality the second. Each year 500,000 plants generated in their crossing program are screened for resistance to various diseases, insects, and nematodes culling to 10,000 to produce breeder seed of forty to fifty new varieties, and 20,000 are transplanted to the field for further research. At the end of three years only one per cent is selected to be used in the crossing program.

Dr. Johnson is concerned about the Wisconsin Agricultural Extension Service emphasis on pre-bud stage harvesting of alfalfa starting as early as May 20th in Wisconsin. This vegetative stage is high in protein and digestibility, but lower in yield. Fiber is missing causing the rations to be too hot. The up-to-five cuttings in Wisconsin must be haylage, as it cannot be dried properly for baling and thus competes with corn silage. The cows may burn out faster and need to be replaced sooner. The genetic base is concentrated into the dairy strains that can produce a phenomenal amount of milk.

Some farmers have used wheat straw to stimulate the cows rumen with fiber in order to maintain proper milk quality. Cal/West Seeds now experiments with what Dr. Johnson calls "relaxed cut" or three cuttings up to "aggressive cut" or five cuttings. The aggressive cut causes more soil compaction and lower total yield. The resulting stress requires an earlier crop rotation than from three cuttings. Three cuttings are criticized for lodging tendencies which Cal/West Seeds is eliminating through use of acquired European varieties. Dr. Johnson believes that fiber must be added back to alfalfa by returning to harvesting at the ten per cent bud stage. This is a more natural feed than using wheat straw as an ingredient, and more milk production per acre is the result. Most of today's farmers do not measure profits per acre believing they can only produce a profit with high cost-intensive milk production.

•　•　•

The original Hoard's dairy farm was called Prospect Farm. It has been designated by the United States Department of the Interior to be on the National Register of Historic Places. On November 1, 1887, William Dempster Hoard purchased the first registered Guernsey in Jefferson County. The name of the animal was Bonnibel, the 1168th Guernsey in the Guernsey registry. Hoard's Dairyman staff believe that W. D. Hoard more than likely kept Bonnibel at his residence in Fort Atkinson. At that time his property took up nearly a city block. He owned a large home and would have had horse stables. The stable-barn would have housed the Guernsey cattle until 1899 when he purchased his farm. Today this herd is the oldest continuously registered Guernsey herd in the United Sates with over 300 cows on a land base of 550 acres. Sand-bedded free stall housing and a milking center were established in 2007. The cows are milked three times daily averaging over 19,500 pounds of milk each on a rolling annualized basis.

The registered Guernsey herd was expanded in 2007 and 2008 with 150 registered Guernsey animals purchased throughout the United States.

51

This was to fill the new sand-bedded free stall housing barn. In the fall of 2009 the Hoard's Dairyman Farm was milking 265 cows with a total of 330 cows on test. The adjustments to the expansion and a recovering milk price put the farm in a position for further expansion of the dairy herd. However, the inability to find an adequate number of affordable Guernsey animals that met their health and other requirements brought about the decision to expand through the inclusion of another breed. Hoard's farm managers also felt the Guernsey was a challenge to get bred compared to other breeds as well as being more susceptible to metabolic and infectious diseases.

Torkelson Cheese is their milk buyer making mostly Muenster and Mexican-style cheese, both of which require higher milk solids. This prompted Hoard's decision to purchase forty Jersey cows rather than Holsteins. These are the first animals in the herd since November 1877 that are not registered Guernseys. The Jerseys are housed in the old tie stall barn now converted to free stalls. The two breeds of cows are thus kept separate, but use the same milking parlor. The editorial in the November 2009 issue of *Hoard's Dairyman* states: "Guernseys continue to be an important part of our long range plans for now. In fact, we just purchased another ten Guernsey cows. We will watch energy-corrected milk production efficiency closely for all cows as well as preg[nancy] rates, vet costs, and other factors in an effort to make a careful decision about the best cows for our business."

By using artificial insemination starting as early as 1940, the Hoard's Dairyman Farm dairy herd was probably the first in the world to be cleared of trichomoniasis – a venereal disease of cattle infected with the small single-celled motile protozoan *Trichomonas fetus* which causes abortions of fetuses just a few weeks into pregnancy, as well as delayed conception leading to full term calves. Neither the carrier bull nor the infected cow shows any outward symptoms of infection. The continued use of their farm as a scientific proving ground, as well as relying upon experienced opinion and university research, has garnered confidence and trust in *Hoard's Dairyman* throughout the world. Today the magazine explores international dairy farming and dairy economics, and is the most respected farm magazine of any kind in the world.

Hoard was encouraged by others in his family to launch a national publication devoted to the dairy industry. They initially published *Hoard's Dairyman* as part of the *Jefferson County Union*. It was so well accepted with its use of expert input that its prestige and influence helped create the stand-alone publication with its first edition on January 23, 1885. In downtown Fort Atkinson you can still find the weekly newspaper office and *Hoard's Dairyman* editorial staff in the same building. By 1914 *Hoard's Dairyman* so permeated the dairy state that the *West Salem Non-Pareil Journal* offered an annual subscription for its newspaper for a dollar or *Hoard's Dairyman* for a dollar. If you bought both it was $1.75. West Salem is over 150 miles from Fort Atkinson.

Hoard's Dairyman has a circulation in the United States of around 75,000 and Canadian circulation of approximately 5000. The magazine has subscribers in over sixty countries and is also published in Japanese and Spanish. Over one hundred employees work at Hoard's home office in Fort Atkinson. Continuing from its legacy, the magazine remains focused on scientific information about challenges facing its dairy audience. Researchers, educators, veterinarians, consultants, farm finance experts, and other national or international experts make up to two-thirds of the authors in each issue. All of the magazine's excellent editorial staff were raised on dairy farms and are actively involved in the activities and management on the Hoard's Dairyman Registered Guernsey dairy farm. *Hoard's Dairyman* editors have made major stands on orderly milk marketing, member-owned dairy co-operatives, animal disease control, promotion of dairy products, and animal improvement programs. They consistently have articles helping dairy farmers better understand their economic environment and how to meet its challenges. *Hoard's*

Dairyman publishes twenty issues annually including a monthly insert for dairy producers in the western United States. There are special publications throughout the year as well as a website (www.hoards.com) with dairy industry news and market information.

W. D. Hoard considered citizenship to be the essence of American freedom. He equated the farmer as the most important class in American society, citing Washington, Adams, Jefferson, Madison, Monroe, and Jackson as farmers. He noted that Webster, Clay, Lincoln, Grant, Garfield, and Sherman also came from the soil. Hoard challenged anyone who did not believe that farming was equal to or superior mentally to any of the arts or sciences. He had the profoundest contempt for those who felt farmers needed only a scant amount of brains. If W. D. Hoard could see his publication today and the mental requirements for dairying he would be even more impressed by the intellectual challenges met by today's dairymen.

W. D. Hoard was also deeply involved in Republican politics. He was a delegate to the Chicago convention in 1880. He was elected Governor of Wisconsin in 1888. Hoard believed education was a necessity and should be taught in the English language used in the United States. He supported the Bennett Law created in Wisconsin requiring all youth between the ages of seven and fourteen to be in school using the English language. The Lutheran and Catholic clergy and the German populace were so angry after passage of this law that Hoard was never re-elected Governor. The clergy eventually realized their wrong-headedness and urged him with their support to run again for Governor or the United States Senate. A much older man at the time, he preferred publishing and declined.

Hoard's continual vocal support for education of youth was recognized. He was appointed to the Board of Regents of the University of Wisconsin in 1907 and then served as President from 1908 to 1911. A bust of Governor Hoard is prominently displayed in front of Agriculture Hall at the University of Wisconsin-Madison.

W. D. Hoard severely criticized farmers for not educating themselves and enhancing their knowledge through any means possible, claiming it had a dramatic effect on their prosperity. He spent his life trying to help others help themselves, and this commitment resulted in constant demand for him as a speaker and spokesman for the dairy cow. Hoard remarked that the dairy cow is the foster mother of the human race and as a mother is "entitled to the consideration that maternity deserves."

In the 1890s Governor Hoard was a familiar fixture at Canadian dairy conventions. When he was unable to speak at the Dairymen's Association of Canada, the convention was described as a tame event by Toronto's *Canadian Farmer*. "His fund of information, his high ideals of service, his eloquence, and his rare gift of being able to interpret a crucial point by an apt story, held his audience as few speakers are able to do. There was never a vacant seat when Hoard spoke. People in other callings as well as dairymen and farmers, would flock to the convention halls to hear him. He was a strong advocate of better farming and better dairying and perhaps more than any other speaker at those early gatherings he was responsible for the advancement this country made in progressive dairying."

After Governor Hoard passed away on November 22, 1918, there were many articles praising his contributions to humanity and to the dairy cow. The above quote from the *Canadian Farmer* is a partial example of the respect accorded him. He was lauded in publications throughout the entire United States, from New York State and City, Philadelphia, the Midwest, even Los Angeles and San Francisco. Excerpts from a sampling of these comments that best illustrate Governor Hoard follow:

> When Governor Hoard founded the publication that bears his name, the farmers of the state of Wisconsin were on the verge of exhausting the fertility of their soil by continuous wheat grazing, as was the custom in those days. He steered them by means of his dairy publication from the plow, wisely,

to the cow, thereby saving both the state and the farmers from immense losses that were staring them in the face....

The transition from wheat growers to butter and cheese makers carried with it the restoration of the crop yielding ability of the farms and the prosperity of the farmers, and by this act made Wisconsin the leading dairy state of the United States....

He often made the remark that there could be no permanent agriculture without livestock and especially dairy livestock which, together with feeds grown for best development and maintenance, such as alfalfa and clover were also permanent factors in the building and the permanent maintenance of the soil....

Governor Hoard loved cows, talked and wrote about cows, and defended them. He bred and raised cows, he manufactured their milk into dairy products, and he labored indefatigably to the end that their product might reach into every home through a progressing and flourishing dairy industry....

The point we would like to make is that this man, raised under humble conditions, self-taught to study and think, made himself a master in his line through loyalty to a great idea and faith in the intelligence and higher feeling of the plain common people.....

Governor Hoard was a leader of men. His vision was broad comprehensive and clear. He was a great student of nature, possessed unusual powers of reasoning, and arrived at definite, conclusive results.

Let us conclude with the remarks of George William Rankin in his *The Life of William Dempster Hoard* written in 1925:

The race of men who lived contemporary with William Dempster Hoard recognized in him the idealist, the master mind, the true American, who, by the virtue of his vision, his intellect, his fidelity of purpose, and his power of leadership, elevated every standard of our national life.

And so God gave us this rare soul as our leader and our exemplar. We shall not look upon his like again, but millions of beings gestating in the future, will steer their course aright by the beacon of knowledge that he kindled. He demonstrated that the result of yesterday's battle never arose to defeat today's, if yesterday's battle was righteous.

William Dempster Hoard, the father of modern dairy farming, single handedly altered the course of American and international dairying practices. In the next chapter we will examine how his visions influenced Wisconsin agriculture.

Chapter Six:

Wisconsin Guernsey Pioneers

The first recorded transfer of a Guernsey into Wisconsin was in March 1881. The cattle were brought by train from Massachusetts to Harvard, Illinois, at which point they were led a distance of perhaps 20 miles across the frozen ice of Lake Geneva to their owner, N. K. Fairbank, a prominent Chicago meat packer. The farm's manager, Mr. W. H. Lawrence, began weighing each cow's productivity in 1883 and in 1892 used the churn butter test on each cow to determine the butterfat produced. In 1893 Mr. Fairbank exhibited his registered Guernsey cow named Materna, registry number 11334, at the Columbian World's Exposition in Chicago, where she won both the 90 day test and came in first place in the show ring. The herd was dispersed in 1903, and W. D. Hoard was one of the purchasers. The hand-written records of the Fairbank herd are archived at the Wisconsin College of Agriculture Library.

At the Wisconsin State Historical Society in Madison are 155 letter books of W. D. Hoard's correspondence.

Other memorable Wisconsin firsts included the making of the first Wisconsin cheese in 1840 in Jefferson County by a Mrs. Pickett and her fourteen year old son, whose cows were brought in from Ohio. The first Guernsey was shown at the Wisconsin State Fair in 1886 by Mr. I. J. Clapp of Kenosha. There was no competition.

Filled cheese was a product in which four pounds of lard or sometimes even tallow was added to a hundred pounds of milk as a substitute for insufficient butterfat needed to produce cheese. Such a practice was widely used in 1890 in Wisconsin. Canada had a strict law prohibiting this process and took away Wisconsin's overseas market in England. W. D. Hoard worried about Wisconsin legislation which would legitimatize such adulteration. Since most Wisconsin cheese was consumed outside the state such adulteration could have had a devastating effect on the new industry. Hoard said people wanted "honest cheese."

In 1895 Wisconsin's legislature banned the addition of any color to oleomargarine as well as the manufacture and sale of filled cheese, and required labeling of cheese made from skim milk. Oleomargarine was first developed by a Parisian chemist, Hippolyte MegeMouries in 1867. It was patented in the United States in 1873 and by 1880 there were fifteen U.S. factories producing it.

The first Guernsey Breeder's Association was organized in 1900 at the Wisconsin Dairyman's Association convention in Watertown. It was called the Western Guernsey Breeders Association as it was comprised of members from several Midwest states. In 1921 it became an association of Illinois and Wisconsin breeders, and then in 1925 it became an organization solely for Wisconsin Guernsey breeders.

The Wisconsin Dairyman's Association held its 38th annual meeting in West Salem, Wisconsin, on February 9th and 10th, 1910. The report by A. J. Glover, the second editor of *Hoard's Dairyman,* included this excerpt:

The dairy farmers of Wisconsin are beginning to appreciate the power of the mind which above everything else brings success. Too many farmers are deficient in clear, comprehensive thinking. In the past farmers have not been good readers or thinkers. They are reading now, I am glad to say, and they are thinking hard and have solved, during the past twenty years, many of the problems that have confronted the dairyman.

I can remember when we knew little about the dairy cow, her breeding, the product she produced, and the growing of the proper crops for her feeding. We knew practically nothing of the analysis of milk and of feeds; farmers were feeding almost anything and everything they grew. They were feeding rations of corn meal and timothy hay and expected to get milk in large quantities, composed very largely of elements not contained in corn or timothy hay to any extent. It was almost like putting wheat in a threshing machine and expecting oats at the other end. The farmer began to learn of the breeding and feeding of animals and began to see the difference in the form of animals. They realized that the beef and the dairy cow not only did not resemble each other in conformation, but each of these animals was created for a distinct purpose. The dairy animal had no place to put high priced beef because she had the wrong conformation. The farmer came to realize the dairy cow was a manufacturer internally of milk from her feed. The dairy cow needed large nostrils, a large heart, and large lungs, large digestive capacity, and a large udder. She must inhale large quantities of pure wholesome air. That led to the subject of better ventilation of our barns, and purer and healthier conditions. We came to learn that the cow must have a strong heart and big lungs, because we soon determined when we began to look inside of this dairy cow, that the milk was elaborated directly from the blood; that the blood passes from the lungs to the udder and back through the so called milk veins to the heart and lungs, and the lungs must be able to purify the blood as it passed through them.

At this 38th annual meeting, it was brought to the attention of those assembled that W. D. Hoard was not present. The Wisconsin Dairymen's Association was very much a part of Hoard's life and passion, and hanging at the front of the meeting room was a picture of the former Wisconsin Governor. The association forwarded the following to him: "The Wisconsin Dairymen's Association, in convention assembled, sends heartiest congratulations to Governor and Mrs. W. D. Hoard upon this fiftieth anniversary of their marriage. We today wish to express our growing appreciation of those years of usefulness and the indelible imprint of that splendid record has left upon two generations making the name of Hoard the most widely known in the state, and always an inspiration to broader and better citizenship."

The Wisconsin Dairymen's Association believed that their state possessed all the ideal requirements for the production of milk: climate, an environment for luxurious grasses and legumes, and energetic and intelligent farmers. They believed more milk and less meat was by far healthier.

At this 38th meeting in West Salem, the Dairymen's Ten Commandments were officially decreed:

1. Thou shalt call each cow by name, in a gentle and loving manner, for the Boss will not hold him guiltless that taketh her name in vain.
2. Remember the Sabbath Day, and do only such work as seemth necessary.
3. Six days thou shalt labor and do all thy chores, but the seventh day is Sunday, and the cleaning of stables and all unnecessary work should be dropped, so that thy son and thy daughter, thy man servant and thy maid-servant may attend church.
4. Honor and respect thy Kingly sire, that thy days may be long upon the land which the Lord thy God giveth thee.
5. Thou shalt not swear.

6. Thou shalt not scold.

7. Thou shalt not curry thy cattle with the milking stool.

8. Thou shalt look well to the comforts of thy cattle.

9. Thou shalt not bear false witness against thy neighbor's herd, for verily it heapeth coals of fire on thine own head.

10. Covet not thine neighbor's herd, for verily thou hast made thy selection and verily thou shalt prosper if thou stay by thy choice.

• • •

In the mid 1950s when my father made himself a chute for channeling straw from the threshing machine blower into the mouth of the baler to instantly bale straw, I thought it the height of ingenuity. Straw was no longer wasted but was available for immediate storage, and the dirty job of later removing straw from a stack was eliminated. Farmers in the dairy industry have, by necessity, been the generators of ideas and thought unequaled on a regular, steady, consistent basis by anyone.

There can be no accomplishment or establishment created and enduring that has not been shaped by many hands working both separately and cooperatively. Such is true with the establishment of the Guernsey breed of dairy cow in the United States. For a thorough synopsis of the many pioneers throughout the country no better source can be recommended than *The Guernsey Breed* edited and compiled by C. B. Harding in the year 2000.

One early pioneer was Charles L. Hill (1869-1957), a prominent Guernsey breeder and historian from Rosendale, Wisconsin. After 1888 he devoted much of his working life to the importation of Guernsey cattle. He became a member of the Executive Committee of the American Guernsey Cattle Club in 1896, and he was President between 1912 and 1914. He is the author of *The Guernsey Breed* (1917) and *The History of Wisconsin Guernseys* (1948). These books provide detailed data on the very earliest importations and the establishment of the breed in the United States. Hill was very active with his own Guernsey herd. His oral recordings on dairying are archived in the Wisconsin State Historical Society in Madison.

I had always been aware that the West Salem Guernsey Sales Pavilion was the largest of its kind in the United States and that more Guernsey cattle were sold and shipped to and from West Salem in the early to mid 1900's than any other place in the nation. As a young man I spent a lot of time at this Guernsey Pavilion as Father had been in charge of sales for decades. Years later I wrote an article for the West Salem Historical Society newsletter about the sights and smells of the Guernsey Pavilion at sales time. The article was so well received I was encouraged to proceed further. The idea was rather appealing, and I was much surprised when initial inquiries turned up two extraordinary Guernsey pioneers from West Salem.

Attorney Harry Griswold of West Salem told of his Great Grandfather claiming you could make a wonderful living with one silo and forty acres. Great Grandfather Henry Daniel Griswold and his sons Harry and Clinton were prominent in local, state and national Guernsey circles. An invaluable archive Attorney Griswold offered me was the perusal of numerous daily cash books of Henry Griswold beginning January 1, 1877, when he began farming, until his health failed him in 1933. Not only did they represent fifty-six years of continuous daily financial entries, but they also held a cornucopia of information from being a beginning farmer, to creating a solid enterprise, through retirement.

The other surprise was the discovery of a book entitled *Queen Vashti* by Adoniram Judson Phillips. This is the biography of a registered Guernsey cow of prominence by the name of Queen Vashti paired with the philosophy of the author. A. J. Phillips was a West Salem entrepreneur who developed his own strains of cold-hardy apples and was the first serious producer of registered Guernsey cattle in La Crosse County.

Adoniram J. Phillips and Henry D. Griswold lived during the same time frame and environment, and like W. D. Hoard they both came from the farm environment of the eastern United States. Phillips hailed from Pennsylvania and Griswold from Connecticut. Each man was highly educated for that period and enjoyed writing and reading poetry. They were hired by the Institutes of Agriculture in Wisconsin and Minnesota to travel throughout those states teaching farmers, based on their knowledge and experience. The Institutes were sponsored by the major universities of those states prior to the creation of the farm extension service. Both men were charter members of the Wisconsin Guernsey Breeders in 1900, whose twenty-six charter members also included W. D. Hoard and Charles L. Hill. H. D. Griswold and A. J. Phillips were charter members of the La Crosse County Guernsey Breeders in 1907.

Our second and third pioneers are the spirit and foundation that made their community a special part of the American Guernsey experience.

Chapter Seven:

Adoniram Judson Phillips

"But who shall speak for those whose mouths are dumb! To poor brave brutes, with patient eyes, and feet that go and come to do our bidding, toiling on withoutaward or fee; wearing their very lives away, poor things, for you and me."

– A. J. Phillips

The educator best known for his propagation of cold-hardy apples, and who furthered the popularity of the registered Guernsey into the Midwest, was born October 17, 1833, in Chester County, Pennsylvania. A. J. Phillips was the son of a Baptist Minister, and both of his grandfathers fought in the Revolutionary War. He moved to Watertown, Wisconsin in 1849 and in 1855 settled in Big Creek near Sparta. His wife, Avis Buttles

Phillips, was born December 20, 1841, in New York State, and when she was seven her family travelled west to East Troy, Wisconsin. A. J. and Avis married December 12, 1861, and shortly thereafter made their home in West Salem. They had been married fifty-six years when he passed away in 1917. She died in 1932 having lived for seventy years in West Salem. The best apple A. J. Phillips ever propagated was named Avista after his wife.

Mr. and Mrs. Phillips had six children all of whom succeeded in careers away from the home farmstead. The two oldest, girls named Mamie and Lulu, both taught school for seven years and then married farmers. Mark worked as a mail carrier between Chicago and Minneapolis. George became a railroad contractor in Indiana and Will a dentist in La Crosse. Charles attended Agriculture College and ran the Mindoro Creamery.

This cooperative creamery is the oldest in continuous operation in Wisconsin and still produces blue and Gorgonzola cheeses. To get the Mindoro Creamery butter to the West Salem railroad, it was ultimately decided that the best route would entail cutting through the uppermost point of Phillips Ridge. The cut was begun in 1907 using only hand tools and wheelbarrows – the terrain was too steep for horses and mules. The ridge was assumed to be composed primarily of relatively soft, manageable sandstone, but a deep underlying layer of hard Ordovician dolomite rock was exposed. Thus the efforts in 1907 and 1908 required some dynamiting. Once completed, the cut measured 74 feet deep, 25 feet wide, and 86 feet long. Fourteen thousand cubic feet of rock and other debris were taken by wheelbarrows over rough uneven planks down the hill. The task was so demanding that many a man took only one trip down before walking off the job for good. If he managed to persevere long enough to tip over his load three times, he was fired! The final cost to the taxpayers of La Crosse County was $11,241.29. After completion the cut became a spot for community gatherings and picnics. Its picturesque setting has since garnered tourists from the throughout the United States.

Mindoro Cut being excavated from Farmington Township side

Today travel from West Salem on Highway 16 past Lake Neshonoc then north on highway 108 for four miles, at which point the curving road begins to meander sharply uphill for another mile through ever-increasingly high hills. Suddenly you come upon Mindoro Cut, now considered to be the largest hand-hewn cut through a hill for a road in the United States. The Cut was placed on the Wisconsin Register of Historic Places in time for its centennial celebration in 2007 and is now on the National Historic Register. A plaque explaining its significance has been erected at the site.

We spent much time in the Register of Deeds office in La Crosse in hopes of identifying the exact location of Phillip's apple and dairy farm and were surprised to find the name A. J. Phillips referenced all over several plat maps. He purchased numerous acreages throughout the northern portions of the township of Hamilton and several lots in the Leonard Addition of West Salem. Here it was noted that he also served as legal representative on several mortgages. Going toward the town of Mindoro from West Salem, at a sharp angle to the right of Mindoro Cut runs a road which rises steeply uphill for 400 to 500 feet leading to a farm on the top which is surprisingly level for all that height. In modern times this road was named McClintock Road. It was on these heights that A. J. Phillips propagated his 1000 apple trees, and Queen Vashti and the other registered Guernsey cattle had their home. This precise location for the Phillips farm we assume to be correct. Mr. Phillips said his farm was the highest place in La Crosse County, and a thorough study of old plat maps and knowledge of the entire locale makes this site the only reasonable location. He named his homestead Phillips Ridge. He purchased the land from Joseph Ariel on November 1, 1870. He sold it November 21, 1878, to M. L. Tourtellotte, and on December 20 of the same year he rented the farm back from him.

Mr. Tourtellotte, along with Oscar F. Elwell and Thomas Leonard, laid out the original plat of the Village of West Salem in 1858. In that year the Chicago, Milwaukee, & St. Paul railroad was built through the Town of Hamilton. Leonard donated to the railroad ten acres of land lying east and northeast of a spot where he wanted them to erect a depot. A twenty-acre plat, surveyed by H. I. Bliss of La Crosse, became known as "Leonard's Addition," the foundation for what was to become West Salem. The grid-like streets included Main, Franklin, Hamilton, and Jefferson intersected by Melville, Church, Leonard, and Mill. The first frame building in the village was a general mercantile store built by Frank Burgett in 1857. The first hotel was built that same year on the corner of Main and Leonard streets by Thomas Dutcher. The first saloon started by John Hommell was also on the corner of those streets. Dr. William Stanley became the village's first physician, arriving in June of 1858. The first drug store was started by A. K. Viets in 1863. The Post Office was established in 1860 with Edward Walker appointed Postmaster. Byron A. Viets succeeded him in 1861 followed by William Van Zandt in 1863. In 1863 Wisconsin Governor J.M. Rusk appointed Phillips to be Postmaster and he remained in that position until 1878. Phillips sold the first money order to Simeon Mahlum August 8, 1871, the payee being Thompson & Co. of Beloit, Wisconsin. The total number of money orders from the West Salem post office was 10,444 from that first sale until 1881. The population growth of the village was slow and sporadic, but had nearly 300 people by 1881. The railroad which was instrumental in establishing the village in 1858 was vital to the prosperity of the new community. Between October 1, 1880, and April 1, 1881, 125 railroad cars of livestock originated from West Salem. On the last Tuesday of March 1889 the Wisconsin State Senate formally declared West Salem to be a municipal corporation. The West Salem Centennial in 1951 and the 150th Anniversary celebration in 2001 were based solely on a house built by Thomas Leonard on the site where a high school was later built in 1917. This first dwelling was built seven years before the original plat and thirty-eight years prior to West Salem's legal founding!

A. J. Phillips was a charter member and Secretary of the Wisconsin State Horticultural Society. In an article for the 1894 *Wisconsin Agriculturist* entitled "Wisconsin as a Fruit State," he advocated apple growing in Wisconsin as more profitable than growing fruit in southern or western states. He said: "It takes more investigating and greater care in selecting to secure varieties for central and northern Wisconsin than it does in more favorable locations.... We have varieties that have withstood the test in 35 degrees to 45 degrees below zero. We feel confident in planting and recommending the same to others similarly located." In a paper and address presented to the Wisconsin Horticulture Society for the summer and winter of 1882 and 1883, Mr. Phillips reported on prospects for the season's fruit crop. He mentioned that he lived on a bluff 400 to 500 feet above the valley below, his soil being clay with hard subsoil. He stated that while there was frost on the hill, his fruit was not injured by it. He said there was an eight to eleven degree warmer temperature on the bluff than in the valley below.

A survey of internet entries for A.J. Phillips shows him mainly remembered today as a horticulturist and apple progenitor *par excellence*. As Secretary of the Wisconsin State Horticulture Society, he not only kept records of all meetings and proceedings but countersigned all deeds, leases and conveyances. He presented many lectures and participated in discussions over the years on cold-climate apple propagation at very elevated heights, particularly of interest to Minnesota growers. His father had experimented with apple seedlings in the mid 1800's, and A.J. claimed that the Wealthy apple tree produced the best fence posts! He enjoyed feeding apples to his registered Guernsey cattle. According to Phillips: "Planting an orchard is like writing your autobiography and going around the country telling people how to breed good dairy cows is working for posterity."

Joseph Moran, a native of New York, came to West Salem in the 1860's to give his sons a better chance in the world. He bought a farm to raise apples. After hearing they could not be grown in Wisconsin, he prepared to move until he heard of a successful nursery in Springville, Vernon County. Having no transportation other than his own legs, he walked thirty-two miles to Springville, purchased one hundred apple trees of which eighty were one year old, and returned home with the trees strapped to his back, starting out the very next morning after he had arrived. Those trees produced an abundance of apples for him and his family. Around 1890 Moran found an apple seedling sixty rods away from his orchard and from any other apple tree. He built a fence around it to protect the new to-be tree. Eight years later this tree provided Moran, now over eighty years old, and his three little grandchildren ample fruit to eat. His friend A. J. Phillips exhibited apples from this seedling tree at the annual meeting of the Minnesota Horticulture Society for four years.

In West Salem, Phillips was a neighbor of Phil McConnell. Together they imported the first registered Guernsey in La Crosse County, Cadet, whose registry number was 1740. She was purchased April 10, 1888 from Mr. Gordon of Koskonong, Wisconsin.

The first registered Guernsey imported into Monroe County, contiguous to the east of La Crosse County, was Yeksa, registry number 2426. She was the mother of Queen Vashti. Yeksa was purchased by F. M. Foster of Sparta on April 16, 1886, as a young calf for $150.

The sire of Queen Vashti was Puck, number 1257. Sir Champion, registry number 16, was the sire of both Puck and Yeksa. Queen Vashti's grandfather on both the paternal and maternal side was the same. When Governor Hoard saw Yeksa and Puck at the Monroe County fair he predicted that they and their ancestors would fix a type and individuality that would make a mark in the Guernsey world. Yeksa's productivity as a two year old convinced the Fosters that the Guernsey was the breed of the future.

A. J. PHILIPS

Owner of Queen Vashti for twelve years.

Queen Vashti was born the last part of July, 1889 near Sparta, Wisconsin at Riverside Farm owned by A. T. Foster and his wife Henrietta. All of the Foster calves were fed warm milk almost every day until they were a year old, as the Fosters believed it was beneficial to good health and growth. They believed in being with their animals as much as possible and treated them with kindness. Henrietta Foster was a woman who understood dairy husbandry to the very depths of her being. Although confined to a wheelchair she made many trips to the barn to be with the animals she loved. When dairy animals were raised by others, especially by those who were negligent or cruel, the altered disposition of a single animal could have a negative effect on the rest of the animals in the herd.

There were many, notable and otherwise, who praised Henrietta Foster. Mr. I. J. Clapp said that Mrs. Foster's great foresight and intelligent work in breeding and writing for farm journals had done more for the Guernsey breed than any advertising could have done. Reverend C. L. McKee of West Salem, Wisconsin said she belonged to a class of breeder who went beyond the ordinary and had intellect and discernment sufficient to fix a type in the mind and devise it from the selected individual. She could ignore accepted standards and go beyond them. She wrote under the pen name "A Farmer's Wife" for the Minneapolis publication *Farm, Stock, and Home*. For several years she wrote for *Hoard's Dairyman* under the editor W. D. Hoard. Hoard said she had a remarkable and ready faculty of expressing her thoughts; that her thought instinctively took the place around the center purpose like iron filings around a magnet. He appreciated her efforts on behalf of *Hoard's Dairyman*.

Mrs. Foster had to seek the dry climate of Oklahoma because of her health; the Fosters initially rented out their farm, including their livestock. During the next year, Yeksa died from weed poisoning and Queen Vashti's first calf was killed by wild dogs. These negligent, preventable circumstances convinced the Fosters to sell their farm. The Fosters were well aware of Phillip's reputation as a prize-winning apple grower, and they believed he would provide an excellent home for Queen Vashti and her sire Puck. Phillips had heard Governor Hoard praise the Yeksa family at the Monroe County fair and expressed an interest. At first Phillips refused Puck, preferring a cheaper yearling bull, but Mr. Foster convinced him that a properly cared for four-to-ten year old bull of Puck's genetic quality was preferable to that of a cheaper young bull. A. J. Phillips purchased Puck and Queen Vashti from them and owned her for twelve years. Phillips eventually wrote a book entitled *Queen Vashti* and dedicated it to "Mrs. Henrietta

T. Foster of Tecumseh, Oklahoma, to whose good advice, genius, and ability in fixing types in animals, I am indebted for my success in handling animals."

Henrietta Foster worked tirelessly for Oklahoma's moral and humane education law. She and Leslie B. Niblack of Guthrie enacted that law through the Legislative Assembly of the Territory of Oklahoma on March 4, 1905, which required every teacher, under penalty of not receiving pay for services, to teach morality in its broadest sense for the purpose of elevating and refining the character of school children up to the highest plane of life. Not less than one-half hour per week was to be devoted to the humane treatment of animals and birds. No experiments upon any living creature were to be carried out in the schools of the Territory of Oklahoma. All prior laws in conflict with this act were repealed.

A circular by Mrs. Foster included the following: "Educating the head alone will not lessen crime. The most harmful criminals are those whose heads have been highly educated. Educating the heart refines and elevates the soul. The public school is the factory of good citizenship. It is a fruitless effort reforming men and women who may pass their bad attitudes and conduct unto future generations. It is impossible to teach old dogs new tricks."

Queen Vashti was written as if told by the Queen herself, and chronicled both her life and the life and philosophy of A. J. Phillips, guardian and protector of "dumb" animals who could not speak for themselves. It presented a backdrop of the environment and the livelihood of farmers in the closing years of the 19th and on into the new century. No copyright or publishing date was provided in *Queen Vashti*. However, the last dates mentioned in the text were for Rigolette going on official test January 1, 1906, with her production to August 1, 1906. From this and scattered other bits it seems safe to say the book was published near the end of 1906 or in 1907.

QUEEN VASHTI 6051.
Dam of Salems King, Yeksa's Queen, Queen Deelte and Suffiency at 12 years of age.

Phillips said his book *Queen Vashti* was created so that every chapter would be helpful to the youth of the United States of America with the hope of making the world better and happier. The foundations of the book were kindness and truth. Phillips believed nothing was substantial and permanent without truth, and its success was molded by daily efforts of speaking truth with ones neighbor. His beliefs: "any day is lost when the descending sun views no kindly action done, speak gently, let no harsh words mar the good that may be done." All of the chapters of *Queen Vashti* begin with a poem. Here is the poem which begins Chapter 26, page 284:

> Truth crushed to earth shall rise again;
> The eternal years of god are hers;
> But Error, wounded, writhes in pain,
> And dies among his worshipers.

This sentiment starts Chapter 29, page 329:

> Give fools their gold and knaves their power,
> Let fortune's bubbles rise and fall;
> Who sows a field or trains a flower,
> Or plants a tree, is more than all.

According to A. J. Phillips, cattle of the Channel Islands (Guernsey, Jersey, and Alderney) had close contact with the human race and were cared for mainly by women. Through this they acquired a high level of refinement and intelligence making them much more responsive to kind treatment, wherein they exhibited a greater appreciation of such treatment. He urged everyone to be kind to all harmless creatures the Creator had made. It was deplorable that the supposed most perfect of God's creatures could be taught to be kind and humane only through appeal to the sense of monetary gain. Cowards are cruel, but the brave love mercy and delight to save. Kindness to dairy animals begat kindness in return. God implanted in all creatures the love of liberty and the freedom to roam at will.

It was commonly accepted in those days that a mother cow should drink the first of her milk as it had a good effect on her system. A cow was not to be milked dry for the first three days after calving, and the extra colostrum milk after the first milking and nursing was fed in a pail to the other calves. On the fourth day after calving the mother was separated from her calf and joined the rest of the milking herd. Phillips' calf-raising program included sucking the mother for three days, followed by ten days of feeding a mixture of skim milk and whole milk, after which time skim milk was mixed with soybean oil until the calf was a year old.

· · ·

Phillips bought the first cream separator in La Crosse County, a Baby De Laval. According to Mrs. Clint Griswold people came from near and far to examine his cream separator. At the Wisconsin State Dairymen's Association meeting Mr. Phillips told of the wide range of 22 points down to 16 on his cream test at the creamery. He had sent a sample to be tested by Professor Henry at the University of Wisconsin, Madison, but it leaked and was unusable. He subsequently told the cream hauler to get another sample to send but was told not to bother as his cream sample was up to 22 points. Governor Hoard stood and said that was the quickest return he had heard of except when a man placed an ad in a paper for a boy to do chores and that night his wife gave birth to twin sons!

Phillips purchased a four year old bull named Vidette, registry number 1874, from H. D. Griswold. The bull was gentle and easy to handle – he stated that Mr. Griswold always handled him carefully, resulting in an easy disposition.

As Phillips' renown grew so did his responsibilities apart from dairying and cultivating apples. Here was a man born in 1833 who came to Wisconsin in 1849, married in 1861, became West Salem postmaster in 1863, purchased an active lumberyard in West Salem in 1868, and was Treasurer of the town of Hamilton in 1868 and Hamilton Town Clerk from 1870 to 1873. J.M. Rusk became America's first Secretary of Agriculture, and he requested Phillips to work with him for a year in the Agriculture Department in Washington D.C. To that end Phillips rented his farm to Ole Berg. While in Washington he visited his old home in Chester County Pennsylvania near Penningtonville (later named Atglen), and there he met S. C. Kent who at that time imported more Guernsey cattle than anyone in America.

In La Crosse, Phillips helped start the Inter-State Fair which included the areas of northeastern Iowa, southeastern Minnesota, and western Wisconsin. At the first Inter-State Fair in 1890 Phillips took in $50 in premium awards from his Guernsey cattle, apples, and horses. That same summer he purchased a registered Guernsey cow from H. D. Griswold named Guilford. Henry Daniel Griswold and A. J. Phillips were very close friends. At the annual County Fair in West Salem on September 2, 1902, Fair Secretary A. J. Phillips displayed the "famous" Guernsey herd of twenty cows belonging to H. D. Griswold which in the prior year had earned over one hundred dollars each for their owner. Phillips said: "This entire herd is the result of straightforward breeding on dairy lines, by a man who is a plain but very intelligent farmer."

At the Minnesota State Fair Phillips received the Herd Premium Award even though there was no competition. Judge Dr. B. M. Wood of Mankato said the Guernsey cattle were so outstanding they deserved the award! The Walworth County Fair in Elkhorn, Wisconsin was the largest county fair in the United States. Phillips showed at this fair as well as at both the Wisconsin and Minnesota state fairs, encompassing nine hundred miles, $400 in premiums, and $200 in expenses. This certainly represented a major commitment in both monetary terms and endurance around 1900.

While attending the Wisconsin Farmers Institute in the spring of 1886, Phillips received a letter from his hometown of West Salem requesting facts needed to organize a creamery association. He brought home the information and helped organize what became the West Salem Co-op Creamery. Although there was competition from another creamery in town as well as from one in the near-by town Barre Mills, the co-op sold over six million pounds of butter between 1890 and 1900. Most of the sales went to Philadelphia, Boston, and New York. At the 29th annual Wisconsin Dairyman's Association meeting held February 13-15, 1901, Mr. Phillips presented a paper entitled "Facts from a Gathered Cream Creamery." The subject of the paper was the West Salem Co-op Creamery. Not only did Phillips report on this, but he provided very detailed financial data on individual profit margins per pound of butter throughout the years. He was asked about how those margins were obtained by ex- governor Hoard, among others.

Over a thirty-five year period A. J. Phillips attended farm meetings in eleven states. The largest crowds were for the North Dakota Agricultural

College's Tri-State Grain Growers' Association held in Fargo. Anywhere from 800 to 1500 farmers from Minnesota and North Dakota attended each session. At the annual January meetings Phillips estimated that fully eighty percent of the attendees wore sheepskin overcoats. For three years he led discussions on fruits and dairy. He introduced the farmers to the Guernsey breed. He would argue that the female in both humans and dairy was the prevalent indicator of future generations. An authority on breeding usually gave a counter argument in favor of the male influence!

J. J. Hill of Minneapolis, president of the Great Northern Railway and a close friend of Phillips, imported over eight hundred bulls of dairy and beef breeds from Scotland and northern England, many costing as much as $300 each. He gave away these animals to farmers along his rail lines in Minnesota and North Dakota with instructions on farming practices and self-reliance. He also provided these farmers with purebred hogs to improve their swine herd inheritance traits.

Every dairyman has an animal philosophy and method that differs some-what from that of every other dairy farmer. A. J. Phillips believed strong lung capacity and good constitutions for dairy cows were created by good care including growing and pasturing on hilly land. This caused every mus-cle to be brought into use sometime during the day. Several times in *Queen Vashti* Phillips extolled the virtues of having Guernsey cows on hilly land. He claimed to pasture on the highest hill in La Crosse County.

Queen Deette was a registered Guernsey cow owned by A. J. Phillips. She was the first Guernsey in Wisconsin to get into the "Advanced Registry" of the American Guernsey Cattle Club. Advanced Registry was a special production testing program for only the best animals in the breed that met a minimum standard of milk and butterfat production. The testing was more rigorous than the once a month visit of the milk tester. This daughter of Queen Vashti produced 14,501 pounds of milk and 669 pounds of butterfat in twelve months of official test in 1903. In seven consecutive days from June 1 to June 7, 1903, being milked by her favorite milker John Hanson, and tested by Roy T. Harris, an official tester from the University of Wisconsin College of Agriculture, she produced 413.1 pounds of milk with a butterfat percentage test of 3.92 for 16.2 pounds of butterfat. The daily pounds of milk ranged from 61.2 down to 57. Any Guernsey breeder worth his salt would have been happy with that production in 1963, sixty years later!

Phillips' reputation as a producer of top Guernsey animals did not go unnoticed. Queen Deette's bull calf, registry number 6477, was sold to a breeder named Yeaton in Ilwaco, Washington. Campbell's King, registry number 4951, grandson of Queen Vashti, was sold to the Kansas Agricultural College in Manhattan, Kansas as a sire for "common" cows to study the effects of a good purebred sire. A published report indicated that several of his offspring were excellent heifers.

A.J. Phillips attributed all of his success in dairy farming to his parents, his wife who nurtured their six children, and Governors Hoard and Rusk. Queen Vashti's picture hung next to the pictures of the two Governors in his home. The pure air and drinking water of La Crosse County along with the lung capacity, strong legs and constitution provided by the steep hills, resulted in high quality milk with plenty of solids and butterfat, and longevity and good health of his Guernsey cattle. This, Phillips claimed, was living proof of Queen Vashti's good productive health at the age of seventeen years.

Except for Queen Vashti and two bull calves, Phillips sold his herd to A. H. Sagendorph of Spencer, Massachusetts. He brought Queen Vashti to his home in West Salem near the railroad tracks. Phillips continually emphasized that superior blood lines and plenty of fine treatment were the two basic elements of good production. In 1901 at twelve years of age Queen Vashti, under the ownership and management of A.J. Phillips, had produced over 80,000 pounds of milk, 5000 pounds of butter, and seven offspring. For Phillips, she averaged around 11,500 pounds of milk per lactation.

A.J. Phillips ended his dairy farming with the sale of Queen Vashti for $300 and the bull Primitive for $200. They were also sold to Mr. Sagendorph of Spencer, Massachusetts with virtually all his prized Guernsey herd at the end going to this gentleman. On the first day of the trip east to her new home and barely out of the station in West Salem, Queen Vashti gave birth to Phrosia, No. 14532. Phillips visited Queen Vashti in Massachusetts in February 1906, staying five days and milking her while there.

Queen Vashti was the 174th registered Guernsey to qualify for Advanced Registry completing her record at fourteen years of age. An article in *Hoard's Dairyman* entitled "The Story of a Cow" was about Queen Vashti. Queen Vashti, as you remember, was a daughter of Yeksa. By 1906 more cows of the Yeksa family made large official records than any other family of Guernsey cows in the world! Actually the most cows from *any* cow family qualifying for Advanced Registry came from the Yeksa family. Two animals each produced over 14,000 pounds of milk and 700 pounds of butterfat. One of these became the only cow to produce over 800 pounds of butterfat in Advanced Registry and the first cow in the world to produce over 1000 pounds of butterfat in a single year.

Inbreeding was the success of the Yeksa family, and "blood will tell" was the philosophy of Henrietta Foster and Mr. Phillips. It was believed that if an animal failed to meet high productivity, it was not because of all the Yeksa blood, but because of too much inheritance from blood it ought not to have had.

We close now with another aspect of the life of A. J. Phillips as Justice of the Peace. The partial headline and story from the *West Salem Nonpareil - Journal* dated May 8, 1914, reads:

WALTER JONES COMMITS AWFUL DEED – PULLS GUN ON LOCAL JUSTICE A. J. PHILLIPS FOR REFUSING BAIL AND A FEW MINUTES LATER SHOOTS AND KILLS A MAN AGAINST WHOM HE HOLDS OLD GRUDGE, RUNS AMOK IS SOON OVERPOWERED

One of the most cold blooded murders in the history of the county occurred last Saturday night about eleven o'clock on South Leonard Street near the Cullman Lumber and Supply Company office. Twice before Jones had tried murder that night. Twice he tried to kill Justice of the Peace A. J. Phillips, for a fancied wrong in issuing a warrant for his arrest. Twice the justice saved his life through his knowledge of the mad man's desire.

The village of West Salem was aroused to fever pitch over the revolting details of the killing. Officers found it necessary early Sunday morning to take Jones to La Crosse to save him from the possible vengeance of a mob.

The man was not intoxicated when he fired three shots at his victim. The district attorney has talked with him and is satisfied that he is sane.

The murder victim was William Voeck who had in July 1913 heard screams across the street from his home ran over to find the killers wife savagely beaten. Jones drove Voeck away with a loaded shotgun. After his wife procured an arrest warrant he escaped to La Crosse not to return until the night of the murder.

Chapter Eight:

The Griswold Family

Our third pioneer Henry Daniel Griswold was born on a farm in Guilford, Connecticut March 7, 1853, the eldest of either nine or ten children – records are inconsistent. Guilford was a small town southeast of New Haven and near the shores of Long Island Sound. He graduated from high school at the Guilford Institute and studied for two winter terms at the New York Preparatory School in Claverack.

His father had an excellent reputation as a farmer. A quote from Henry praised his father: "My father was one of the best farmers of his time and I was early taught the habits of industry, economy, and careful thorough work." In April of 1874, Henry's father gave him $100 to start farming in the west in either Wisconsin or Minnesota. Leaving Caroline his betrothed to join him at a later date, he wrote this poem to his family upon his departure:

THE SAILOR BOY'S FAREWELL

Wait, wait ye winds while I repeat
A parting sign on to the fleet,
Whose station is at home.
Waft the sea boys simple prayer,
And let it oft be whispered there,
When in the far lands I roam.

Farewell to Father – revered hulk!
In spite of metal, spite of bulk,
His cable soon may slip.
Yet, while the parting tear is moist,
The flag of gratitude I'll Hoist
In duty to the ship.

Farewell to Mother – first class she!
Who launched us on life's stormy sea,
And rigged us fore and aft!
May providence her timbers spare,
And keep the hull in good repair,
To tow the smaller craft!

Farewell to sister – lovely yacht!
But whether she'll be manned or not
I cannot yet foresee.
May some good ship a tender prove,
Well found in stores of truth and love,
And take her under lee!
Farewell to George – the jolly boat!
And all the little craft afloat
In homes delightful bay,
When the arrive at sailing age,
May wisdom give the weather gauge,
And guide them on their way!

Farewell to all! On to life's rude main,
Perhaps we ne'er shall meet again,
Through stress of stormy weather:
But, summoned by the Board above,
We'll harbor in the port of love,
And all be moored together!

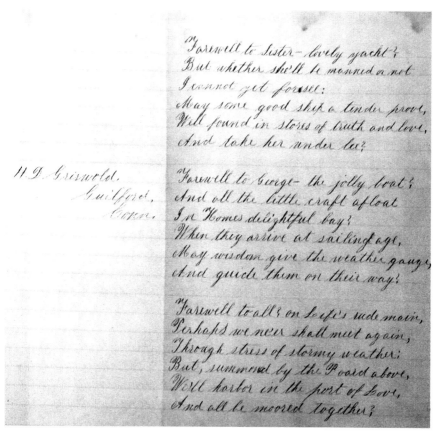

"Farewell to Sister – lovely yacht!
But whether she'll be manned or not
I cannot yet foresee:
May some good ship a tender prove,
Well found in stores of truth and love,
And take her under lee?

H. D. Griswold,
Guilford,
Conn.

"Farewell to George – the jolly boat!
And all the little craft afloat
In Home's delightful bay?
When they arrive at sailing age,
May wisdom give the weather gauge,
And guide them on their way?

"Farewell to all! on Life's rude main,
Perhaps we never shall meet again,
Through stress of stormy weather:
But, summoned by the Board above,
We'll harbor in the port of Love,
And all be moored together?

Original version of The Sailor Boy's Farewell

Henry Daniel Griswold soon found that at the price he could afford, all the desired quality of land in Wisconsin and Minnesota had been taken. He formed a partnership with an individual he met in Wisconsin and they moved to the southeast corner of Dakota Territory near Vermillion. The crops of their first harvest season were devoured by grasshoppers. Years later his grandson, Don Griswold, speculated about Henry's trip to West Salem driving his oxen through Minnesota as being very slow and dispiriting. Henry preferred cheaper oxen to horses as he was experienced with them from his youth in Connecticut. Darkened by defeat he most likely received solace from his early morning Bible reading, which he always did throughout his life.

Henry ended this disastrous episode by settling with the William L. Dudley family in West Salem, Wisconsin. The Dudley and Griswold families had common ancestors, and they came together from England to Connecticut in 1636. Griswold is to this day a very prominent family name in Connecticut. Henry taught school at Oakhurst during the winter, a position that Dudley secured for him, and worked on the Dudley farm in the summer. Years later Henry loved telling stories to his grandson, especially about teaching "mischievous, overgrown" roughnecks at Oakhurst School, but he never mentioned anything about South Dakota or Minnesota. The ox yoke and iron tether stake were stored above the hog house and forgotten. His niece said that awful place in South Dakota seared his soul and complicated his life.

The ox yoke used by Henry Daniel Griswold on his journey out of the Dakota Territory to West Salem. Also shown are the journals he kept starting in 1877.

William Lee Dudley was also a native of Guilford, Connecticut, and he came to Wisconsin in 1855 then to West Salem in 1858, the same year as the railroad. He became a farmer, eventually accumulating 500 acres, part of which is now the present Arne Marking farm as well as land today owned by Maple Grove Country Club. He built a Congregational church and cemetery on his property. He had two sons and two daughters including Jennie born in

1853 and a son named Wilbur. When Wilbur married Marian Bailey, William bought them a farm later known as the Raymond Knutson farm situated a half mile from West Salem.

On November 8, 1877, Henry married Jennie Lee Dudley, William's daughter. He and his wife received a farm of forty acres directly east of Wilbur's as a wedding gift. This land was on the edge of West Salem and is now part of the village with a housing development on it. Henry and Jennie had five children. Mary, the first born died at six months, and their surviving four sons were Robert, Harry, Clinton, and John. Two days after the birth of John their fourth son on April 28, 1891, Jennie died. Always mindful of the forty acre wedding gift, Jennie made Henry promise that he would provide all four sons with a college education. Henry was ahead of his time in the pursuit of knowledge and it is doubtful that he would have done otherwise. Robert and John received engineering degrees from the University of Wisconsin. They settled in New York and New Jersey. Harry and Clinton became successful breeders of registered Guernsey cattle.

William L. Dudley told Henry shortly after Jennie's death that he had better find a wife and mother for his four sons. Henry wrote to his former sweetheart in Connecticut, Caroline Parker. Since Henry had last known her she had become a school teacher. The letter was inadvertently dropped by the mailman in a snow bank and was not discovered until spring by a student. The ink was smeared, but enough of the message survived to be understood. Playing it cool, she advised Henry he could come east to call on her. He obediently accepted her invitation. They were married at the Guilford Congregational Church April 4, 1892. This was eighteen years after Henry first left Connecticut. They had one daughter, Katharine, born September 16, 1894. Katharine became a college teacher and retired in Pikeville, Kentucky.

Henry tried potato farming for the John A. Salzer Company. He soon realized that potato farming could not be depended upon for a decent living. He also found this depleted the fertility of the land. He attended Farmers Institutes and Dairymen conventions before deciding on dairying as a farm profession.

Henry Griswold became known as the "man who kept forty cows on forty acres." He believed that size was not too small for an adequate living and not too big for proper management. Henry said, "Less acres and more intelligent thorough methods is the crying need of the times." H. D. Griswold was progressive in his methods and a teacher to other farmers. Writing on his farm stationery probably in 1909 he pointed out that he was the first in western Wisconsin to use the Babcock butterfat test. He was the first to ventilate his barn using the King system. He was the first to test for tuberculosis. He was one of the first to put up a silo. By using the waste of dairy animals to increase the fertility of his soil he exclaimed that he harvested 200 tons of well-eared mature corn into his silo from only ten acres of land.

Henry Daniel Griswold conducted Farmers Institutes for the University of Wisconsin and the University of Minnesota serving throughout the states from 1907 through 1920. He was President of the Wisconsin Dairymen's Association in 1912 and 1913. He was a member of the Wisconsin State Fair Board from 1914 to 1924. He received plaques and recognition for his contributions to agriculture from the University of Wisconsin and Wisconsin Livestock Breeders Association.

The University of Wisconsin sent a letter to H. Griswold requesting his presence at a ceremony to award him a plaque and give him recognition. Henry jokingly asked the University which H. Griswold did they want?

Harry W. Griswold, born on the family farm on May 19, 1886, was the second son of Henry and Jennie Griswold. He graduated from West Salem High School and the University of Wisconsin Farm Short Course. In the spring of 1906 Harry began working for Henry at the rate of $20 a month, plus room and board, and in 1911 he rented the family farm from his father who had moved to West Salem. He established a milk bottling and distribution center on his farm. He was a charter member of the La Crosse County Guernsey Breeders

Association and served at different times as Secretary-Treasurer and President. He was in charge of the sales committee for the Association. He was also a private promoter of registered Guernsey sales in his own right, partnering with Raymond Knutson and selling throughout the entire United States. In 1914 when the American Guernsey Cattle Club revised its scorecard, he and W.D. Hoard were two of the six members on the committee responsible for that revision.

Harry continued his father's profound commitment to education and community service. He was a member of the West Salem School Board from 1912 to 1929. He served on the Wisconsin Board of Vocational Education from 1930 to 1936. He was a Wisconsin state senator from 1932 to 1936. As a delegate to the Republican State Convention in 1934 he received endorsement from twenty-three counties to become governor. He became a member of The United States House of Representatives January 3, 1939. He remained there until his death on July 4, 1939. Harry had a shortened but illustrious career.

A eulogy from U. S. Senator Alexander Wiley, the Father of the Saint Lawrence Seaway:

> Harry Griswold was honest in thought and deed, a clear and straight thinker. He was a student of government, believing in our system of government. There was nothing demagogic in Harry Griswold. He was not afraid of being with the minority.
>
> Though he was a newcomer to Washington, Mr. Griswold's ability already had him singled out as a legislator of outstanding caliber. His activity on the Rivers and Harbors committee had already met with favorable comment.
>
> His opinion in farm matters was highly regarded in Congress because of his wide experience in farm activities as a member of several livestock breeder's associations and as president of the Guernsey Breeders' Association and the La Crosse county Breeders.
>
> His qualifications as a representative were exceptional. His counsel and friendship were both valued and will be missed by his many friends in Washington and Wisconsin.

The Henry Daniel Griswold Family in later years

Mary Sybil Bailey of Mansfield, Massachusetts had an aunt who was married to Wilbur Dudley, brother-in-law of Henry Griswold. During a summer visit with her aunt she met H. W. Griswold and they decided to marry. Harry and Mary had five daughters and one son Donald, who was born August 6, 1914. Even with the Guernsey dairy legacy, Don Griswold, as he was always known, could not find it in him to continue in his father's and grandfather's footsteps. At the advice of his Uncle Clinton Griswold who served on the draft board from 1940 to 1966, Don enlisted in the army. The officer candidate school class he enrolled in was the same as that of Clark Gable. They passed each other in the hallways but never knew each other. After graduation Don served in photo intelligence in the Aleutian Islands. He was discharged in the summer of 1945 with the rank of Captain in the U. S. Army Air Corp.

In September of 1945 he purchased the *West Salem Nonpareil — Journal* and changed the name to the *West Salem Journal*. His competitor to own the newspaper was "Lefty" Johnson, who before World War II had been the newspaper's printer while Don was a reporter. The surviving wife and daughter of Colonel Glen W. Garlock, the paper's owner and a Lieutenant Colonel in WWI, sold it to Don. Lefty opened a print shop where Don's son Harry had his attorney's office from 1980 until the summer of 2011. Don sold the *West Salem Journal* on July 1, 1971. He purchased the *Sauk Centre Herald* in Minnesota, which he sold upon his retirement in 1988.

Gail Twining married Don Griswold, and her sister Jean married Tim Johnson. Stepping aside for a moment from the Griswold family, it is interesting to note that Jean and Tim's son Jay Johnson was selected for the United States Naval Academy beginning in the fall of 1964. He made the navy his career and became Acting Chief of Naval Operations when his predecessor committed suicide. President William Jefferson Clinton appointed him Chief of Naval Operations on his 50th birthday June 5, 1996. In 2008 he began working for General Dynamics and became President and Chief Executive Officer on June 10, 2009.

Don and Gail Griswold had four sons: Harry, the attorney in West Salem, John, a physician in Baltimore, Paul who perished in a fire in Sauk Centre, and Dan.

Dan was director of the CATO Institute's Herbert A. Stiefel Center for Trade Policy Studies for 15 years. The CATO Institute is a libertarian think tank in Washington D. C. He has a journalism degree from the University of Wisconsin and a degree in the politics of the world economy from the London School of Economics. He has authored major studies on globalization, trade, and immigration. In September of 2009 Daniel Griswold published his book *Mad About Trade* through CATO. On their web site CATO states: "This much-needed antidote to a rising tide of protectionist sentiment in the United States offers a free spirited defense of free trade and tells the underreported story of how a more global U. S. economy has created better jobs and higher living standards for American workers." In 2012 Dan decided to maximize his administrative skills and became President of the National Association of Foreign Trade Zones in Washington D. C.

In an e-mail to me in August 2008 Dan wrote the following:

> I read several of my Grandpa Harry's speeches in the Congressional Record when I worked for a member of Congress in 1981-83. It is one of those funny ironies in life that I now make my living in part by criticizing the same federal protection and subsidies for dairy farmers that my Grandpa Harry advocated when he was in office. "The American market for the American farmer" was one of his catch phrases.

Clinton or C. D. Griswold, a prominent and respected dairy farmer with registered Guernsey cattle, was the other dairy-farming son of Henry Daniel Griswold. Clint Griswold attended Beloit College for two years before transferring to the University at Madison and completing an economics degree in 1910. He purchased his farm in 1913 next to the original 500 acres owned by William Dudley, and he farmed there all his life. The house on his farm was built in 1858 by William Hull, who also built the Congregational Church and the home of Pulitzer-winning author Hamlin Garland. Clint married Ada Richmond in November 1915.

Ada Richmond Griswold received a degree in chemistry from The University of Wisconsin in 1912 and served as vice-president of her class. She was named to the Mortar Board, an honorary society for outstanding women. After her marriage to Clint, the rich Guernsey milk produced by their cows (and helped undoubtedly by her chemistry background) soon established Ada to be the "Cottage Cheese Lady." She provided the Bodega restaurant in La Crosse and everyone else in the West Salem community with her special product. One day a truck with "A. J. HERMAN" printed on its door entered their yard and began unloading equipment. Clint became alarmed and left the dinner table to find out what was happening. Ada had saved enough money from the sale of cottage cheese to provide her husband Clint with a hay loader and hay rake. The hay loader was a high contraption on two steel wheels that used "teeth" on its moving conveyer driven by the wheels to bring loose hay onto the wagon. Clint had previously used a pitchfork to throw the hay onto his wagons.

Clint and Ada had two children, Clinton and Florence. Both have degrees from the University of Wisconsin, Clinton in chemistry and Florence in zoology. Clinton did not pursue farming but worked in the oil industry. Florence had a career in what is now known as Meritor Hospital in Madison. She is in her eighties and still attends all University of Wisconsin home football games, as she has done since her college days.

Florence fondly related to me some incidents in the life of her parents. Her mother Ada felt there must be something wrong because the farm men would never come to *their* home when settling up the threshing financing at the end of the season. Clint shyly had to explain that beer was part of the settling-up process – something Ada did not allow. Beer was on the menu at the Griswold home following the next year's threshing season!

One Monday forenoon Clint asked Ada if pie was on the menu for dinner. Dinner was (still is!) always at high noon on the dairy farm. Ada pointed out that Monday was wash day, and if she was washing clothes how could she possibly make pie for dinner? Well, Clint said that he bet Ella Young would have pie for her men that noon. Ada immediately phoned my grandmother to find if this was true. Yes indeed it was. A subsequent phone call revealed the pie to be leftovers from a prior baking day. Clint sure knew how to work the system!

Florence's friends from West Salem enjoyed coming to the farm and "rubbering" on the party line. Everyone's phone would ring on the rural party line when anyone on the line received a call. Each phone had a unique ring based on longs and shorts. Ours was one long and two shorts. When calling someone on your line you did not go through the operator, rather you would twirl the crank three times for a long and one time for a short with appropriate pauses. Propriety meant you would stay off the line when it was not your call. "Rubbering" meant you were not following accepted practice!

Clint served on the La Crosse County Guernsey Breeders Board and the Tri-state Breeders Co-op sire selection committee. He and Ada together received an honorary plaque for their many contributions to agriculture by the College of Agriculture of the University of Wisconsin. The farm was sold in the 1970's.

Clinton Dudley and Ada Griswold receiving a Testimonial given by the Faculty of the College of Agriculture with the approval of the Regents of the University [of Wisconsin] as partners in the betterment of farm, family and community, dedicated to the service of youth, agriculture, church and school. Award given in 1960.

Florence commented often on the frugality required of her Grandfather Henry Daniel Griswold in order to survive in farming and the effect it had on his children. What follows next is an in-depth examination of his financial legacy.

Chapter Nine:

H. D. Griswold Economics

"Less acres and more intelligent thorough methods
is the crying need of the time."

– H. D. Griswold

The farmstead of the Henry Daniel Griswold family

Farmers have always had the reputation for throwing all income and disbursement receipts into a shoebox. They knew neither their profitability nor their loss. Henry Daniel Griswold was an exceptional exception to this!

My father kept daybooks of farm income and expenses used primarily for tax purposes when he farmed beginning in the 1930s through retirement in 1967. Henry Daniel Griswold began his daybook January 1, 1877, when he began farming. His daybooks included every penny that passed through his hands for personal as well as for business expenditures. Reading through his entries spanning over fifty years could be considered an economic study of farm life during that period of rural Wisconsin history.

Economics is essentially nothing more than the study of everything you might do financially on an individual basis, to the study of what a firm, or a farm operation like Henry Daniel Griswold's, does (called micro-economics), to what a country or even the entire world does (called macro-economics). Since everything we do has a financial outcome we can look at what H. D. Griswold did through this framework and get some idea of the life and times of that era.

Remember that Henry Griswold left home in 1874 with $100 from his father. He left Dakota Territory a defeated man with a pair of oxen and a wagon which his partner provided. The loss of Henry's crop and the personal despondency he felt as he traveled to Wisconsin from the Dakota Territory is something La Crosse County, Wisconsin farmers would never have to endure, owing to their lush valleys and adequate rainfall conducive to successful dairy farming. My father said that there had always been a reasonable harvest during his lifetime. Henry came to West Salem seeking out William Dudley, who originally was from Henry's home community of Guilford, Connecticut. He lived with the Dudley family, taught school, and worked on their farm in the summer. On November 8, 1877, he married Jennie Lee Dudley and received a forty acre farm, including buildings, as a wedding present from his father-in-law.

Keep in mind that what his cash books illustrate is what life was like over a century ago when our nation was primarily made up of farmers, craftsmen, and traders. The six figure tractors and combines with global positioning systems used by today's farmers might have cabs replete with surround sound and air conditioning. Sophisticated computer monitors on many of today's combines provide yield and moisture level during harvest. That stored data guided by the GPS can provide the proper seeding and fertilizer placement for the computerized seed drill the following spring. Dairy farms today may have thousands of milk cows. At the World Dairy Expo in Madison, Wisconsin in 2011 an exhibit featured a milking system wherein a cow walked onto the milking platform, was fed grain, and was milked by a computerized system totally devoid of human intervention. For today's farmer there is mobile communication, instant messaging, international travel, plus the expectation of government protection should the need arise; these things now are all standard fare, not one of which could even be imagined a century ago. Travel with me as we encounter notable "firsts" during the farming lifetime of Henry Daniel Griswold and his contemporaries: the use of electricity, telephones, and motorized transportation. In the grand scheme of historical context, this is but a blink of an eye ago.

It is tempting to expect more information from a cash entry in this survey. These cash books, however, are not diaries. A severe application of both thought and imagination is required in the interpretation of many of Henry's entries!

Unlike many other daybooks, H. D. Griswold's begins with a balance sheet which was dated January 1, 1877. There were $417.11 in assets and no liabilities. This balance sheet was a little more sophisticated than you might think, as it included receivables and accrued earnings not yet received. Henry owned a wagon he valued at $85, a plough at $15, and one-half interest in a seeder worth $20. He had a $125 deposit at Batavian Bank with accrued interest of $13.05 and another deposit of $40. He had a receivable of

$75 from W. S. Dudley for oxen and another receivable of $40 from School District No. 2. He had $4.06 cash on his person.

In January 1877 his only income was twenty-five cents that he found. He gave to charity sixteen cents, bought a diary for $1.25, had his hair cut for thirty cents and two teeth filled for two dollars. Yes, dentists filled cavities in 1877!

Henry began February with sixty cents in cash. Remember his daybook was cash in and cash out and did not include bank deposits or liabilities. He received $50 from the school district for teaching and paid Mrs. Hauser $10 for board which meant meals. He paid Murphy eight dollars for teaching him something (again, Henry's wording!). He purchased fine boots for $5 and coarse boots for $4, as well as seven yards of cloth for two pair of pants and twelve yards for three shirts, box collars, and cuffs for sixty-five cents, and an "ornate" account book for seventy cents. This account book remains in good shape more than 130 years later.

With no March income Henry purchased onion seed for three dollars and an ax for $1.65.

On April 13 he received payment in full from School District No. 2 of $140 and settled his board arrears with Mrs. Hauser of $30. During the month Henry paid $2.50 to have his pants and shirts made. He paid five cents for some apples. For farming he purchased strawberry plants and seed potatoes. Farm supplies bought included harnesses, halters, a whip, curry comb and brush, hand saw, hammer, brace and three bits, a square and one pound nails, a clevis, a spade, a hoe, an iron rake, a manure fork, a screw wrench, and bolts. He paid Mr. Dudley $50 on account. Personal items included a hair cut, ink, school cards, and a collar button.

He paid four boys a total of $3.37 for weeding in May. Mrs. Johnson was paid $20 for board. The month's most interesting purchases were strychnine for seventy-five cents and Paris green for fifty cents, both common rodent poisons. Assuming the receivable from School District No. 2 was a loan made on November 25, 1876, at five percent per annum, he received the $40 back with 98 cents interest for 178 days. He received another $400 for teaching.

The only income from June was a post office money order from home for $50. Five dollars for a church pew and a one-cent stamp were the most interesting entries.

We have looked at Henry's first half year in daily record keeping and farming. Two things come to mind. One is the informal system of lending and borrowing occurring. Henry was doing both. You will notice this pattern throughout our survey. Another is the bare bones necessities he needed to acquire for an earnest start in farming. Here is a man with basically nothing but the desire to succeed. As is evident from his records, for his first farming season he raised only cash crops. In July, Henry purchased a hay rake from Fritz Miller for seventy-five cents, paid Mr. Servais two dollars for helping hay and gave George four cents. Only $4.12 was spent and no income was received.

The meticulous daybooks of H. D. Griswold

Costs in August were for bag string, timothy seed, a bushel basket, and hired labor for cutting and binding grain.

In September Henry received the first fruits from his farming. He sold 35 bushels of wheat for $35.10, four bushels of onions for $1.60, and four head of cabbage for twenty-eight cents. He received $300 from home of which $100 was deposited in the Batavian Bank. There was a new high of forty-four disbursements in September for $289.95, including a suit of clothes for $40, no doubt for his wedding, and the bank deposit. Without the monetary loans from home, Henry would have found the going tough indeed.

Below is a chart of cash movement for the first nine months of Henry Daniel Griswold's farming career which is a simple example of his cash flows:

DATE	CASH IN	CASH OUT	FARM SALES	BORROWED	DEPOSITS & RECEIVABLES
JAN 1, 1877	$ 4.06	$ -			$ 293.05
JAN 1877	$ 0.25	$ 3.71			
FEB 1877	$ 50.00	$ 28.35			
MAR 1877	$ -	$ 4.65			
APR 1877	$ 140.00	$ 143.20			
MAY 1877	$ 440.98	$ 450.00			
JUNE 1877	$ 50.00	$ 29.01		$ 50.00	
JULY 1877	$ -	$ 4.12			
AUG 1877	$ -	$ 22.20			
SEPT 1877	$ 236.98	$ 189.95	$ 36.98	$ 300.00	$ 100.00
FIRST NINE MONTHS	$ 922.27	$ 875.19	$ 36.98	$ 350.00	$ 393.05

With his impending marriage to Jennie Dudley in November, Henry was buying groceries and not paying Mrs. Johnson for board, having settled with her for the final time on October 1 for $43.03. That month 38 bushels of onions sold for ten dollars, 64 head of cabbage for $2.47 and a later combination of the two brought in $2.85. Miscellaneous proceeds of eighty cents included five cents that he found. He lent Lewis five dollars and gave Reverend Clark a dollar for his silver anniversary. The first livestock Henry obtained were five six-week old pigs, for which he paid $5.

In November, 1877 Lewis returned the five dollars he had borrowed the prior month. Henry sold sixteen bushels of 25# wheat for a total of $15.40. He received payment for his oxen and cashed in a certificate of deposit from Batavian Bank for a total of $140.25 including interest. He paid $200 for a team of horses. He purchased 15 bushels of wild Russian wheat for $1.65 per bushel, 22 bushels of Odessa wheat for $1.35 per bushel, 1300 pounds of hay for $5.20, 390 pounds of corn for $2.75, and 1072 pounds of oats for $11.75. Personal expenses for November were for food, clothes, and wallpapering for the dining room and bedroom.

There was no income in December and expenses totaled $8.15. He had only seventy-five cents in his pocket at the end of the year, but much to his consternation there should have been thirty-six cents more according to his precise calculations!

Henry kept a separate listing of payables and receivables which were crossed out when settled. As of January 1, 1878, Henry Daniel Griswold had total assets valued at $720. He had an account of $25 he owed, plus a $350 loan from his father, John E. Griswold, with interest at six percent per annum with accrued interest owed of $11. Net worth was $334 not including the wedding present of a forty acre farm.

Now he had the means to farm in earnest.

The working assets in the beginning of 1878 included $50 at Batavian Bank and, of course, seventy-five cents. We could dwell on all the items of each month hereafter, but we have gotten a pretty good idea from studying 1877. From this point forward we will look only at items that are interesting and major trends while trying our best to understand the cash entries and their underlying economic meaning.

Speaking of interesting entries, in the 1878 cash diary of January 29 we see an earning of fifteen cents for picking onions. In Wisconsin in January, one can only think of onions either frozen or rotting in the ground. Whatever "picking" onions means, Henry earned fifteen cents for his labor. Crop inventory sales were $31.05. A round trip ticket to La Crosse, less than fifteen miles away, cost sixty-five cents. Headache pills were purchased for ten cents. At the end of the month Henry purchased a 248 pound hog for $9.92, which was probably butchered for home consumption.

With only $1.01 available February 1, Henry withdrew his money from the Batavian Bank. He paid $21.50 interest expense to his father and gave his wife Jennie $10. During March he sold two bags of oats for a dollar, a bag of corn for 25 cents, 15 bushels of 35# wheat for $13.50, and three bushels of potatoes for a total of 60 cents. Monthly proceeds were $44.07. Monthly expenses were $25.12. These included binder string for five cents, fasteners for thirty cents, paint for two dollars and a paint brush for $1.25, a looking glass for 40 cents, a stove pipe for 40 cents, a bench screw for 75 cents, and crackers for five cents. April proceeds for three bags of oats and one of corn were $1.85. This was not much less than the corn planter purchased for $2.75, which was less than the $3.25 paid for three fruit trees. Three lemons were purchased for ten cents. Being married perhaps bolstered Henry's culinary expectations! There was no income in May but $3.35 in cash expenses including 73 cents for 14 pounds of nails and a Sunday school donation of eight cents.

During 1878 Henry received income from selling four hogs, four of the five piglets he purchased back in Oct 1877, weighing a total of 1305 pounds at two and a quarter cents per pound, plus income from the sale of crops and produce. He hired out himself and his team of horses for three days for a total income of $6. He earned $2.25 for two days of setting fence. He spent one and a half days threshing for Mr. Lovejoy earning $3. Total proceeds from farming ranged from $244 to $264 depending on interpretation of income. A listed expense to two individuals was added into income. Expenses for the year exceeded $310. Nothing was listed for entertainment or reading. We can only imagine the hard manual labor and deprivation from our point of view. However, the solitude, the beautiful bluffs and being at one with nature before the urban sprawl of today must have been magnificent and soul sustaining.

The balance sheet for January 1, 1879, had working farm assets of $548 and liabilities of $420.50. The operating net worth of $127.50 was a drop of $206.50 or 62% from the year before. This balance sheet was from Henry's own stern calculation. The horses were still valued at $200. Tools were valued at $20, and the harnesses, wagon, bob sleigh, and other equipment totaled $185. The rest of the assets included livestock, produce, and grain. The liabilities were $60 in bills owed in addition to the loan from his father.

In 1879 Henry established himself in the very labor intensive dairy and egg production businesses. Four dozen eggs sold in January grossed a total of fifty cents. He purchased a Jersey heifer from Bradley in February for seventeen dollars and another heifer from Lutz for $15. On April 9 he paid Atkinson two dollars to use his bull for stud services.

Henry rented a post office box for sixty cents for a year. Among the more interesting purchases was a baby carriage for two dollars on April 5. Butter cost fifteen cents a pound – he bought fifteen pounds during the year. Suspenders cost him forty cents. Dried beef and fish were ten cents a pound. One donation was for eleven cents. Receipts on hogs sold were at the rate of three cents a pound. There was borrowing from and repayment to his wife Jennie in amounts between four and ten dollars throughout the year. The daybook contained only items where cash was involved. We cannot know personal consumption of items produced or of items traded in kind for food or other essentials such as the chickens to produce the eggs. In 1879, Henry sold three loads of straw to Cargill, a company which must have had a great impact in rural La Crosse County and West Salem after it moved its headquarters to La Crosse in 1875.

W. W. Cargill and Sons had started in 1865 with a single grain storage warehouse in Conover, Iowa. New country grain elevators were built piggybacking the railroad expansion routes throughout the newly settled prairie states, where Mr. Cargill harvested and processed grain and built storage facilities, including major grain terminals in Duluth and Minneapolis. In La Crosse, Wisconsin, located on the Mississippi River, the Milwaukee Railroad and the Southern Minnesota Railroad connection proved irresistible to William Wallace Cargill, and he moved his family and national headquarters there in 1875 where it remained until 1913. During that time Cargill expanded into flour milling, coal, farming, real estate, their own railroad, lumber, and innovation in financing and the moving and storing of grain. W. W. Cargill and his brothers created what would eventually become one of the world's most prominent agricultural commodity giants. The Cargill motto in 1865 "our word is our bond" was reaffirmed as its guiding principle in 1995, as it had become a global leader in nourishing people through innovation and technology.

Henry and Jennie lived within a half mile of West Salem in the Township of Hamilton, which completely surrounded the town. In 1880 the population of Hamilton Town as they called it was listed at 1661 by the U. S. Census Archives, with nothing listed for West Salem. West Salem had no official census record in 1880 because it wasn't formally recognized by the state legislature until the last day of March 1889. In 1880 La Crosse County, including the city of La Crosse, had a population of 27,073, of which 9953 were foreign born, primarily Scandinavians and Germans. Hamilton Town in the 1890 census had a population of 1400, West Salem a population of 542, and La Crosse County 38,801 with 12,953 foreign born.

On January 1, 1880, Henry Griswold's total assets were $665, an increase of $117 over the prior year. Liabilities were $40.50 less than in the prior year and totaled $380, with only ten dollars in bills payable. Farm operating net worth was $285 higher than at the beginning of 1879, but still less than it had been in the beginning of 1878. In January 1880 the Griswold's made several Sunday school payments ranging from three to six cents. In February a note for $20 plus $1.50 in interest was paid to Marietta Lee. A significant income of $11.80 was earned in March for hauling grain for the Sharpless Estate. Harness mending in 1880 cost anywhere between a nickel and a dime. A sofa purchase in March cost $1.50. In May stockings and lace were 95 cents, and the same amount was spent for a calico dress. Much calico, muslin, flannel, thread, buttons, denim, hook eyes, ribbon, and dress lining were purchased for a dress made by someone for the labor cost of $3.15.

Other interesting entries included an ox muzzle and cabbage plants each costing fifteen cents, a pair of shoes for $1.65, and a door frame for $1.25. Henry purchased insurance on the house and furniture for $8. A threshing fee of $13.50 was paid to McClintock. He paid $5.20 for yearling pasture rent. Church pew rent was ten dollars. Henry paid fifty cents for a ticket to the county fair. In November the sale of thirteen hogs at four cents a pound yielded $124.50. Henry sold many cabbages, potatoes, and onions that he harvested. He earned $12 for six days work at the Sharpless Estate.

Henry borrowed $20.50 from Carrie, the older sister of Jennie, on October 28. Barely a month went by in 1880 wherein Henry was not involved in borrowing or lending money. Borrowing and lending of small sums of money between individuals was a major necessity in the economy of these early farming communities. To compare frugality and necessity today with that over a century ago begs the question. Today's is a much looser financial environment, almost courting disaster!

At the end of 1880 property taxes of $25.53 were paid on his 40 acre farm. Finally some outside reading material was purchased: $4.90 for a newspaper to be received in 1881. Operating net worth at the beginning of 1881 was $473. Assets were livestock, grains, tools, and equipment. Debt to

Henry's father was $300 and other liabilities $20. Assets increased by $128 and net worth by $188. This minor increase was for one year of hard manual labor and no teaching income as there had been in 1877. Overall operating farm assets and net worth did increase by 19% and 66% respectively and debt reduced by 16%. Under the circumstances this was an extraordinary accomplishment.

On January 25, 1881, a household sewing machine was purchased for $35. On the 27th *Uncle Tom's Cabin* was purchased for twenty-five cents. On January 31, $50 was paid to J. E. Griswold on the note. In February corsets were purchased for $1.25 and baby shoes for 35 cents. Seven hundred feet of lumber cost $2.10. Costs for living and farming were interspersed and quite regular. On March 5 baby shoes cost one dollar. Another 700 feet of lumber was purchased on March 9. It seems amazing that cinnamon and coffee were available in a small isolated rural community in 1881; coffee was 25 cents a pound, the same as crackers, and cinnamon was ten cents. May's purchases included six lemons for 15 cents, a sulky cultivator for $33, and 150 cabbage plants for 75 cents. In June a horse hay rake cost $6.50 and a hat for Jennie $5. Strawberries were ten cents a quart. In October, seven sewing machine needles cost twenty-five cents. Shoes for their son Robbie cost seventy-five cents. In December, a well was dug for ten dollars. Railroad tickets also represented a major expense: a 500-mile ticket for $15, a ticket from the state line to Chicago for $1.60, and a ticket from Chicago to Springfield for $9.25.

Proceeds during the year included eggs bringing in ten cents per dozen, potatoes 45 cents per bushel, a bag of corn thirty cents, and a gallon of sorghum forty cents. Henry sold eight dressed hogs at $6.80 per cwt. and received $142.59. He also sold sixteen pounds of butter for twenty-five cents per pound grossing four dollars. They were making butter! In July they received $9.65 for an old horse, and later another horse was sold for a dollar. This was probably the original team purchased for two hundred dollars.

We are now entering a more integrated and complex farming operation with an expanding family. In December 1881 there were sixty-two cash entries. Henry created no more year-end balance sheets. So many tools and operating items had been purchased that their true value with or without depreciation expense was too fuzzy to be worth the effort. Livestock, as with the horses, would lose value while newborns enhanced value. In this rustic period value could only be determined when entering the market place.

In 1882 Henry Daniel Griswold traveled extensively. On January 23 he traveled by rail to a location undecipherable from his handwriting, continuing on to the Illinois towns of Galesville, Meridian, Springfield, ending up in Grand Rapids, Michigan. The rail trip from Springfield to Grand Rapids cost $20.50. From Grand Rapids he went to Chicago on January 30. He rode a "bus" in Chicago for fifty cents and spent $1.61 to get back to the state line. There is nothing indicating if he traveled alone or with others or the purpose for the trip. Was this for business or personal enlightenment?

In March Henry sold corn and oats for $160 and a bushel of clover seed for $3.75. Receipts for butter averaged between twenty-five and thirty cents a pound. Butter, grain, potatoes, hogs, and eggs were the primary sources of income in 1882. He sent a money order, presumably to his father, for $100 and paid $50 on a note to W. I. Dudley. His entries for cash on his farming operation were now almost on a daily basis.

Some interesting entries included a doctor bill in March for $2.75 and a pair of shoes for Jennie in April for the same amount. Henry worked one day whitewashing for someone and earned two dollars. He sold 183 bushels of oats for $64.10. Several entries during winter months were for dried apples at fifty cents per purchase. In April a chamber pot was bought for a dollar. Henry and his horses earned two dollars for a day of work on April 26. Shoe polish cost twenty-five cents, the same amount paid to Miller in May for cleaning his oats. Two pairs of baby shoes were purchased on June 26 for $2.40, and two dollars for baby pictures. Dress facing, pins, buttons, thread, gingham, trimming, stockings, hats, and shoes were bought in June. In September cinnamon and cloves were purchased at fifteen cents each as well as a corset for a dollar. Wallpaper was acquired on several occasions throughout the year at seventy-five cents a roll.

Domestic enhancement continued in 1883: over twenty-three yards of rag carpet were purchased at fifty cents per yard. Ten yards of calico were purchased at eight cents per yard and four yards of cotton cloth for nine cents per yard. In June Jennie had a dress made for six dollars and bought shoes for $2.50. Robbie and Dad got a hair cut for twenty-five cents each. A tombstone cost fifteen dollars – the same price as church pew rent. Five to ten cents was occasionally given for Sunday school, and a dollar was donated for church repair in August. They received five dollars for renting Jennie's organ to someone. Jennie's watch was repaired for $1.75 and Henry's for $1.50. Eighty-eight cents was spent for twenty-five pounds of buckwheat, ten cents for lemons. In October teeth were pulled for a dollar. Three years of house insurance came to eight dollars.

How was the price of a commodity determined? Were there differences in the quality in what Henry sold such that he might get either a premium or a reduction when quality or size was not up to standards? Would 1883 standards be relevant today? Butter price fluctuated somewhat over time: twenty-three cents per pound for butter sold at the beginning of 1883 was less than the twenty-five to thirty cents the prior year, but by March it was back to twenty-five cents a pound. Eggs sold for fifteen cents a dozen on March 9 and 12.5 cents on March 19. Potato receipts from the crop of 1882 were mostly between forty and forty-five cents per bushel, except for the "small" potatoes sold in April for twenty cents a bushel. The fall crop of potatoes brought twenty-five cents per bushel and 189 head of cabbage brought four cents per head. Grain sales of 275 bushels netted $112.85. Seven hogs averaging 233 pounds each brought proceeds of $57.03 and sale of two steers brought in $52.50.

Henry had established himself as a farmer and family man by 1884. Operating equipment had been paid for. Income and expense items through 1889 were similar to those of the recent past. The lowest price received for eggs was ten cents a dozen and for butter fifteen cents a pound. Sales volume was very small during these years. One can only wonder at the extreme pressure on the family for financial survival. Toiletries and conveniences that are taken for granted today as absolute necessities were sparse at best. Payments on the Dudley debt and to his father continued during this time.

In 1887 Henry expanded from the inherited forty acres to sixty. With the purchase of the twenty acres of land, it was necessary to cover the accrued interests of Snyder's mortgage of $7.75, of which $7.50 was reimbursed by J. H. Miller. On April 30, Henry paid fifty dollars to "John Miller on his place." From this we can assume that Snyder had originally purchased the land from John Miller on a land contract, which is a legal document of sale between the original owner and the purchaser with title remaining in the hands of the seller until paid in full. On May 21, 1887, Henry paid eighty-five cents to record a deed. On June 8, 1887, a newspaper ad was placed for one dollar on the Miller house and three acres, which were sold on August 27 for one thousand dollars. He promptly paid $850 in two installments to Dudley and another one hundred dollars October 21. What did Dudley provide or pay for that never was entered into the cash book – perhaps the twenty acres?

In 1888 Henry paid W. P. Hitchcock twenty-five dollars for twenty-five bushels of wheat. He also borrowed $125 from him with a note. In December 1888 a windmill was purchased for eighty dollars. On March 30, 1889, Henry sold two acres of land to the La Crosse County Agricultural Society for $600, and he put $400 of this money into the "Salem Bank." The "Salem Bank" was in Alex Johnson's drugstore on Leonard Street, the main street through town.

On May 20, 1889, Henry helped create the foundation not only for his sons' registered Guernsey enterprises but also for putting La Crosse County on the map as the Guernsey capital of the United States by spending $175 for two registered Guernsey calves. One was undoubtedly Vidette, a bull whose name means a sentry positioned beyond an army's outpost. The other was a female whose offspring was the first animal Henry registered with the American Guernsey Cattle Club on June 9, 1892, for a cost of $2.05.

Henry's thirst for current events and knowledge beyond his immediate sphere of the coulee region in western Wisconsin was supported by his December subscription to *Hoard's Dairyman* for $1.05. He spent $1.35 for the *Milwaukee Sentinel* to begin in January 1891. He also spent one dollar for the *West Salem Journal*. On August 31, 1890, sixty cents was spent for two tickets to the circus.

When Prof. Steven Moulton Babcock, dairy chemist of the University of Wisconsin, first arrived at the University in January 1888, Dean H. L. Russell assigned him the task of creating a low cost and workable test for butterfat that could be carried out by farmers and creamery operators working without a laboratory. Later, Dean Russell stated: "By means of the Babcock test, dairying has been developed from one of the most haphazard industries to an exact and attractive business enterprise." This test gave farmers throughout the world the opportunity to be compensated fairly for their milk. The first bulletin announcing this successful butterfat test was published in July, 1890. Scientific advancement has now produced a protein content test to go along with the Babcock butterfat test.

Henry Daniel Griswold was a leader unafraid to be progressive, and he was the first in the area to test the productivity of his dairy cows. He purchased a butterfat milk tester in December, 1891, costing $8.08 plus freight and paid twenty-five cents for the sulfuric acid used in the milk testing. He was enthusiastic and inspiring enough to engage his friends to follow his lead. In 1892 he received twenty-five cents from individuals for doing their milk testing.

In 1891 cash proceeds were $998.21 and cash outflow was $1370.74 necessitating borrowing $250, which represented twenty-five percent of the entire operating farm revenue. Henry also borrowed $300 from H. Dickinson and $50 from W. L. Dudley. A new barn cost $109. Butter sales were 2031.5 pounds for $388.93 or 34% of gross farm operating proceeds.

· · ·

This cash book is a most intimate diary of Henry and Jennie's life together. Two days after the birth of their fourth son John, Jennie passed away on April 30, 1891. While reading Henry's subsequent entries you can almost feel the poignancy of this loss and the effect on their family. Domestic labor for the remainder of 1891 was $150, and for many years afterward Emma Wehrs was paid for work in the home.

In 1892, farm operating proceeds were $1287.46. Cash outflow of $1403.76 included Jennie's gravestone for $74. The trip east in April of 1892 to woo and marry Caroline Parker cost $128.47 or ten per cent of sales, necessitating borrowing $100 from Jennie's sister Carrie and $50 from Dickinson.

In 1893, the sale of 2931.5 pounds of butter for $609.24 accounted for fifty-three percent of gross operating proceeds. Henry rented out Vidette, his registered Guernsey bull, for stud service to A. J. Phillips for an extended period for fifty dollars beginning March 10, 1893. Henry spent $27.93 to go to the Columbian Exposition in Chicago.

Proceeds of land and wood lot sold in 1897 for $550 were used to repay Carrie $400, and the cemetery received $150.

I have prepared a ten year summary of receipts and expenses from 1888 through 1897 which begins and ends on a calendar year basis. The monetary cost of borrowing is included:

PROCEEDS:

BUTTER	$4462.46
GARDEN CROPS	2809.28
LIVESTOCK	2166.92
GRAIN	928.24
LABOR	576.97
MISCELLANEOUS	532.13

TOTAL OPERATING RECEIPTS $11476.00

OPERATING EXPENSES:

HIRED HELP	$2214.59
ROUTINE	1859.39
FEED AND GRINDING	930.51
TAXES	657.73
INTEREST	306.88

TOTAL OPERATING EXPENSES $ 5969.10

LIVING EXPENSES:

GROCERIES AND SUNDRY ITEMS	$2248.21
HIRED HELP	1117.20
CHURCH AND CHARITY	348.22
MAJOR TRIPS	205.34
DOCTOR	202.20

TOTAL LIVING EXPENSES $ 4121.17

AMOUNT REMAINING AFTER EXPENSES $ 1385.73

INVESTMENTS:

LIVESTOCK	$1212.71	
IMPROVEMENTS	746.52	
EQUIPMENT	179.55	
TOTAL CAPITAL INVESTED		$2138.78
LESS TWO ACRES OF LAND SOLD	600.00	
NET CAPITAL INVESTED		$1538.78
NET SHORTAGE OF CASH AFTER TEN YEARS		$ 153.00

According to Henry Daniel Griswold's records 27,542.25 pounds of butter were produced over the ten years. Of this, 25,104.75 pounds were sold for $4462.46 at an average of 17.8 cents per pound, and 2437.5 pounds of butter were for personal consumption or bartered. If none were bartered, roughly twenty pounds of butter were consumed by family and hired help per month.

Garden crop proceeds were $2718.18 from potatoes and $91.10 from strawberries. Corn and oats proceeds were $841.04. Henry's labor for others totaled $576.97 but stopped after 1890. Dairy husbandry is very labor intensive and requires close scrutiny. Hiring out ones own labor at this point of increased involvement would be counter productive.

Labor expense both for farm and the home was one-third of the total of both operating and living expenses. Simple hand labor was needed in all areas of the early farm operation. This was especially true following the loss of the young family's mother. Extra help within the home also freed up needed labor for the farm operation.

Routine operating expenses including dry goods were considered an operating expense, even though some clothes and other items were for domestic use. The cost of producing butter consumed and/or bartered was hidden in the operating expenses. During this period of farming, much consumption was of products produced on the farm, including eggs, meat, grains, potatoes, strawberries, and other garden crops. Bartering between parties of food products would have been routine and did not get into a cash book.

The financial statement items noted above could be examined individually for more insight; however, they definitely were not typical of the everyday pioneer farmer. Henry was very progressive and more educated than his contemporaries. He was willing to read and learn at a time when most farmers refused. He was an early subscriber to *Hoard's Dairyman*, the *Milwaukee Sentinel*, and *Harper's Magazine*.

Henry's desire to produce the best butter most efficiently inspired him to continue the enhancement of his dairy herd through further investment in registered Guernsey cattle. On March 12, 1903, Henry purchased two Guernsey calves from Mr. Charles L. Hill, the Guernsey importer, for $225 plus $9.45 shipping. This huge investment in registered Guernsey animals represented almost twenty percent of annual proceeds. Below are the recorded cash book entries of registered Guernsey purchases and later sales, especially of bulls after he became established as a prominent breeder of registered Guernsey cattle.

H.D. Griswold Registered Guernsey Transactions				
Date	**Purchases**	**Related**	**Sales**	**Counter Party**
		Cost		
May, 1889	$ 175.00	$ 2.05		
February, 1893	$ 75.00	$ 3.85		George C. Hill
January, 1894		$ 5.30	$ 25.00	G. G. Hitchcock
March, 1903	$ 225.00	$ 9.45		Charles L. Hill
March, 1903		$ 3.05	$ 50.00	Moran
July, 1903	$ 50.10	$ 3.15		Reitbrock
July, 1903		$ 3.25	$ 25.00	Dederic Wehrs
January, 1906		$ 5.05	$ 100.00	
February, 1906	$ 85.10	$ 5.25		
June, 1906	$ 175.00	$ 8.88		
July, 1906	$ 165.15	$ 10.44		Solverson

October, 1906	$ 155.00	$ 10.44		Solverson
March, 1907			$ 125.00	A. J. Phillips
May, 1907		$ 5.00	$ 50.00	
May, 1907	$ 250.10			
July, 1907	$ 100.00	$ 10.03		
July, 1907			$ 125.00	G. G. Hitchcock
September, 1907			$ 150.00	Nuttleman
December, 1907			$ 75.00	W. J. Dawson
December, 1907	$ 200.00	$ 8.13		Biern
May, 1908		$ 1.03	$ 100.00	J. Heitman
August, 1908		$ 3.02	$ 125.00	Forrest - Henry
September, 1908		$ 3.02	$ 100.00	Trimbell
September, 1908		$ 3.02	$ 100.00	G. G. Hitchcock
September, 1908		$ 3.02	$ 100.00	Banub
September, 1908	$ 1,200.00	$ 53.35		Kimball
September, 1908		$ 2.06	$ 150.00	Christensen
September, 1908		$ 1.03	$ 100.00	Harry Griswold
December, 1908		$ 10.30	$ 75.00	Erdyman
January, 1909		$ 9.06	$ 490.00	Tobey
February, 1909		$ 6.04	$ 250.00	
March, 1909		$ 3.02	$ 140.00	
June, 1909		$ 3.02	$ 75.00	Hulda
July, 1909		$ 3.02	$ 125.00	Ashburn
August, 1909		$ 3.02	$ 45.00	
October, 1909		$ 3.02	$ 75.00	
November, 1909		$ 3.02	$ 133.00	
January, 1910			$ 89.00	
July, 1910			$ 65.00	

Much of Henry's cream was now sold to Armstrong, the proprietor of a hotel in West Salem. Other small amounts were sold privately, with the rest sold to his creamery. Whenever Henry received his monthly income from the creamery he used part of the proceeds to buy butter.

In 1901 Henry built the first silo in La Crosse County. He eventually helped construct silos for many neighbors, including my Grandfather. The following is a table listing the cost of this silo:

LA CROSSE COUNTY'S FIRST SILO	
ITEM	**COST**
"Silage Book"	$ 0.10
3 rolls silo paper	$ 20.10
Silo lumber	$ 76.50
Stone	$ 50.00
225 pound of nails	$ 6.60
Lumber	$ 15.80
4 barrels of cement	$ 6.00
10 barrels of lime	$ 7.00
3 "loads" of sand	$ 0.50
"Silo" nails	$ 3.50
Mason work	$ 3.50
Other labor	$ 2.25
300 feet of lumber	$ 6.60
4 barrels of cement	$ 12.00
Silo ventilator	$ 6.00
Siding	$ 2.05
Iron steps	$ 0.70
Paint	$ 5.00
Silo Total	$ 224.20
Ross Cutter	$ 79.10
Shipping	$ 11.00
Cutter Total	$ 90.10

Corn silage was to become a major feed input for the dairy cattle, requiring the purchase of a corn planter for ten dollars on May 16, 1902. The newly-built silo did not have enough capacity for the herd; therefore a Kalamazoo silo was purchased for $121.36 plus $21.60 for freight in June of that year. On September 10 Henry paid Ray Lewis fifty dollars for filling his two silos. Corn silage gave the farmer for the first time an efficient high energy feed. To balance the ration, protein and dietary supplements were required; these were usually purchased. Now more dairy animals could be fed per acre of crop land.

In January of 1902, Henry purchased 4425 pounds of wheat bran for $40.45, less than a penny a pound. In purchasing feed supplements for his dairy herd, Henry Daniel Griswold was way ahead of his time. Forward pricing or purchase became popular in the mid 20th century when adequate dry storage was available on the farm or farm elevator. We do not know whether Henry's purchase was for later delivery, but we do know he guaranteed access to his wheat bran and oil meal at favorable prices. Private enterprise and individual decision-making by those capable of sound business practices are and have always been the foundation of prosperity. Wheat bran was the most consistent feed purchase. High protein cottonseed oil meal was also purchased in large quantities, but not as often. The table on page 122 documents the bulk grain purchases from 1902 through 1909.

On June 5, 1902, Henry purchased a cream aerator for $4.15. Also in June Henry purchased tuberculosis test instruments for five dollars and a mowing machine for $36.50. In 1902, Mr. Baker, a hotel proprietor in West Salem, bought a large proportion of Henry's cream. In 1901 and 1902 Henry rented the fairgrounds for $65 per year. William Oldenburg owned a general store in West Salem where Henry kept an account, paying Oldenburg in amounts ranging up to one hundred fifty dollars. When Henry paid for things on account, there is no way ever to know what he purchased or its purpose. It should be understood that we only have a glimpse into his proceedings, unfortunately no way to fill in the blanks.

H. D. Griswold Bulk Grain Purchases				
DATE	GRAIN	POUNDS	COST	COST PER POUND
JAN. 1902	Wheat Bran	4425	$ 40.25	0.9 cents
APR. 1902	Oil Meal	500	$ 7.50	1.5 cents
SEPT. 1902	Wheat Bran	12000	$ 85.50	0.7125 cents
OCT. 1902	Oil Meal	6000	$ 79.50	1.325 cents
OCT. 1905	Wheat Bran	25000	$ 165.63	0.6625 cents
FEB. 1907	Wheat Bran	2000	$ 21.00	1.05 cents
FEB. 1907	Oil Meal	3000	$ 42.00	1.4 cents
OCT. 1907	Oil Meal	16000	$ 224.00	1.4 cents
APR. 1909	Wheat Bran	2000	$ 23.00	1.15 cents
MAY 1909	Wheat Bran	1000	$ 12.50	1.25 cents
AUG. 1909	Oil Meal	1000	$ 17.50	1.75 cents
AUG. 1909	Wheat Bran	2000	$ 22.00	1.10 cents
SEPT. 1909	Wheat Bran	1400	$ 15.92	1.137 cents

Henry's annualized receipts from milk production increased by ninety-five per cent between 1900 and 1903. On March 9, 1903, Henry sold 15,240 pounds of hay for $45.72 or six dollars per ton. On July 1 Henry purchased a buggy and harness from Kimball for $53.50. On August 15, 1903, Henry received his first salary of $25 plus $15.28 for expenses from the Wisconsin Institute. Henry invested considerable money in his sons' college education.

In 1904, Henry paid his first telephone bill, totaling $16.50.

In 1905, a trip on the Mindoro stage coach cost forty cents. Horses continued to be a primary source of productive power in American farming until after World War II. An ensilage cutter was purchased for $90.15 in mid-September. On October 5 Ole Knudsen and his team of horses received $5.65 for helping harvest corn for the silo. In October of that year, 254 bushels of potatoes were sold at forty cents per bushel for total revenues of $101.50. Every week milk and cream were sold to a local hotel. On November 15 a corn binder was purchased from Asmus for forty dollars. Tuberculin was purchased for $3.55 in November. On December 1 he bought clover seed for $16.75.

In 1905 Henry also received $2.50 for an article he submitted to *The Farmer,* the Minnesota state farm publication. In June Henry paid $326 for a house in West Salem. On September 2, 1905, Rob received a wedding present from his dad of fifty dollars. A suit for Harry cost sixteen dollars and Clinton's was eleven dollars and fifty cents.

On January 5, 1906 sixteen hogs were sold averaging 236.25 pounds per hog with total proceeds of $177.65. Henry had cakes of ice sawed every winter. This winter he paid $7.80 for 522 cakes. In the spring of 1906 Henry began paying his son Harry twenty dollars per month in wages. On July 12 seven tons of hay was purchased for $4.30 per ton.

On January 26 and 27, 1906, Henry paid one hundred dollars plus $19.90 in interest to complete the house purchase in West Salem. That same month he began renting it out at the rate of twelve dollars a month. In mid-February he paid $14.59 for a visit to Madison and Fort Atkinson. Did Henry visit Hoard's Dairyman? We will never know! Late in August he spent $4.50 visiting Wisconsin Dells.

The La Crosse County hotbed of registered Guernsey activity owes its genesis to Henry Daniel Griswold and later to his son Harry who turned cattle jockeying into a serious profession. The La Crosse County Guernsey Breeders Association was founded in 1907 with father and son being instrumental in its creation. On March 20, 1907, Henry's records show in book four, page 109 the payment of his first dollar in annual dues.

The financial records for 1907 were unusual in their scope. Expenses included eight hundred dollars to Harry for his inheritance, three hundred dollars for Clint's education, and $362 paid on notes. Telephone expenses for the whole year were eighteen dollars. Capital expenditures included $97 for a new windmill and $35 for a water tank. On December 14, a typewriter was purchased from G. I. Tofson for $55. Farm proceeds were $4636.75, of which $2534.69 was from cream and milk, $1269.75 from cattle sales, and $832.31 from miscellaneous farm sales. He also received $144 for renting out his home in West Salem.

In February 1908 Henry received $106.50 for expenses and $135 for four and a half days work from the Minnesota Institute of Agriculture. He received another eight dollars from them in March, and in April there was a ninety dollar final payment.

In June 1908, Henry purchased 5575 pounds of hay for $27.87 (or ten dollars per ton) and a manure spreader for $120. Several days' labor for silo filling came to $1.50 per man day.

To promote his registered Guernsey cattle, Henry paid the American Guernsey Cattle Club for advertising on October 26, 1908. He was setting the precedent for being as much of a seller of registered Guernsey cattle as he was for dairy production. This became the standard of the La Crosse County Guernsey establishment well into the middle of the twentieth century.

In 1908 operating receipts were $4559.43 with $4075.99 from the dairy operation. This was divided into cream sales of $2372.32 and cattle sales of $1703.67. Henry also received income from the Minnesota Institute of Agriculture totaling $362.76. On October 24 he purchased fourteen cow stanchions for twenty-one dollars plus ninety cents for shipping.

In 1909 most of the cream went to the Pure Food Company which specialized in ice cream. He continued his sales to a local hotel and various individuals. The winter's Institute teaching proceeds amounted to $159. In September he purchased the cereal "Cream of Wheat" for fifteen cents. In November entries included thirty cents for toilet paper and "fixture" and five cents for Borax. In May he had "circulators" printed for $2.50.

The first entries for what appear to be a motorized vehicle were $1.96 for fourteen gallons of gasoline on September 8th and seventy-five cents for a dry battery on the 9th. Another ten gallons of gasoline was purchased on the 10th for $1.40.

The year 1909 was the first year that Henry's revenues from cattle exceeded his revenues from dairy products he produced. Cattle sales were $2370 and cream sales were $1894.97. These combined were 92% of gross sales of $4643.36. At one time he sold over $4000 of cream annually. He was milking less but selling more breeding stock. He had property taxes of $172.61 and a bank note of $300. Fairground rent cost $130 in October.

On March 7, 1910, Henry became fifty-seven years of age and began his post farming career. He spent $25 at a Guernsey meeting. On April 1 Henry spent one hundred dollars to purchase a share in the West Salem Farmer's Store. He traveled to Denver and Portland near the end of July at a cost of $227.85. Piano tuning cost him five dollars. Institute teaching netted him $337.66 in 1910 and he was reimbursed for expenses of $43.02. During the year he earned seventy-one dollars as a census taker.

Hydro-power from the La Crosse River was the source of electricity in the West Salem area in the beginning. Henry's first use was recorded with an October 1st entry for $12.50 for "lights" from Swarthout. Swarthout later sold its water power generating plant to Northern States Power Company, which is now Xcel Energy.

In 1910 Henry bought more land for $2500, and he paid $1000 on his mortgage. He received $1200 from sale of land to Horman, and he paid off his bank note with proceeds of $1500 from his New York mortgage. Whether the New York mortgage had something to do with family inheritance, and what the other transactions of land purchase and sale mean in the big picture, are more than likely not significant for our purposes.

In 1910, Henry rented his farm to his son Harry. He still had major college expenses for Clint, John and Katharine. Included below are the major cash movements from 1910 thru 1920.

H. D. Griswold Retirement Revenues & Education Expenses Starting in 1910				
Year	Farm Rent	Institute Income	College Expense	Real Estate Tax
1910	$ 1,420.00	$ 337.66	$ 635.00	$ 194.42
1911	$ 1,150.00	$ 382.50	$ 625.00	$ 288.73
1912	$ 1,150.00	$ 445.00	$ 554.40	$ 301.98
1913	$ 1,100.00	$ 392.50	$ 669.80	$ 275.55
1914	$ 1,200.00	$ 477.25	$ 538.42	$ 307.14
1915	$ 1,200.00	$ 450.00	$ 545.10	$ 278.26
1916	$ 1,200.00	$ 455.00	$ 568.40	$ 323.32
1917	$ 1,200.00	$ 542.50	$ 308.32	$ 341.06
1918	$ 1,200.00	$ 457.50	$ -	$ 310.89
1919	$ 300.00	$ 385.00	$ -	$ 473.92
1920	$ -	$ 420.00	$ -	$ -

In 1911, Henry paid interest expense of $153.39 during the year. Even after retirement he had debt. During the year he put in a bathroom at a cost of $167. Annual cost for "lights" was $15.10. Henry sold land to the Hamilton Cemetery in 1912 for $50.

From 1877 thru 1912 the cost of a haircut never varied from twenty-five cents. Only when beard trimming and shaving were involved was the cost more. Beginning in 1913 hair cuts were either thirty or thirty-five cents. In 1913 overalls cost seventy-five cents. Living in town now involved paying an annual water tax of two dollars.

In 1913, Henry borrowed $500 on a one-year note. It is hard to imagine him surviving financially had he not received the forty acre farm as a wedding present.

In 1914 Henry received $20 as a livestock judge. His most intensive work for the Wisconsin Farm Institute began in 1914: he made presentations in Sauk City, Madison, Black River Falls, Amory, Roberts, Antigo, Tomah, Reedsburg, Richland Center, Marshfield, and Osseo. Major expenses in 1914 were $150 in interest expense and $107.32 for two trips to New York.

On November 20, 1915, he gave a wedding present to Clint of $50. On December 28, he borrowed $300 from Clint. By 1915 hair cuts cost forty cents each.

In 1916 Henry earned $112.50 from "street work." He paid $123.35 in interest expense. World War I produced the first "temporary" federal income tax, thus in 1917 Henry paid $1.23 in federal income taxes. That "temporary" tax is still with us! Henry paid ten dollars in both November and December to purchase Liberty Bonds. He gave one dollar to the Red Cross and ten dollars to the YMCA. He earned $30 as a livestock judge and $5 for work at a Guernsey picnic. Henry spent $151.57 for a trip east. Hair cuts in the last half of 1917 were fifty cents.

He received $30 for six days work at the Wisconsin State Fair in 1918 and $25.90 for work for the school district. He borrowed an additional $200 during the year, but paid $780 for War Bonds and $38.05 for war thrift stamps. He gave one dollar to the Salvation Army and six dollars to the Red Cross. On January 21, 1918, Henry paid $330 for three calves for Clint.

On January 14, 1919, Henry received $300 less $30 for penalty for a net of $270 from the sale of his war bonds. On the same date he borrowed $250 from the bank and paid farm property taxes of $473.92. This is 52.4% higher than the prior year and constitutes 39.5% of total farm rental income. This might have been a good reason to sell the farm to his son Harry, which he did on April 9, 1919, receiving a down payment of $2000; this sum Henry immediately paid to S. R. Wakefield on his own mortgage. Below are the payments by Harry to his father.

YEAR	PRINCIPAL	INTEREST
1920	$ 200.00	$ 820.00
1921	$ 200.00	$ 812.00
1922	$ 200.00	$ 804.00
1923	$ 200.00	$ 696.00
1924	$ 200.00	$ 788.00
1925	-	$ 780.00
1926	$ 400.00	$ 772.00
1927	$ 200.00	$ 764.00
1928	$ 200.00	$ 756.00
1929	$ 200.00	$ 740.00
1930	$ 200.00	$ 732.00
1931	$ 200.00	$ 900.00
1932	-	$ 724.00

On May 3, Henry spent $20.60 for the contract and abstract on his farm. On July 29, he created his will for a cost of ten dollars. It was and still is in society's best interest not to have an inheritance tax when an operating family farm passes from one generation to the next for the same purpose. The three heifer calves he had purchased for Clint the prior year were sold to him for one dollar. On December 18 Henry donated ten dollars for Armenian relief.

On May 7, 1920, Henry paid Dr. Wakefield $7.50 for X-rays on his teeth. Henry was now on the Wisconsin State Fair Board, and on September 12, after earning $35 for seven days work at the Wisconsin State Fair, he purchased a set of false teeth for $75. A sofa cost $20.35, and hair cuts were now sixty cents. 1920 was the last year Henry worked for the Wisconsin State Agriculture Institute, where he earned $420 for his work. He purchased $400 in bank stock. He borrowed $200 which was sent to his daughter Katharine.

In 1921, Henry's interest expense was at an all time low of $7.45. The bank note of $200 was paid off. 1922 was the first year that Henry paid no interest expense – he was 68 years old!

He cashed in his United States War Bonds and purchased eleven shares of Empire Gas & Electric for $1012. In January, 1928, Henry spent an even $500 for more Empire stock. In 1931 Henry received $9.33 every month from his Empire stock which calculates to a 7.5% dividend rate. In June 1932 Henry received his last dividend from Empire. There was no indication of his having disposed of the stock.

• • •

We now close the fascinating farm history chronicled in Henry Daniel Griswold's financial day books. The entries stopped in 1933. Henry passed away on February 23rd of that year. To summarize is best left to Henry from a hand-written memo on his formal stationery with the heading "SHOWDOWN FARM GUERNSEYS of West Salem, Wisconsin". We estimate it was written in 1909.

> I was the first in this part of the state to use the Babcock test, and by its use have raised the average [butterfat production]. I was the first to put in the King system of ventilation, the first to test my cattle for tuberculosis, and one of the first to put up a silo. I believe in using business methods in farming as well as in any other line of business. I keep strict account

of everything. The farm has increased in fertility as shown by the fact that this year we put in the silo 200 tons of well eared mature corn from ten acres of land.

The income from the farm [provided] a meager living until last year when receipts from the products of sixty acres reached $4600.

I have four boys. The oldest has graduated from the Engineering course at Madison. The second has graduated from the Agriculture course. The third is taking his third year at the University, and the fourth will enter the University next year.

Less acres and more intelligent thorough methods is the crying need of the time.

I was born on a farm in Guilford, Connecticut, in 1853 of old New England stock. My father was one of the best farmers of his time and I was early taught the habits of industry, economy, and careful thorough work. I came to Wisconsin in 1874 and worked on a farm by the month two summers and taught school the winters. I settled on the farm I now have which consisted of forty acres. I could not get a living from 40 acres farmed in the general way of mixed farming. I took up potato farming for the John A. Salzer Company. I soon realized that potato growing could not be depended upon nor could the fertility of the farm be kept up.

I attended Farmers Institutes and Dairyman Conventions and took up dairying in earnest. I purchased a full blood [an old fashioned way of saying Purebred] sire. That was 20 years ago. I have kept full blood sires ever since and by careful selection, care, and good feeding have increased my income from year to year. We now have 60 acres and milk 20 to 25 cows.

Chapter Ten:

H. D. Griswold Management

"The dairyman must have lots of patience; 'hoping all things, enduring all things.' Thought and study brings out the best in the dairyman. Satisfaction in things accomplished makes it all worth while."

– H. D. Griswold

Henry Daniel Griswold

In the beginning of the twentieth century the only method for the state universities in Minnesota and Wisconsin to disseminate knowledge to farmers was through their sponsorship of Farm Institutes with classes run by educated farm practitioners. Most farmers were first or second generation immigrants with scant practical experience in farming and, as W. D. Hoard learned to his frustration, in many cases possessed a lack of interest and trust in formal knowledge. Henry Daniel Griswold had both the practical experience to be respected for his accomplishments in farming and the educational skills needed to communicate with these farmers and to interact with them in a classroom situation.

Farmers Institutes At Turn Of Century

H. D. Griswold and Ida Tilson travelling in winter for
Farm Institute lecture presentations

This chapter includes speeches and excerpts from his presentations at the Wisconsin Farmers Institutes. They offer an intimate insight into what farming was like in the early years of the twentieth century. A surprising number of concepts apply as well today as they did then.

HENRY DANIEL GRISWOLD PRESENTATIONS FOR THE WISCONSIN FARMERS INSTITUTE TAKEN FROM ON-LINE ARCHIVES OF THE UNIVERSITY OF WISCONSIN AGRICULTURAL LIBRARY:

EXPERIENCE IN BUILDING UP A HERD OF PROFITABLE DAIRY COWS

After hearing from Governor Hoard and others, H. D. Griswold, with 50 good acres of land and 4 or 5 dual purpose cows, decided to emphasize cream and butter production to better enhance his profitability. He chose purebred Guernsey dairy animals and used the Babcock butterfat test. From his heifers he kept the best and culled the rest. His average yield of butter per cow when he began testing in 1891 was 265 pounds per cow, increasing to 315 pounds in 1892, and staying above that amount with an average 350.7 pounds over a ten year period. The best year was 1897 with 392 pounds of butterfat on average, thus proving the efficacy of testing and using high quality purebred Guernsey bulls. The animals had a uniformity of appearance pleasing to the eye according to him. He stated that his average butterfat production was 400 pounds if heifers were not included in his report. Fifty years later average production was no better for many dairy farmers. Henry did not buy any heifers and was on his third purebred Guernsey bull when giving the following presentation.

> "There is, in my opinion, a great advantage in raising one's own cows. If one buys, one is liable to bring in some disease; then a new cow is strange to the place, and her fright scares the rest. My calves are pets from the start, and by the time they are grown, every conceivable noise that four healthy boys make they are used to; and when we milk, whether the boys laugh or whether they scrap, the cow chews her cud and gives down her milk just the same.
>
> Don't sell the best cows, no matter what the price offered. What is a cow worth that will give one seventy dollars a year clear profit? And after you have raised a nice heifer, don't sell her until you have tried her and found what she can do."

Henry's whitewashed barn was ventilated according to Professor King's plan. The stalls were 7 to 8 feet in width and equipped with a chain on each side for fastening around the cow's neck. Henry considered the dairy cow to be delicate and poorly designed for the long, hard winters of Wisconsin. She paid big returns for kindness, good feed, and warm, comfortable stables. The cows were milked first thing in the morning while eating a balanced ration of ground corn and oats, plus bran and either soybean or cottonseed oil meal. Ten to twelve pounds of grain were fed per day with care not to overfeed. The animals had access to unlimited quantities of corn stover. Henry did not have a silo as yet but was planning one when he wrote this essay. Grain was again fed at evening milking with all the hay they would consume overnight. Pastured cows were fed little grain until the pasture was short or not adequate, at which time access to grain was gradually increased. This old potato farmer also fed some culled potatoes. Having adequate water was a major problem – there were no individual water cups for the cows, so they needed to be taken from the stalls to the watering tank. By experimenting, Henry learned that copious amounts of water were essential for maximum production. He determined that a sick cow confined to the barn drank 100 pounds a day. Cold-weather exposed animals drank and produced less, so he kept producing animals indoors during inclement weather and made sure water was abundantly available.

"The best cow last year made 504 pounds of butter; the poorest, 200 pounds. The herd numbered eighteen. The best ten cows averaged 400 pounds per cow." Henry used average costs per head in ascertaining his profit margin, making no distinction to the fact that higher productivity required more quality inputs. Average cost was $30 per cow and average butter proceeds amounted to $65 per cow. Excessive moisture in the pasture that year caused a reduction in production, but a higher price brought in more proceeds than when production was better. The economics of scarcity was more profound without adequate cooling, storage, and transportation, at least when considered from today's vantage point. Skim milk was fed to the hogs, as it was a non-marketable source of cheap protein and other nutrients, with the added bonus of being a natural de-wormer. Cooling milk for urban consumption was not readily available in 1900.

Henry advocated weighing and testing so that a buyer would be willing to purchase a quality animal, but he did not advocate purchasing for the reasons given above. While the work of dairying was confining, he reasoned that earnings were made every day. He advocated patience and perseverance to overcome the discouragement that came with the inevitable setbacks.

HERD IMPROVEMENT by H. D. Griswold *

Henry Griswold used the example of a factory to describe milk production: a dairy cow consuming raw materials to produce milk is basically an animal factory. He explained that a manufacturer spent years of study and thought and invested considerable sums of money in perfecting his machine. The farmer, on the other hand, paid no attention to perfecting his dairy machine. He chided the farmers of 1908 that the process was simple and the returns large. Henry pointed out that the average Wisconsin dairy herd was a mixed lot with one cow having dairy capacity and the other an inferior dairy breed, such as shorthorn, thus worthless. He urged weighing and testing milk, culling poor producers, and studying the dairy breeds to decide on the line of breeding best suited for one's own environment. Henry continued by saying that farmers should pick a purebred sire with an ancestry of cows that have done good work. Do not be afraid to pay a premium as it will be the best investment you can make. Raise heifers carefully and take pride in them. Take more time with your dairy animals and less time with the field work. You can afford to do this, he said. With ups and downs over 17 years Henry boasted that the milk income gave his family the comforts of home and provided college for his children. The study and development of farm animals was a pleasure for the whole family.

In 1907 Henry's average receipts per cow totaled $147: $120 for cream, $15 for a calf at birth, and $12 average value of skim milk per cow. The average cost of feed was $44 for 21 cows including three heifers. One of his cows in 11 lactations had produced over 103,000 pounds of milk. He did not put a value on overhead costs or measure the hours of labor required or return per hour. (In the 1950s my father informed me that my time did not matter, as it should be available at all times for the enterprise.) At this time, Henry had two silos holding about 200 tons total, and corn silage was fed the entire year. Before Henry had silos, he had 18 cows with $1100 cream income. This was doubled to $2200 from 24 cows after he fed silage. Grain was not fed in the summer. The part that flummoxed some of his listeners was that his two-year-old heifers all produced 300 pounds of butter in the first lactation. After seventeen years of carefully selecting purebred Guernsey sires, he did not need to cull for productivity. He rejected many heifers in the beginning, but through production testing and strict culling unproductive strains were eliminated. At the second national dairy show in 1907, Henry's bull Endymion, No. 8916 A. G. C. C., was the Grand Champion.

A COW PER ACRE by Henry Daniel Griswold *

"In the first place, the land must be good, and in a high state of fertility. Big crops of corn saved in the silo, alfalfa hay cutting three crops in a season, successfully cured, sugar beets or mangels, will produce an immense amount of cow feed per acre. Oats and peas sown together and cut for hay, followed by rape, also yield large amounts of feed. Pasturing is a wasteful method on high-priced land. The silo and soiling crops will support more cattle than pasturing.

Our large farms are for the most part poorly tilled, robbed of their fertility because the owner will not keep the necessary amount of stock or needed help to work them properly."

Henry theorized that in those days it was not possible to purchase one or two hundred acres at one hundred dollars per acre and expect to eventually pay for it. Purchasing a few acres and using careful thought and study, much as a college-educated professional does in his specialty, would be more successful.

> "The advantages of a small farm are many. The hauling of manure and of crops is carried on much faster on account of the shorter distance. In using a manure spreader, a team and man will haul two loads forty rods in the same time required to haul one load two hundred rods. The same is true in nearly all the hauling. Less fencing is required, less feed has to be furnished, smaller amounts of capital, smaller taxes and general expenses are proportionally less."

Henry loved his little farm and family. By being next to town he saved time and money; being several miles from supplies and using horses as the main travel method would have required a long list, no mistakes, and plenty of time. With a small farm and a growing family he eventually eliminated the need for hired help. Furthermore, with a small farm he could control the work instead of the work controlling him. Henry advised shoring up the sacredness of the farm home by putting in a heating plant, a water system and sewage. He felt this was a better investment than more land. He said his land was "there from creation and will be there till the end of time." It was his "in trust to cultivate and improve for those that shall come after." Henry felt that the quiet, independent life of a dairy farmer would create possibilities unknown yet at that time. Perhaps it is for the best that he can't see the housing development on it now!

It took ten acres of land with well-matured corn to fill both of Henry's silos. This amounted to half the feed for his stock. One silo was 18 feet in diameter and 32 feet deep and the other 12 feet in diameter and 24 feet deep.

The corn-planting method was one seed per six inches in the row with the rows 3 feet 8 inches apart. It was drilled and not checked. Henry felt pastures consumed too much energy in navigating and would tire the cow before she had enough to eat. The silo was the only way, he concluded, that he could support one cow per acre of land. However, if he had to choose between a top quality registered bull or a silo, Henry would choose the bull.

THE COW – HOW TO FEED HER by H. D. Griswold*

"Farmers must be a student of agriculture over many years, adjust themselves to conditions, and adapt to new ways. Every season and soil is different creating differing feed values for the same crop. Each farmer must be a student of his own conditions and surroundings. Alfalfa and clover must be cut early and cured carefully to preserve the leaves and blossoms. Over ripe fibrous hay is unpalatable and will only be picked over and have fewer nutrients. Corn silage can be fed summer and winter, tastes good to the cow, and produces the most per acre. Farm feeds lack adequate protein and must be supplemented. Wheat bran is both high in protein, easily digested, and laxative. That and high protein meals balanced properly and fed carefully will provide healthy stock and good milk production. The more corn in the silage and the better quality the hay will lower the grain needed to balance the ration. Do not over feed to put fat in the productive animal and do not under feed. Each animal is different and must be fed accordingly. Feed to make sure the bowels never become too loose or constipated. A good, warm, well-ventilated stable saves feed. Pastures should have supplemental feed to achieve good nutrition and production. Have salt in small, adequate quantities. Have plenty of clear, pure water at moderate temperatures. Feed at the same time night and mornings. Love is a necessary ingredient given to the cow if you want her to produce well."

THE FARM HOME by Mrs. H. D. Griswold, published March 12, 1912*

According to Mrs. Griswold, the most serious problem and "stupendous fact" for the farm home was the farmer. When the mistress of the home had grasped and solved that successfully, she could rest assured of victory over all other problems. Mrs. Griswold's essay which follows focused on individuals rather than the physical assets of a farm home.

> "Farm men tend to be inflexible and of hard to convince temperament. They have an aversion once the clean clothes are on in the morning to washing up and cleaning up even if going to meet people in town as a waste of time. Her lament is for the farmer to see himself as others see him. While the farm denim so firmly attached to the farmer's soul is suitable and useful, it is an eyesore. At the time it was hard to employ and keep a dressmaker. If it were not for the mail order house or department store, the woman would be embarrassed by the lack of proper dress.

> A farmer is often forgetful and gets so involved in conversation in his community with like minded people he may forget to come home. There is many a traveling salesman invading the farm yard. Many products sold do not do what they say they will and as can happen 'A fool and her money are soon parted.' Love, pet, and praise your farmer husband as you can catch a fly a lot better with molasses rather than vinegar. A smile is better than a frown even when it is hard because of weariness or disappointment. Husbands and wives should tolerate each others whims, and support each other emotionally. It pays to be stingy. To buy tickets to every entertainment and church supper, to contribute to every worthy object would soon cripple people of moderate means. A kindly but firm 'No,' is often the most effective word in the language. Take time away from the work to enhance your well being. Others can fill in for a week. You can never read enough to gain in breadth of thought and expression as you can by the time away. A family united has strength in union while one divided is weak."

FARM MANAGEMENT by H. D. Griswold, written in 1912

Henry Daniel Griswold invoked biblical history to claim that the earth was prepared for man before he was created.

> "Man was given dominion over the earth and all living things upon it. The brain and the hands were to be applied to the application 'in the sweat of thy brow shalt thou eat bread.' The first farm management that history records was that of Adam. He made some mistakes: he raised fruit and he also raised Cain, and ever since this time man has been making mistakes, raising fruit and raising Cain.

> To be a success as a farm manager a farmer must have good common sense and a good wife. If he has the first, it will naturally follow he will have the last. The love of outdoor life of soil preparation, plant and animal life and all the things that contribute to it are a necessity."

Henry recommended a two-man operation as a better organizational tool than one man, such that by working together any job that came along could be handled. He also recommended using the best of everything to produce the healthiest product in demand by the consumer.

> "Always keep tools housed when not in use. Keep enough stock of some kind to consume the products of the farm on the farm; keep enough, but not more than you can keep well. Keep the best. Do not think you must raise everything, things that do not pay are best left to some one else. Do your own buying and selling as much as possible; pay cash and pay promptly."

Henry urged the farmer to keep his farmstead attractive and in good repair. He stressed the importance of adequately helping your wife and providing for her needs as well as for modern conveniences. She should be in charge of the home and treated with respect and dignity. Henry believed in 1912 that more and more women would manage farms and manage them successfully.

FERTILIZERS ON OUR FARMS by H. D. Griswold, written in 1913

Henry did not believe commercial fertilizers were necessary since the manure and other methods of enhancing fertility were used on Wisconsin dairy farms. He recommended more livestock intensity to produce stable manure for fertilizer. He felt farms were too large, as farmers were more interested in obtaining land than livestock. With high-quality stock more money could be made at home feeding the livestock than by selling grain and hay. He lamented the loss of the fertility from the liquid part of the manure. Henry recommended tight gutters and floors with enough absorbents to take up the liquid and hold it to save the nitrogen and other ingredients needed for the land. He advocated getting the product to the field as soon as possible after it was produced. "Do not let animals run and stand in creek beds, but keep them where their fertilizer can be saved for crop land." Clover needed to be seeded several times in many cases to get a proper stand. Henry recommended legumes to capture nitrogen from the air as well as for keeping the soil loose.

THE GUERNSEY as written by H. D. Griswold in 1913

"The assumption is that the present race of Guernsey cattle came to the Isle of Guernsey from France. Breeding animals for dairy quality has created excellent milk cows of a uniform type. 193 Guernseys were registered at the time of the establishment of the American Guernsey Breeders' Association in 1877. The Columbian Exposition in 1893 and the Pan-American Exposition proved the worth of the Guernsey by winning over all competition. At this writing, there are 39,500 Guernsey cattle in the United States. Wisconsin leads with 3000 located in 43 counties. New York is second with 2340, and Pennsylvania third with 2,066. These were also the three leading dairy states in the country."

Henry advised using the purebred Guernsey bull to enhance productivity up to 50%. For purchasing he recommended heifer calves rather than expensive cows with good records that would not fit into the environment and habits of the new owner. Henry's average production per cow at this time was 430 pounds of butterfat.

THE DAIRY SIRE by H. D. Griswold*

"The extra cost of a purebred sire pays for itself within three years. Never purchase the bull without establishing that high production is on both sides of the bull's family tree for generations. The bull's mother should have the type and quality for easy handling and longevity. A bull old enough to have progeny of his own is of use in how well increased productivity is transferred. Seven day records and fair premiums are irrelevant. Do not inbreed. Feed the bull for good breeding condition by keeping him healthy and not fat. Do not let him run with the herd. Keep him in a box stall."

FARM ACCOUNTS by H. D. Griswold, written in 1915*

"Farmers do not come by bookkeeping naturally. He loves the outdoors, works hard, and at the end of the day has no appetite for accounts. Once started a farmer sees its value and accounting CEASES to be a burden. It becomes a source of interest and even of pleasure. Farmers have a tendency TO PUT OFF paying accounts. Every farmer should pay his bills promptly. This will enhance his business reputation and simplify his bookkeeping. Habits are easily formed. Create the habit of sitting down at your desk after the day's work is done and writing down the day's accounts soon becomes a regular routine and is done as a matter of course. Using memory does not work and can create hard feelings if there is no verification of transactions. Never co-sign a note. This is a foolish custom and can result in serious loss."

*BUILDING A PRODUCTIVE DAIRY HERD
by H. D. Griswold, written in 1915*

"The cow you buy simply to give milk for a year or two is not respected as highly as one born on your farm, raised under your care, loved, nourished into being a mature animal of profit and beauty. If a prize winner and your work is connected with it, there is satisfaction greater than any dollar value.

When away for a period of time, the real dairyman is most interested in the welfare of the herd and young stock and not the cream check. Fads and fancy come and go. Many a good cow has been sacrificed to the ideal of color, conformity, and type. Never lose sight of productivity as being the main purpose of a cow. Let the millionaire do as he pleases. The man of business should look first to production and hold lightly to the minor things. Some lines of breeding are less resistant to disease and certain weaknesses. Be careful in selection.

In purchasing purebred sires, which is the only kind to buy, it is vital to choose one with uniform high productivity over many generations rather than phenomenal records of individual animals. Never purchase under-sized bulls as the offspring will be the same and it will limit the sale of offspring. Inbreeding can cause disaster and deterioration in many cases."

The following speech was probably presented in the winter of 1916 to the Wisconsin Farmer's Institute. It summarized H. D. Griswold's entire farming experience. For the full understanding of his philosophy, it is presented in its entirety in his own words rather than paraphrased.

FACTORS AFFECTING FARM INCOME

"The first and most important factor affecting the farm income is the man himself. He should be a master of the farm and not a servant to the farm. In any other business, the man fits himself for his work before he begins, and after that is constantly on the watch for new ideas and methods. He advertises his business and strives at all times to give his customers a good article and an honest deal. He anticipates their wants. He keeps strict account of his business and takes time to read and to attend meetings of men in his line of work.

The successful farmer today does not so much depend on brawn and muscle as in former years. He is thinking more, studying more, how shall he manage his soil to keep up its fertility, the crops to raise for the most profit, and he plans far ahead in the arrangement of crops to keep a rotation and use his land to the best advantage. He is studying the breeding of stock to produce the best horses, the most productive cows, the most economical pork, and hens that lay in the winter.

He must also be a man of skill and ability and resource. Nor can he leave his work to hired help but must be the master of the farm himself. He must be in personal touch with the work to be done. Time is precious, and every day's work should be planned ahead so there need be no delay. Changes in the weather necessitate change of plans, and many a time have I wakened in the night to hear it raining and at once commence to change the program for the next day's work.

Nothing thrives without care. It is the business of the farmer to know when the mare is due to foal, the cow to calve, the sow to farrow, and to see to it that they are properly cared for. Many animals die at birth and the cause is laid to luck, when the real cause is sheer neglect. Indifference, ignorance, and intemperance, are the main reasons for poverty on our farms. Eternal vigilance is the price of success.

Every farmer should be in touch with our University and the work they are doing. They can test his soil and tell him what it needs and help him in many ways, and they are ready and anxious to help him if he will give them the chance.

If you have a county representative, use him. If you have an agricultural school, use it. Make the most of these opportunities. And have a simple system of bookkeeping so that you know your business. Every other business man does. Why not you?

A good wife is a necessity. A bachelor never amounts to much in a farm or anywhere else. The wife many times is the better farmer, and thus many a good farmer has been made out of very poor material. She is mistress of the house, and can by wise management add greatly to the farm income, or she can be a burden that no farmer can carry and prosper. Boys and girls should not be counted as factors in the farm income. Their business is to go to school. It is right and proper that they should help what they can, but do not let a few dollars stand in the way of their education. Teach them to work, but don't work them too hard.

Instead of buying more land or putting money in the bank, put a little more into working capital in the shape of better stock and equipment. Have good horses and mares if possible of good type and blood, and breed them to the best sires. They can do a large amount of work and at the same time raise valuable colts that will add materially to the income of the farm. Keep good cows. Belong to a test association, and know your business, and cull out the poor unprofitable cows. Build up your herd by using a full blood sire of one of the recognized dairy breeds. Stick to one line of breeding and have a herd that is good to look at, that brings you a margin of profit above the cost of feed and brings a good price when you have one to sell. One of the most serious losses today is the feeding of crops to poor stock. There are farms in this state of 100 acres or less where the sales of milk and cream are over two thousand dollars per year, and the sale of stock is much more. There is no excuse for a farmer keeping poor hogs; study to produce the most hog with the least expenses for feed. One farmer in this state this last winter, even with the poorest corn crop in the history of the state, raised and sold fifty sows that brought him at auction on average of over sixty dollars each and an equal number of male pigs that brought him nearly as much. Poultry can be made a source of considerable income. Give them a properly constructed house and feed and care for them right so they will produce eggs in winter when the price is good and they will bring good profit for feed and small capital invested. But the way most farmers keep them there is little or no profit.

A silo is a strong factor in the farm income. Last fall the man with the silo could save his corn crop and use it, although it was badly frosted, and immature, and get good feed out of it. With a silo the corn can be all saved from the field and we have for winter milk production a feed that comes the nearest to grass feed of anything we can get. Also the summer silo is a great help to tide over dry spells when the pasture is short. Where tillable land is used for pasture there is much of the pasture grass trampled and soiled and wasted, and if the same land were put in corn, and that corn saved in the silo, very much more feed and milk could be secured from the same acreage. Alfalfa, I am satisfied can be grown in nearly all parts of the state. It will in most places need lime and inoculation, but it is well worth the time and expense required because it will furnish the protein of our dairy feeds which we are now buying outside the state and for which we are spending a large amount of money. Therefore the raising of alfalfa means a large factor in the farm income.

Seed grains can be made a source of special profit. It costs no more to raise the corn, and if by saving out the best and fire drying it you get two or three dollars per bushel instead of fifty or seventy-five cents, you are surely getting big pay for the extra work.

The same is true of oats or barley or potatoes. Sow and plant the best seeds, prepare the ground in the best possible shape, plant in season, and do not be satisfied with anything but the best, for therein lies the most profit.

Good fruit is also a source of profit, but it is of no use to set it out about special crops. Agents of canning factories, sugar beet factories, tobacco factories, and many others are only interested in their own profits. If a farmer has the help and suitable conditions and the crop can be handled without interfering with other crops, a small acreage may (remember, however, that special crops are soil robbers) handled at a profit. Plenty of good livestock must be the basis of all permanent agriculture.

Hired help: That farmer is fortunate who has help of his own. If he has a son who will stay with him, give that son so good a chance at home that no one else can tempt him away. If he must hire, then hire good men and give the men a good show. I have worked as a hired man and I have employed men. There are two sides to the question. A hired man today must be a different man than was employed when work was done more by hand. Today the man must be able to handle horses and machinery. If he is skillful with horses and in the proper care of machines, he can do much more work in a day and do it better and is consequently more profitable and worth more wage. If he takes an interest and does not have to be told everything, for instance, a farmer set his hired man to plowing while he went away for the afternoon on other business. The plow caught a root, and broke the beam. The man promptly took out the broken beam, used it for a pattern, hewed out a new beam from an oak fence post, fitted it in, and was plowing again when the owner came home. Such a man is worth more than a man who sits down and waits for someone to fix it for him. The best men are the cheapest in the end, and a poor man is dear at any price. One man worked for me eight years and others for long terms. After a man is used to your ways and methods, he is much more valuable. Therefore, pay him accordingly, treat him like a man and talk over the work with him. If he can give you some good ideas, use them, and above all, give him enough to eat!

We are getting more and more machinery for farm work. Some are of great help and some are good under certain conditions therefore the farmer should be careful in what he buys. A tractor may be all right on large level farms, but for the small farmer on side hill land had better stick to his horses. Be sure before you buy that the machine will pay you under your conditions. The farmers have spent large sums of money for machinery they did not need or was not adapted for their particular use. A machine that is only used one day in a year the farmer can hire much cheaper than to own it. But have those that you are sure you need, get the best, and keep them in good repair, especially have plenty of small tools. Keep all tools and machinery under cover when not in use and cleaned up after using. Machinery is injured more by neglect than by actual use. I have a potato planter that has been in use every year for thirty years with practically nothing spent for repairs, which is in good condition now because it has always been under cover when not in use and has never been lent.

One farmer in crossing his neighbor's farm and meeting him said: "I found fifty dollars lying in the grass behind the straw stack." It was in the shape of a mowing machine.

Drive the work and don't let the work drive you. One man can handle three or four horses just as well as two and do proportionally more work. Get the horses out early in the morning in the busy season. Let others do the chores, but the men who use the horses must get in full days.

Marketing: So far as possible the farmer should market his own product. Advertising what he has to sell he must do if he wishes to bring his product before the public. Then he must put on the market a first class article. The public today is demanding quality as never before. If we wish to succeed we must put up the very best that brings the price. You cannot force anyone to buy poor stuff. In all the co-operative companies that have made any marked success there has been a cooperative movement to produce better, cleaner, more uniform and a more honest product.

Every farmer today is making his own reputation. My brother, what kind of a reputation are you making for yourself? Because upon it will depend one of the vital factors affecting your farm income."

Henry's insistence in the very early 1900's to be a man of business, first echoing much of what was said by W. D. Hoard, is in sharp contrast to many over the generations who simply demanded their right to farm regardless of the consequences.

Chapter Eleven:

La Crosse County Guernsey Breeders

The La Crosse County Guernsey Breeders' Association was organized March 20, 1907, when thirty farmers interested in Guernsey cattle met at the La Crosse County Bank. Ray Lewis was elected Chairman, Harry W. Griswold was elected Secretary and William Dudley elected as Treasurer. W. J. Hanson and Harry Jewett formed the rest of the executive committee. Henry Daniel Griswold and A. J. Phillips were among the twenty-four founding members.

The Constitution of the Association stated its objective: "to promote the breeding and improvement of high grade and pure bred Guernsey cattle in La Crosse County and to aid its members in buying, using, and selling first-class animals ... The annual membership shall consist of men interested in the object of this Association and paying the required dues."

An interesting concept in Article 4 was the requirement of a vice-president for each township in the county. This indicated a hoped-for increase in the Guernsey population in the county, while circumventing the problematic and cumbersome transportation and communication methods of the times. In Section 7 of the by-laws each township vice-president was not only to look after the interests of the association but also to call meetings on his own to advance those interests.

Section 2 of the by-laws stated, "It shall be the privilege of every member to improve his herd of cattle by mating his cows exclusively to purebred Guernsey bulls and doing as much as he can to care for his herd in an up-to-date manner."

On March 4, 1908, the first meeting since inception was held, with the re-election of the same officers. A discussion of the work in progress in testing for tuberculosis was held.

On February 20, 1909, the third annual meeting was held. The Dairy Institute was discussed. An offer to hold the annual meeting of the Western Wisconsin Guernsey Breeders at the H. D. Griswold farm was made. The offices of secretary and treasurer were combined and held by H. W. Griswold. Ray Lewis was re-elected President.

On March 10, 1910, the fourth annual meeting was held. The executive committee was instructed to hire a competent individual to test for tuberculosis beginning by fall. The executive committee was charged to solicit funds to make up the deficit in the treasury. Adolph Nuttleman was elected President and Harry Jewett Secretary-Treasurer.

On March 4, 1911, the fifth annual meeting was held with all officers re-elected. The executive committee was instructed to look into the feasibility of having a fall sale. A plan to have a sale pavilion was even discussed.

The sixth annual meeting was held March 9, 1912. Special presentations were given on Guernsey cattle, abortion, and alfalfa. Nothing special was of note from 1913 to 1916. The missing Secretary's reports from 1917 through 1920 coinciding with World War I leads to speculation about the community environment during that time.

Clinton Griswold was President when the meeting was called to order on February 16, 1921. There was a report on a cattle sale on March 24, 1920. H. D. Sandman was secretary and Herman Bonsack, treasurer. L. E. Jewett, a prominent county Guernsey executive for the next forty years, was in charge of the new calf club project. The secretary was charged with getting the Inter-State Fair to create a dairy department.

1923 Guernsey parade in downtown West Salem

From 1921 through 1924, my grandfather Edward Young was chairman of the sale auditing committee, and H. W. Griswold was chairman of the sales committee. The annual meeting on February 24, 1924, saw the adoption of a county show herd with Adolph Nuttleman, A. S. Hyzer, and Emil Miller appointed to create the herd. Assignments were made to supervise the judging of Guernsey cattle at the Inter-State Fair. It was adopted that one percent of the gross proceeds of the cattle sale be used for advertising, a show herd, and other expenses. The executive committee was instructed to organize a summer picnic.

When the annual meeting was held on February 16, 1925, the sales manager was instructed to find room for the animals to be sold. A committee of three, M B. Lee, Vilas Young, and P. A. Larson, was appointed by the president to establish a market for Guernsey milk in La Crosse.

At the 1926 annual meeting it was agreed to hire a bookkeeper for the cattle sales. It was agreed to charge sale consignors fifty cents per head per day up to sale day for care and feed. My father was elected Secretary in 1926, a position he held for 32 years until the annual meeting in 1958.

At the 1927 annual meeting it was decided to join the state association. In 1928 M. B. Lee became president, replacing Clinton Griswold who had held that office since before 1921.

On June 13, 1928 the La Crosse County Guernsey Breeders' Association turned over all assets to La Crosse County Guernsey Breeders' Inc. Twenty-six members voted in favor and none against. This corporation was formed under Chapter 180 of the Wisconsin statutes of 1927 and was recorded in volume seven of Miscellaneous Records, page 166, Document Number 276019.

The first meeting of the corporation directors was held the same date on June 13, 1928. Incorporators of the corporation were listed as M. B. Lee, Vilas Young, Homer Wolf, L.E. Jewett, J. J. Bean, and L. T. Lee. There were thirty-five members at the time of the incorporation receiving certificates of membership. A committee of three was appointed to take charge of the dairy parade at the Wisconsin State Guernsey Picnic to be held in West Salem June 28, 1928. Guest speakers were to be the retailer and Guernsey breeder J. C. Penney and the Governor of Wisconsin.

The second director's meeting of the La Crosse County Guernsey Breeders' Inc. was held September 16, 1928, in the Village of West Salem. H. W. Griswold, sales manager, discussed history and progress of the cattle sales and methods of improvement. President M. B. Lee appointed L. E. Jewett, Elmer H. Larson, and Vilas Young as the sales committee. A discussion ensued about purchasing the O. G. Clark & Co. sales barn, and an understanding of the cost of a possible purchase was established. The sales committee and sales manager were to work together in seeking a purchase.

The third meeting of the La Crosse County Guernsey Breeders' Inc. Board of Directors was held October 31, 1928. A motion was passed to purchase the barn of Jacob W. Patterson for $6800 with the sum of $500 to be paid November 1 and $6300 upon receipt of clear title. It was also passed to borrow $3000 from Bert Dayl for a period of five years at a rate of six per cent, with the first mortgage provided to the lender. At a meeting of the directors held December 31, 1928, H. W. Griswold was hired to be sales manager for the March 29, 1929 sale.

The second annual meeting of the members of the new corporation was held February 19, 1929. The fifth meeting of the directors was held immediately thereafter with M. B. Lee as president, L. E. Jewett as vice-president and Vilas Young as secretary-treasurer.

At the seventh meeting of the directors held September 14, 1929, it was approved to charge sale consignors seventy-five cents per head per day to the day of the sale with the time of care not to exceed seven days. Thirty days after each sale the sales manager was required to supply the Board of Directors with a detailed report on the sale. At the eighth meeting of the Board held December 21, 1929, the charge of care and feeding was reduced back to fifty cents. Ten dollars was to be charged for one freight load of cattle and fifteen dollars for an express load.

The third annual meeting of the La Crosse County Guernsey Breeders' Inc. was held February 1, 1930. A rule was passed that any member found using oleomargarine on his table would be expelled from the Association! In order to promote the Guernsey breed, it was decided to award a deserving youth a registered Guernsey calf to show and to become the foundation of his or her registered Guernsey herd. It was also agreed that any profits in excess of $400 from the two annual sales were to be returned to consignors according to the value of the animal consigned. A committee was formed to consider the possibility of putting on an annual dairy show in the pavilion.

The fourth annual meeting of the La Crosse County Guernsey Breeders' Inc. was held February 10, 1931. It was noted that bulls of inferior productivity were being purchased because of their lower cost during that time of low milk prices. The members proposed to petition the state legislature to exempt a purebred bull from property tax provided proper registry papers were provided. Annual dues were increased from one dollar to two dollars and fifty cents. The University of Wisconsin had stopped blood testing for abortion, and the members resolved to petition the University to continue this valuable program. The fourteenth meeting of directors elected H. W. Griswold, president, L. E. Jewett, vice-president, and Vilas Young, secretary-treasurer.

At the fifth annual meeting held February 6, 1932, it was decided to give each county member an annual subscription to the *Guernsey Breeders Journal*. Preparation was made for a silver anniversary celebration.

The 27th meeting of the Board of Directors held March 23, 1935, called for the purchase of the La Crosse County Sales Company for fifteen hundred dollars. It was unanimously adopted.

Due to the Great Depression there was no Guernsey sale for an extended period. The last report given prior to a regular sale was December 19, 1931, and the last mention of any sale in the records was a combined Guernsey and Holstein bull sale held November 21, 1932. The Guernsey breeders created a private sale committee to continue efforts to sell cattle. At the ninth annual meeting of members dated February 8, 1936, it was voted to resume sales. On February 8, 1936, Adolph Nuttleman replaced H. W. Griswold as president. Griswold, Jewett, and Young had been the three main officers since 1931. Griswold would be elected to the U. S. Congress in November, 1938. The Wisconsin State Guernsey picnic was held in West Salem June 9, 1936.

The spring sale in 1936 as reported by the secretary was so successful that it was voted to have a fall sale. It was voted at the thirty-second Board meeting held January 2, 1937, to have a spring sale April 28 and a fall sale November 17.

At the tenth annual meeting of members held February 17, 1937, the testing committee announced the creation of a Guernsey production testing association. At the thirty-third Board of Directors meeting held immediately thereafter the three principal officers were designated to be the sales committee.

At the forty-second meeting of directors held January 13, 1940, it was established that board members attending the annual state meeting be reimbursed for one night's lodging and one-quarter cent per mile.

The official records of the secretary recorded that there were five sales conducted in 1939. There were a total of seven sales in 1940 with three of those in the spring of the year. There was one spring sale and one fall sale in 1941. The board of directors in January of 1942 adopted a charge of three dollars a head and a four percent commission on all cattle consigned to their sales.

At the fifteenth annual meeting of members held in February, 1942, the Guernsey breeders after making inquiries into the use of artificial breeding adopted a committee of two members from each township to join the Vernon County Breeder Co-op. With the outbreak of World War II, the secretary was instructed to invest $750 in a War Bond.

Grade A milk programs were discussed in 1943. The designation of an "A" was for a higher standard of milk health quality than that regularly sold from a farm, including low bacteria counts and other specific requirements. Today all 65,000 dairy farmers from the fifty states must qualify to produce Grade A milk. Four hundred pages of rules first created in the 1920's dealing with quality controls and milk production processes must be adhered to with assurances to the integrity and continuity of such practices. The integrity of producing milk, including the input from manufacturers and cooperatives provided to the dairy farmer, the production of top quality milk at the farm, the hauling of the milk, the processing including pasteurization, homogenization, and preparing of the milk for sale in its many forms, and not least the assurance at the retail level of proper cooling and dating of this top quality dairy product to assure the public of its healthful and nutritious benefits was only accomplished through many generations of trust among all of the participants. For an excellent understanding read *The Economics of Integrity* by Anna Bernasek published in 2010 by HarperCollins. This book emphasizes the many positive players who over centuries developed trusting relationships we take for granted today that continue to enhance our lives and productivity.

C. D. Griswold reported at the nineteenth annual meeting of members February 9, 1946, that seven "Eastern" bulls were purchased. The secretary was instructed to pay Mr. Griswold for the bulls. Progress was reported on a new Dairy Herd Improvement Association. This milk testing association would provide for a full-time milk tester including the production testing of all breeds of dairy cattle. Tuberculosis and Bangs, formally known as brucellosis, or contagious abortion disease, could be devastating to a dairy herd. Brucellosis and tuberculosis eradication programs had long been sponsored by the La Crosse County Guernsey Breeders' Inc. At the 63rd meeting of the Board of Directors immediately following the members meeting it was mandated that all animals coming through the sales barn must be tested at that time for Bangs. At the urging of Norman Rowe, the West Salem High School agriculture instructor, a Junior Guernsey Association was established.

N. N. Rowe was an agricultural institution unto himself. An orphan and a graduate of the University of Minnesota, he came to West Salem to teach agriculture in the 1920s and was extremely active well into the 1970s. He developed meat judging teams that won national Future Farmer of America trophies in Kansas City. His prowess at creating purebred hog farmers with a national show ring reputation was second to none. Every year for decades he would organize his F.F.A. boys to show purebred hogs at the Wisconsin State Fair. His on-farm tutoring of these projects carried on throughout the year created the best possible animals to be shown and marketed. Mr. Rowe's instruction of many generations of agriculturists enhanced the entire community. He supported and worked hard with the Guernsey breeders during all the years of his tenure. He travelled to get top quality seed potatoes from northern Wisconsin every year for his farm constituency. He held regular night classes for his famers every winter. University of Wisconsin professor Robert Grummer said at one of those night meetings I attended that he would not have bothered to come from Madison except there was no way he would let "Norm" Rowe down. Mr. Rowe encouraged advanced education for his farm boys, and many a doctoral recipient making an advanced science contribution to his country did so because of Mr. Rowe.

1945 Guernsey Youth exhibitors at the La Crosse County Fair

At the 64th Board of Directors meeting held February 23, 1946, the intricacies of multiple leases were discussed. The pavilion itself was owned by the La Crosse County Breeders' Association of which C. D. Griswold was president. They wished to sell the pavilion, and it was agreed by the Guernsey Board to purchase the building for $3000. Two thousand dollars would be borrowed at 3.5% interest. In September of 1946, Harry Martin requested renting the pavilion as a roller skating rink.

At the 27th annual meeting held February 13, 1954, a resolution was adopted to send to the family and keep in record the condolences on the passing of President Adolph Nuttleman, a founding member, periodic president and very active participant for all 47 years of service including financial support in times of need. At the 87th meeting of the Board of Directors held the same day, L. E. Jewett became president and Melvin Schomberg vice-president.

At the 94th Board meeting held October 11, 1956, the rule that profits in excess of $400 be returned to consignors was rescinded. It was costly to administer if strictly adhered to and not in the best interests of the Association.

The 101st meeting of Directors held February 22, 1958, was the last signed by Secretary V. E. Young. He was re-elected to the Board of Directors but refused to continue as secretary-treasurer as he felt it was a time for new ideas. He had served in that position since March 15, 1926, for a total of thirty-two years. My father served on the sales committee for a quarter of a century, during which time there were up to nine sales in a single year. He was one of the founders of the La Crosse County Farm Bureau, served on the Equity Marketing Board, and was president of the West Salem Farmers' Supply and Shipping Association for many years. He served on many state agricultural committees. Most evenings after dairy farm work was done, if he was not attending a meeting, he would be found working at his desk until time for bed. I feel that my father Vilas Edward Young was a truly selfless farm leader at the time of the development of the agricultural infrastructure of the United States. West Salem is but one local community. Multiply this rural community by all those throughout America with their many dedicated leaders – this created the solid infrastructure of American agriculture.

Vilas E. Young

In 1970, La Crosse County Guernsey Breeders' Association, Inc. built a "pump-over" station on West Jefferson Street in West Salem. Milk from La Crosse, Monroe, Jackson, Vernon, and Trempealeau County Guernsey farms was brought daily to this station. The milk was conveyed into tankers each holding twenty-three tons (over 5300 gallons) of milk for shipment to Des Moines, Iowa, where a premium over the regular milk price was received. The station was sold to Golden Guernsey Co-operative July 1, 1972.

As of this writing the original charter of the La Crosse County Guernsey Breeders' Association is still in effect. The centennial of the organization on March 20, 2007, came and went without celebration. There are no longer enough Guernsey dairy farmers left in La Crosse County for viable activity.

The Wisconsin Guernsey Breeders Association still actively serves the area and in 2008 played an essential role in the National Guernsey meeting in Madison, Wisconsin. The national annual meeting is held in Wisconsin every six years or so. It was held in La Crosse in 1997 and is expected to be held there again in either 2013 or 2014, according to Deb Lakey, the influential secretary of the Wisconsin Guernsey Breeders Association. The Great Northern Classic sale in the fall of the year has been replaced by the Upper Midwest Spring Sale and is held annually in West Salem at the La Crosse Inter-State Fairgrounds. This sale is coordinated with the American Guernsey Association, but ninety per cent of the animals originate from Wisconsin, with the rest being from Minnesota and Iowa. The Parrish shows held in West Salem since the early 1900s continue to this day. The original shows, involving several contiguous counties, have been replaced by six Parrish shows throughout Wisconsin, allowing anyone from the state to show at whatever show or shows they prefer.

A mile from where we farmed, the high quality registered Guernsey farm of Don and Kathy Langrehr, Lang Haven Dairy, has gained national prominence. Keeping everything in the family, Kathy's sister married Steve Nuttleman, the great grandson of Adolph Nuttleman, one of the founders of the La Crosse County Guernsey Breeders. Steve and his daughter Alyssa have gained prominence showing registered Guernsey cattle at the World Dairy Expo in Madison, Wisconsin. Alyssa showed the Grand Champion, "Adams Creek Div Mary Kate-ET", in 2011 at the National Junior Show in Louisville, Kentucky.

The Guernsey breed no longer commands the dominant presence it once had. We will examine later what transpired and its implications for the future. We still need to focus on the largest sale pavilion of its kind in the United States.

Chapter Twelve:

ℑhe Pavilion

The "Guernsey Pavilion" of West Salem, Wisconsin, was the largest of its kind in the United States in the twentieth century. It housed upwards of three hundred head of cattle at its capacity in a building so large there were three sets of barn-sized stalls in one facility. The one-story building had overhead storage facilities for grain, hay, straw and repair materials. Attached was the large main sales barn with the sales ring, bleacher seats, food facilities, rest room, furnaces, and managerial and storage facilities for Harry Martin's roller skating rink. This whole plant was across Mill Street directly west of the West Salem Village Park, later known as Emil Miller Park, and within two blocks of the railroad depot. A separate entrance from Mill Street led to a room used for milk testing, which also served as a voting facility.

Years before this incredible complex had even been envisioned, the first sales by the West Salem Guernsey Breeders were held at a barn owned by Charlie Knudson that had been an exhibition barn at the original La Crosse County Fairgrounds just west of the village of West Salem and south of Highway 16. The barn was moved close to the railroad tracks in West Salem in 1904. The Knudson barn was purchased in 1918 by the La Crosse County Guernsey Breeders' Association, the same year construction started on the Pavilion. The first Guernsey sale in the newly completed Pavilion was in March 1920.

In 1922 O. G. Clark and Jacob Patterson, both from the state of Georgia, built modern, well-equipped cattle barns to the south of the Pavilion. They were immediately used as the new cattle holding facilities for sales. These buildings eventually were purchased by the La Crosse County Guernsey Breeders' Inc. in 1946. The Knudson barn was sold to the Town of Hamilton in 1928 for machinery storage.

In September 1946 Harry Martin contracted with the La Crosse County Guernsey Breeders' Inc. to run a roller skating rink in the Pavilion. When no sales were occurring, it was better known by the community as the Martin Roller Rink, with roller skating Friday and Saturday evenings as well as Sunday afternoons. Harry and my father were good buddies, and Harry looked after me on the rink where I spent more time on my butt than upright! Harry kept the facilities clean and warm, made sure all the water pipes did not freeze and cooperated fully when it was time for a cow sale. The Pavilion also was the scene for the annual Fireman's Dance, many 4-H dances, even wedding dances! It was home to plays and other festivities including the infamous "Womanless Wedding" in which male community leaders dressed as ladies performed a wedding ceremony.

A discussion of the Pavilion brings on a warm nostalgic feeling as my mind sifts through the many extraordinary sights and people I encountered there as a young person. Father was in charge of the sales during most of my life growing up on our farm. Sales would usually go late into the evening even though they started promptly at noon. At times the inventory was so large that the sale extended another day. After school on a sales day I would go to the Pavilion to enjoy the atmosphere. I always accompanied father on his frequent trips to the facilities and enjoyed the company of the many people who were part of this fascinating environment.

Upon leaving the Pavilion and walking past the first group of stanchions in the sales barn, I would walk into the barn area and make a sharp right into the corridor leading to Dr. Evenson's veterinary office. The corridor usually smelled of some pink stuff in round cardboard boxes. Near the end of the corridor was Dr. Evenson's office. In winter when the door was closed, I would enjoy the warm steady heat from the miniscule pot-bellied furnace. This was especially enjoyable as the cold cement floor and the un-insulated block exterior of the building made it rather chilly. William Larson, Dr. Evenson's office assistant, sat at an old brown desk. I always remember him wearing a dark button-down sweater. Because space was tight, guests would lean against the long table directly across from the door. "Knuppy," an elderly trucker, could usually be seen there waiting for someone who needed cattle moved. Dr. Evenson was responsible for the health of the cattle going through the Pavilion as well as for making sure all vaccinations and paper work were in order. It was a meeting place for friends and for keeping up with community gossip.

Long before I was born in 1938 there were several cattle sales a year at the Pavilion. I know but little of the sales other than those sponsored by the La Crosse County Guernsey Breeders. Many East Coast dairymen producing milk and compost for the metropolitan market did not raise their own replacement cattle. My father would take cattle "jockeys" who were mainly from New Jersey to meet with potential sellers of dairy cattle from our surrounding Coulee region. These jockeys would buy heifers or mature cows which were ready to freshen (to calve and begin to produce milk). Up through the early 1950s La Crosse County was a major cattle source for the eastern milking market, with railroad carloads of freshening dairy animals leaving West Salem weekly.

When Kathy and I worked in New Jersey in the 1970s, I took my father to visit Mr. Greenberg, an old friend, who was my Dad's major contact in those good old days. When a dairy farmer in our area had a cow for sale, Mr. Greenberg would be brought into the barn to see the animal. He would look but make little or no comment. He would walk slowly about the barn and point to an animal and say, "What about this one?" It invariably was the very best producing cow in the farmer's herd. Before Mr. Greenberg or any of these "cattle jockeys" left the farm, he might have bought the cow the farmer wanted to sell, but most assuredly only if the "best" cow was also part of the deal.

Letters to sales consigners were printed establishing date of auction, health and other requirements as needed to sell cattle. Pictures of "THE PAVILION" were prominent on the letterhead and the return address of the envelope. At age seven or eight, I was properly folding the letter into thirds, and as the pile fell over, I would stuff them into envelopes previously addressed by me. One could only guess about how many letters were needed, thus as the pile of envelopes grew and fell over, we would pack them into boxes and start all over again. Since we also needed to inform potential buyers of the sale, a printer would print on the business side of a penny post card the date of sale and conditions. Using my recently acquired cursive writing skills, I would address the post cards to be mailed, the same as we did the envelopes. Addressing was really a family affair, but to me at that tender age, I felt mighty proud to be included in such matters!

As the time of the sale neared there would be a bustle of activity getting the sale barn ready and answering inquiries. Mom would run out of the house and yell at my Dad, "Long distance!" A long distance call was expensive in those days, and wherever my father was on the farmstead, he would come on the dead run.

On the day of the sale, long white cards at least two feet tall and over a foot wide printed on both sides provided a list of all the Guernseys for sale as well as conditions of the sale. The Pavilion's roller rink was converted to a sale ring loaded with saw dust and roped off at the point of the two doors for entry and exit of the cattle. With this setup, there was never an interruption in the proceedings. The auction ring was surrounded on three sides with bleacher seats going up quite high. At the table in the sales ring, Earl "Feathers" Jewett read the pedigrees, and he and the auctioneer traded tales and inspirational one-liners. There were two "ring men" accepting bids. As most of the cattle were neither halter-trained nor used to being surrounded by such a multitude, there was no end to the cajoling getting them into the ring and turned so the spectators could get a good look.

My favorite memory was when "Unc" (Orrin Young) was helping move animals around the ring. One especially feisty cow came up from behind and belted "Unc" full force with her head. "Unc" fell flat on his ample rump with both legs spread out and the most peculiar expression on his face. Was there deep concern for whatever possible injury my Uncle sustained? The place roared with laughter!

Behind the bleachers was the food stand provided by the West Salem School's band mothers. The offering always included barbeque and ham sandwiches, milk, coffee, soda, and above all many homemade cakes and pies. That fare was worth fighting for!

Time marches on. Cattle numbers dwindle. We sold our registered Guernsey herd in "The Pavilion" on September 2, 1967. Three days later I was in college. The Great Northern Classic was an annual sale held with select high quality registered Guernseys from throughout the Midwest. The last sale in the Pavilion was on August 26, 1972.

The La Crosse County Guernsey Breeders' Association Inc. sold the West Salem Sales Pavilion for $25,000 with possession by John and Leo Hansen of Bangor, Wisconsin on September 1, 1972. Five thousand dollars of the sale proceeds were donated for a newly built Farm Progress Building at the Inter-State Fairgrounds in West Salem, the future home of the Great Northern Classic Sale. The cattle barns were torn down to become parking lots. For a while this once vital part of the Guernsey world and community social events became a grocery store owned by the Hansens. Even that chapter of history closed. Time indeed marches on, and today most of the residents of West Salem remain wholly ignorant of the vibrant beginnings of their now urbanized community.

Chapter Thirteen:

Mid-Century Pioneers

A PRODUCTION PIONEER

Travel from the one-time hotbed of Guernsey activity in West Salem five miles west on Highway 16 and you reach what was arguably once the best producing registered Guernsey herd in the mid twentieth century. The fertile valleys with productive swards of vegetation lying between the magnificent grandeur of the surrounding bluffs are now scarred by Valley View Mall and its associated building frenzy. This inevitable push of "progress" includes a Culver's frozen custard and burger restaurant where once stood the stately brick home of Mary and Bernard Pralle.

Bernard's farming experience began in his youth as a 4-H member. At that time the Pralle family herd was a mixed group of dairy animals. He received a purebred Guernsey from Carl Zoerb as the prize for exhibiting the first place animal in the senior yearling class at the La Crosse Inter-State Fair. Bernard turned this meager beginning into a national and internationally prominent registered Guernsey enterprise. This success emphasized the ideal of the La Crosse County Guernsey Breeders' youth calf program.

Bernard was born May 3, 1920, on the 200-acre family farm purchased by his parents in 1917. His favorite story from his youth is how the family sheep "mowed the lawn" of the nearby Fauver Hill School. The sheep would be driven across the highway to the fenced-in school yard that had a water supply at which they could drink. They would remain there until the lawn was "mowed." The original Pralle farm was split into two parts in 1936 with the building of Highway 16, the major artery connecting West Salem and La Crosse. In the late 1960's the farm was further divided when Interstate 90 was built. The final insult that took the remainder of this productive farm began in the 1970s with the development of an enclosed mall followed later by a much expanded shopping phenomenon.

Bernard and Mary Pralle began their farm operation in 1947. In their first completed year of dairying the herd averaged 350 pounds of butterfat on a 305-day testing basis. When the herd was auctioned on the farm on September 23, 1989, their ninety cows' rolling production for the prior 365 days through August, 1989, was 16,702 pounds of milk, with a 4.5% butterfat test yielding 752 pounds of butterfat and a 3.5% protein average test producing 588 pounds of protein per cow. These records were extraordinary then and perhaps remain so today with the Guernsey being a small minority breed capable of providing the solids, protein, and butterfat required in the making of cheese. The average cow on test today in the United States produces 20,000 pounds per lactation.

Measuring agricultural productivity since 1961 is mindboggling. The International Plant Nutrition Institute states that crop yields per acre more than doubled since 1961, making it possible to feed the world's growing population with only a 27 percent increase in land usage. Without this productivity increase, 292 percent more productive land would have been required to reach the production levels of 2005.

Bernard was influential in establishing protein pricing for milk when the ability to measure protein content in milk first became available. Since protein is an important ingredient in the production of cheese, the Guernsey breed competes favorably with other breeds in marketing milk for cheese production.

By tradition, the farm and its proprietor were always recognized by the name of the man. Mary's influence and contribution to their dairy accomplishments were recognized early on – it was just wrong to mention one of them without the other! The American Guernsey Cattle Club established the Master Breeder Award in 1985. In 1990 the Master Breeder Award went to "Bernard and Mary Pralle," the first award for Wisconsin, but most significantly this represented the first time wherein a husband and wife received the award jointly as a married couple. From 1991 through 1999 no other married couple nor any Wisconsin breeder received that award. The Master Breeder Award in the eleven years between 2000 and 2010 was awarded to seven couples including three from Wisconsin. To emphasize further the changing culture of the Guernsey breed, Jillian Walther, a woman from Garnavillo, Iowa, was elected in 2010 as first vice-president of the American Guernsey Association.

The Pralles' received the American Guernsey Association Gold Star Award twenty-three times, a productivity distinction within the Guernsey breed. As of the end of 2010 this record places them in a fourth-place all-time tie with W.D. Hoard and Sons. Bernard served as Wisconsin State Guernsey Association president and was on the board of directors of the American Guernsey Cattle Club for nine years, including being on the Guernsey Sire Committee all of those years.

After forty-two years of dairy farming, Bernard believed if he ever had to do it all over again, he would keep his herd at forty cows instead of expanding. He did not believe his standard of living was adequately compensated for by more than doubling the size of his herd. With expansion Bernard employed a herdsman devoted exclusively to the dairy animals and needed more inputs resulting in less return per unit of production.

Bernard Pralle

At their Guernsey dispersal sale September 23, 1989, 255 head were sold from 10 a.m. to 5 p.m. Fauver Hill AK Radiance, a five year old cow and the 1987 grand champion at the Wisconsin State Fair and a veteran of the show ring at the World Dairy Expo, was the first to be sold and went to a Michigan buyer for $7,400. In recent times a Guernsey has sold for over $50,000. However, at the 2010 National Guernsey Sale the top animal went for $15,000 and the second for $10,100. The top fifty consignments at the Pralle sale averaged $4153. Fauver Hill Tel Odette, ranked one of the top ten Guernseys in the nation for type and production, was purchased by Phil and Joyce Laesch of Curtis, Wisconsin, for $5200. The Laesch family had worked for the Pralles for three years. When they left to start their own operation they purchased twenty-three head of Pralles' cattle. Fourteen head in the dispersal went to California. Other buyers were from Vermont, Michigan, Ohio, Missouri, Iowa, Minnesota, and Wisconsin. Sixteen cows in the sale were classified excellent and forty three very good. There were six classifications in the Guernsey breed at the time of the sale: excellent, very good, desirable, acceptable, fair, and poor.

It is estimated that perhaps two hundred Guernsey herds throughout the United States had animals purchased from the Pralles during their herd's existence. This does not include the bulls Mary and Bernard sold to artificial insemination stud farms. The Pralles' accomplishments, known throughout the Guernsey world, made them the preferred source for anyone seeking the best animals in the breed.

A PRICING PIONEER

LA CROSSE COUNTY
GUERNSEY-JERSEY BREEDERS

ARE PROUD OF

NORBERT NUTTELMAN

Who Played An Important Role In -

1958 – Marketing the first Guernsey milk to Walker Farms Dairy, Mississippi

1960 – Getting a market in New Orleans and North Carolina

1965 – Securing a market at Leibers Dairy, Nebraska
Building a pump-over station in West Salem

1968 – Marketing milk with A & E, Des Moines, Iowa

1977 – Forming Tri-State Milk Producers with Minnesota and Iowa

1980 – Forming a new Tri-State Milk Cooperative to promote cheese yield
pricing system – 125 members

1984 – Tri-State Milk Cooperative expansion to 635 members in 6 states

For Norbert, the final recognition that the value of milk is in its
components and not in volume, has made all this worthwhile for all
the frustrations and time involved.

THINK POSITIVE – IT PAYS

Our second mid-century pioneer is Norbert Nuttleman, a self-educated gentleman from Barre Mills, a tiny community five miles south of West Salem. He pursued innovative pricing mechanisms for Guernsey milk and selflessly served his community and state. Norbert's calm demeanor with always a gentle smile understated his competence and commanding presence. No situation, regardless of complexity or controversy, seemed to faze him as he competently worked until reaching a satisfactory conclusion.

Norbert was born March 8, 1911. His father died when he was a high school freshman, and Norbert found himself a full-fledged farmer at the age of fifteen in 1926. Norbert met and wooed Edna Rewinkel, a registered nurse at the Lutheran Hospital in Sioux City, Iowa. Edna, whose mother died when she was less than a year old, was a native of Wakefield, Nebraska. In those days with men doing the outside work and women the inside, her father could not properly care for and raise a young child. He arranged for her to live with a nearby family that had no children, and eight to ten years later she was passed on to someone else. He always paid for her care, because without such a monetary agreement, she could have been legally adopted by the care givers. Her father ate dinner with her every Sunday after church and would not tolerate her being adopted by anyone.

After many trips to Sioux City, Iowa, Norbert informed Edna that he could no longer afford to come and visit, and so on January 20, 1937, they were married. The economic depression that hit hard across America and their rural community of Barre Mills created a dependency upon one another for survival. Dairy farming even in the best of times is a tough life, leaving one totally exhausted but contented at the end of a day. Norbert and Edna believed that the best part was "they were with their own!" Neighbors became life-long friends who were depended upon in times both good and devastating. Norbert and Edna, along with my parents, formed the "500 Card Club" with other like-minded farm people. This became a special monthly treat, ending decades later only after too many of the players were no longer alive.

Cream prices during the Depression were only seventeen cents per one hundred pounds. In 1937 Norbert and his brother Harvey created Nuttleman Brothers' Dairy. They competed with fifty other dairy producers selling milk door to door in La Crosse with a Guernsey product of five per cent butterfat milk for five cents a quart. The milk route continued during the war years even with Harvey in the military. The route was abandoned in 1951.

Starting in World War II the United States Government began the milk pricing scheme of paying for milk based on a hundred-weight and not on the components found in the milk. In the early 1960s Milwaukee Golden Guernsey Dairies needed additional milk in the fall months and paid an extra twenty-five cents per hundred pounds premium for milk from registered Guernsey cows. At that time the premium was in excess of five percent over the regular price. The Wisconsin Guernsey farmers found another market at Walker Brothers Dairy in Greenville, Mississippi. Two or three tankers were shipped weekly. Sometimes a tanker went to New Orleans or North Carolina. After Walker Brothers closed, a new market was eventually found at Liebers Dairy in Lincoln, Nebraska.

Due to closures of local milk bottling facilities in the late 1960s, a pump station was constructed in West Salem by the La Crosse County Guernsey Breeders Inc. When Liebers Dairy went out of business, a market was established with Anderson-Erickson of Des Moines, Iowa. Mid-America Dairymen were the middle men in the venture. Within five years of that relationship a dispute arose between them and the Guernsey milk suppliers over milk pricing premiums. Norbert became the prime mover in putting together a farm co-operative to sell Guernsey milk emphasizing its higher protein and butterfat content. The culmination of Norbert's efforts resulted with the Guernsey breeders of Iowa, Minnesota, and Wisconsin creating Tri-State Milk Co-operative in 1977. This venture would not have been successful without Norbert's determination and will. Many years later it was noted that "Norbert Nuttleman served on the Tri-State Milk Co-operative Board. He did a great deal to advance co-operative goals and objectives. He served many years unselfishly for his fellow producer members."

Energy cost increases by 1980-1981 had become too prohibitive for Wisconsin producers to market milk with Anderson-Erickson in Des Moines, thus the Minnesota and Iowa producers split from the co-op to continue supplying Anderson-Erickson. At the same time the new protein test for the content of milk became reliable. The Tri-State Milk Producers Co-op supported a cheese yield pricing system and began selling on that basis beginning March 31, 1982.

In Norbert's words: "The final recognition that the value of milk is in its components and not in volume, has made it worth while for all the frustrations, and time involved in appeasing inter-state shippers, state boards of health, and sweating out bouncing checks and day to day problems. It has all paid off!"

Norbert Nuttleman, needed on the home farm thus cutting short his formal education in the ninth grade, became well educated through extensive reading, community service, and acute observation and analysis of his everyday environment. He was recognized as a member of the American Guernsey Breeders Association in 1944. He served as president of the La Crosse County Guernsey Breeders and was on the Wisconsin State Guernsey Breeders Board of Directors. Norbert served in the Wisconsin State Assembly from 1960 through 1970. During all ten years he served on the Assembly Agriculture Committee, chairing the Committee for a period of time. He served on a fourteen-state agricultural legislative committee during this time, and traveled to the USSR and Chile to gain an understanding of their agriculture and culture. Norbert served as the agricultural representative in the La Crosse Chamber of Commerce. If there was an endeavor or an association to benefit agriculture and the human race, within his ability to participate, Norbert was there. He is, perhaps, among the very last of the American pioneers devoted to the sustenance and improvement of society without asking for anything in return.

Chapter Fourteen:

West Salem's Newspaper

"The Public Press No Less than Public Office is a Public Trust"
The Nonpareil-Journal
West Salem, Wisconsin Friday, December 26, 1913

American newspapers sprang up as soon as settlements were sufficiently large to support one, and the early papers reflected the environment of the community as well as the values and whims of the local editor. The West Salem newspaper was no exception to this: often mere tidbits are enough to evoke a level of understanding of the growing community and its Guernsey experience that could never be gleaned from a scrutiny of the hard facts of its history. The articles were written in a straight forward "tell it like it really is" manner and offer a rich, often amusing portrait of the community and its values packed with colloquialisms unacceptable by today's journalistic standards.

The newspaper masthead was for the most part the "West Salem Journal" or the "West Salem Nonpareil Journal: A Paper of the People, by the People, and for the People." Later after being sold it became "The La Crosse Countryman." The first newspaper in West Salem marked its beginning in the 1880s. A massive fire destroyed downtown West Salem on July 1, 1911. My father and his family ran past the adjoining Nuttleman farm and down the railroad tracks to witness the devastation. The newspaper offices were gone along with all records and archives. The Wisconsin State Historical Archives have nothing of the newspaper prior to that date. There are isolated, aged and worn pre-fire copies still in existence.

The newspapers available have a special value. They not only chronicle the local items of interest, but record world, national, state, and regional news, although undoubtedly colored by local and publisher prejudice. The weekly paper was available to its readers every Thursday. The West Salem newspaper was also a farm paper displaying farm news, advertising, and events with several articles of learned advice as to the best methods of farming. There are preserved and bound copies of these newspapers subsequent to the fire in the offices of River Valley Newspapers Incorporated in West Salem. The oldest, most torn and water-damaged newspaper copies were rescued by Terry Hanson who dug them out of a dumpster and transferred them to the care of the West Salem High School.

The newspapers of the early twentieth century served as the only real news source for rural communities such as West Salem. The La Crosse Tribune was over a dozen miles away and there was no radio. During World War I a local doughboy American soldier writing home would have his letter published in its entirety in the West Salem newspaper. The letter was usually long, short on today's professional analysis, but a fascinating narrative of the European community, culture, and war as witnessed by the soldier.

What follows in this chapter is a potpourri of items taken from the West Salem paper that provide a better understanding of Guernsey history and the community in which their tale unfolds.

The population of West Salem in 1910 was 840.

August 22, 1913:

> Harry Griswold is expected to arrive here from the East with 18 to 20 high-priced Guernsey cows. This will be undoubtedly the first bunch of thoroughbred cows ever brought into this community. The ordinary farmer would throw up his hands in horror if asked to pay what these cows will bring. Mr. Griswold knows the value of good stock and when he finds the cows he wants the price does not stand in the way.

June 5, 1914:

W. F. Miller and the Von der Ohe Brothers won third and fifth place respectively in the Wisconsin State Farm Management contest. These farmers living at the edge of West Salem allowed the newspaper to focus on the communities' many bragging rights including purebred stock sales, "a very productive creamery," horse sales, band, orchestra, author Hamlin Garland, Hotel May, pea-canning factory, Wisconsin Institute conductor Henry Griswold, and the monthly poultry journal called *The Wisconsin Poultryman*. The newspaper claimed that these facts made West Salem famous throughout the nation.

March 27, 1914:

> The Western Wisconsin Guernsey Breeders' Association extravaganza and sale will be held Friday June 14, 1914. A visit to some of the great cows of the breed at the farms of C. D. Griswold, Ray Lewis, Alfred Stubbs, H. W. Griswold and many others is in the forenoon. A lunch at Mr. Stubbs will be at noon and is located four blocks from the depot. At 1 p. m. Charles L. Hill, former President of The American Guernsey Cattle Club will speak on 'Wisconsin as a Guernsey state'. At 2 p. m. William H. Caldwell, Secretary of The American Guernsey Cattle Club will speak on

'Productive Capacity of Guernseys as seen in Public and Official tests'. Professor C. P. Norgord will speak at 3 p. m. on 'alfalfa and clover in relation To Dairying'. Catalogues and hotel reservations will be reserved for all who contact H. W. Griswold. On Saturday, June 20, Guernsey Breeders' from West Salem will hold a sale of seventy-five head of registered Guernseys 'of the highest class ever offered at public sale'. High class registered bulls and a few daughters that are direct descendants of the champion butter cow of the world will be offered at private sale.

The Alfred Stubbs barn was located at 400 North Leonard Street, on grounds now owned by the West Salem School District and the Village of West Salem.

June 1914:

The progressive people of West Salem showed they had recovered from the devastating fire of July 3, 1911. Hotel May is known all over the state and the local band one of the state's best. Purebred dairy and swine, and regular draft horses and poultry sell to every state in the nation. Miller and Nuttleman's hog sales are an annual event. The West Salem Guernsey Breeder's sale held at A. I. Stubbs large round barn brought buyers from near and far arriving on every incoming train for several days prior to the sale. Seating capacity being created to hold 1800 people was pretty well filled up. At one o'clock the gathering was called to order by H. W. Griswold who briefly but clearly stated the purpose of the sale and desires of those interested. They did not look for a record sale, but rather a developing sale - one that would encourage new men and young men to make a start in this great industry and strive for better breeding and more of it. Colonel Geo. A. Bain of Lexington, Kentucky, was auctioneer. There was an estimate of 500 buyers. Sixty-five head sold for $18,450. Private sales the same day brought the total volume to $21,175. Only twelve of the sixty-five head stayed in La Crosse County.

Stubb's Guernsey Barn-W. Salem-Wis.

June 19, 1914:

To continue Wisconsin as the Guernsey capitol of America is one of the purposes of a state-wide campaign which is being carried out this month by the officers and members of the Western Guernsey Association.

Public meetings will be held at the Walter farm, near Walworth, on June 17, at the Gerritt's farm, Waukesha, on the 18th, and in a mammoth tent near A. I. Stubbs' barn in West Salem on the 19th. It is expected that addresses will be given by W. H. Caldwell, secretary of the American Guernsey club; Hugh Van Pelt, Waterloo, Ia.; C. P. Norgord, superintendent of Farmers' Institutes, and George C. Humphrey of the Agricultural Experiment Station.

The big purpose of the movement, of course, will be to encourage the establishment and development of profit-producing herds of Guernsey cattle. Already herds of this noted Channel Island breed have been established in very many counties of the state.

A *GOOD LAUGH* printed in 1914:

The physiological benefits of laughter cannot be overestimated. It shakes up the diaphragm, sets the pulse to beating to a lively measure, stimulates the blood and enlivens the brain. Used with discretion, laughter is as inspiring as a sea breeze, as refreshing as a needed shower. Its moral effect is beyond computation. It is contagious, and will dispel gloom where it peals forth in honest merriment. Indulge now and then in a good laugh. The man who laughs never kills himself.

Friday, February 25, 1916:

BREEDERS ASSOCIATIONS HOLD BIG MEETING:

Three Breeders' Associations, assisted by the Sparta Advancement Association gave one of the finest programs ever held in the interest of live stock in this state and the fine weather coupled with the excellent program attracted a large audience. By 11:30 the Sparta Court House was filled by an enthusiastic gathering of farmers.

Hon. Geo. McKerrow began the program at 10:30 on *Improvement of Livestock in Wisconsin*. He brought out the great value of pure bred sires. He said: "A poor sire is a whole herd and a good one is half of the herd... Form a partnership with your wife and family and greater success and more pleasure will follow."

Mr. Irwin, owner of the world's champion cow and one of the most constructive breeders in the United States with an intensely interesting lecture on *The Dairy cow from a Business Standpoint*. Mr. Irwin compared the dairyman and his cow to the manufacturer and his machine. Competition is also forcing the dairyman to use the most economical and profitable cows. Higher land prices and more keen competition and the man with the scrub cattle will be pushed out of the dairy industry. Mr. Irwin was asked many questions pertaining to feeding which he answered very simply and directly. He said, "The more protein you can feed, the more products you will get, if at the same time you keep the equilibrium of the cow. Do not work the cow at a disadvantage. An automobile will not run without sufficient care, oiling and gasoline. Neither will a cow produce without care, kindness, and plenty of the right kind of feed. A cow that is in fear of her keeper can never do her best work."

JUNE 2, 1916:

At this time when all the papers are commenting on the life work of the great James J. Hill of St. Paul, it is interesting to note what A. J. Phillips said about the great empire builder more than sixteen years ago in his book *QUEEN VASHTI.* Through the courtesy of Mr. Phillips we are enabled to publish a picture of Mr. Hill as it appeared in the book as well as the authors comment:

Another man I want to tell you about, who is a great friend of the people, especially the farmers, is J.J. Hill, President of the Great Northern Railroad. The best address I ever listened to was one he delivered about a year ago at the annual meeting of the Minnesota Agricultural Society in Minneapolis. He tries in every way he can to help the settlers along his line of road in Minnesota and North Dakota to help them improve their herds of cattle, he in two years' time, imported, mostly from the North of England and Scotland, about eight hundred thoroughbred bulls of the beef and dairy breeds, some of them costing more than three hundred dollars each, and gave them to the farmers. He also gave them thoroughbred pigs to improve their hogs. He gave the farmers a lot of good sound advice. He told them to look after their own interests and not allow themselves to be fooled by demagogues. But the best advice he gave them was to educate their children well.

FRIDAY, MARCH 30, 1917:

ADONIRAM JUDSON PHILLIPS died in the La Crosse hospital Thursday, March 22, 1917, having been taken there but a few days before for the better care that he might be given and to minister to his comfort as far as possible, but with little hope of his recovery.

He was born in Chester County, Pa., Oct. 17th 1833, the son of a Baptist minister. He came in 1849 to Watertown, Wis., and later to the western edge of the state, settling in Big Creek, near Sparta in 1855. He was married in 1861 to Miss Avis Buttles and is survived by her and three sons; Charles of Savannah, Ill., W. J. Phillips and Geo. C. Phillips of La Crosse. Among the agriculturists, horticulturists, and dairymen throughout the Northwest and especially in Wisconsin and Minnesota Mr. Phillips was well known as a lecturer at large gatherings including state fairs. He received diplomas from the University of Wisconsin in areas of specialty. He was the avowed and active champion of the dumb brutes and birds uncomplainingly served as humane agent. His actions as well as his writing were for temperance in all things and respect for all life.

S. L. McKee of West Salem, Wisconsin wrote a poetic tribute in the newspaper obituary. This tribute reflects A. J. Phillips' love and creation of poetry which seems to be a common trait of the sturdy pioneers of the dairy farming trade.

FROM THE WEST SALEM NEWSPAPER SOMETIME IN 1920s – also includes adaptation from *THE WISCONSIN FARMER*

Feed costs were more than half the total cost of milk production, and labor was valued at 25 percent of the cost of production, or 26 cents per hour. In 1923, the average cost of producing 100 pounds of milk was $1.96 and each pound of butterfat cost 56 cents to produce. Dairymen received $2.39 per hundred pounds of milk, and 68 cents was received per pound of butter. In 1924, costs were $2.25 per hundred pounds of milk while $2.33 was received. For butter the cost per pound to produce was 62 cents and income 65 cents. Margins dropped from 43 cents for one hundred pounds of milk to six cents and for butter per pound from 12 cents to three cents. The average cost of keeping a cow was $142 per year. Any cow producing less than 200 pounds of butterfat per year was unprofitable. A minimum production of 220 to 250 pounds was considered the minimum objective. During this time dairymen were urged to remove waste from mangers. All feed should be kept sweet by prompt removal of waste from mangers and by occasional washing with a liquid disinfectant prepared and applied in strict accordance with directions printed on the package.

June 7, 1928:

> The state Guernsey Picnic to be held in West Salem June 21, 1928, will have Wisconsin Governor Fred R. Zimmerman, a man worth both seeing and hearing, to deliver an address. The Governor's address is entitled "Wisconsin's Dairy Industry". Also speaking will be a Guernsey Breeder of national fame, J. C. Penney, of Hopewell Junction, New York. The nationally known owner of a great chain store system is also worth hearing and seeing. The J. C. Penney address is entitled "Constructive Plans for Breed Advancement.
>
> For this occasion West Salem will decorate itself and all that it can offer in the way of hospitality will be extended freely. Most of the stores and business places will close during the program so that all may hear our Governor and Mr. Penney. Join with us for the day and remember it is a picnic with a noon picnic lunch. Bring the family and well filled baskets, help yourself to our lawns if you wish or use the park. Plenty of free hot coffee and Guernsey cream will be available. We want you to feel at home and to understand that this is just a social affair without money or price and that it is open to all regardless of cattle possessions or lack of them.
>
> Judging and exhibition of La Crosse County Guernseys is under the leadership of A. O. Collentine of the Wisconsin College of Agriculture and C. B. Finley of the American Guernsey Cattle Club.
>
> Thousands of people from all over Wisconsin are expected to descend on this tiny village. Practically every West Salem businessman contributed generously so that exhibitors

are assured of cash prizes for their time and trouble. After the day's program is complete a four p.m. baseball game is scheduled between Bangor and West Salem. The Rural Letter Carriers Annual Ball featuring Bendel's Orchestra will be held in the Guernsey Pavilion in the evening. "Better top off the day by attending the dance. All your friends will be there.

The population of West Salem was 1027 in 1920 and 1011 in 1930.

JUNE 28, 1928:

2500 people came to West Salem, the prior Thursday, June 21, with excellent weather. By noon the streets were crowded with cars with large groups in shady spots to enjoy a picnic dinner. In the Guernsey Pavilion a dinner was served at noon with one table in the center for the dignitaries. By 1:30 all seats were taken and standing room at a premium. A band concert preceded the welcoming address by F. I. Bolles, mayor of West Salem. Dr. W. A. Munn, Wisconsin state Guernsey President, responded to the welcome with kind comments to the community. Dr. Munn stated that 25 of the 28 county Guernsey Associations were represented at the picnic. Fifteen of the counties had three man judging teams at the event. Dr. Munn said that this 1928 picnic the most successful since the plan was adopted five years prior. The Barron County Quartet, a popular promoter of Wisconsin to other regions, sang parodies on popular songs that boosted farming and Guernsey farmers. J. C. Penney, whose name-sake company operates 1025 stores in 47 states, was the main speaker. Mr. Penney is also President of Penny-Gwin Corporation that owns 125,000 acres of Florida land being subdivided among dairy farmers and developed along original lines. Mr. Penney has one of the greatest Guernsey herds in the world. J. C. Penney began with several stories and then read from a prepared paper. Mr. Penney was raised on a farm and returned to farming in search of better health. He liked livestock and began raising grade Guernseys. He decided raising grades was not constructive work. He switched to purebreds with the goal of building one of the greatest purebred herds in the world. He plans that this herd shall contain not only outstanding individuals, but their produce shall develop along the very best lines of breeding for production and style.

Governor Zimmerman followed Mr. Penney as speaker. He said that Wisconsin farmers had problems unsolvable by millionaires with a watch charm for a farm created by the overflow of chain stores from 47 states. He offered to be employed by Mr. Penney to write his speeches as he could do much better.

1928 ON FEEDING COWS ON PASTURE:

Comments from E. C. Elting of the University of Missouri: Guernseys and Jerseys produce milk with 4.5% butterfat. Blue grass pasture is the warm weather feed which should be supplemented by 3 pounds grain for a cow producing 20 pounds of milk, 4# for 25#, and 5.5# for 30#, 7# for 35# and 8.2# for 40#. Cows producing lower fat milk would require less grain. Blue grass or legume pasture will supply enough protein so that home grown energy-producing feeds such as corn, oats, and barley can be used to supplement the grass. The beginning of the pasture season requires more high energy as from corn. In the late pasture season more emphasis should be on protein and less on energy. It was recommended to have a small field of Sudan grass to help overcome the late summer pasture shortage.

A synopsis of a later article from the newspaper stated that root crops such as beets, turnips, and carrots could be fed in small quantities, but fed after milking to prevent off flavor in the milk. Soybeans offer the dairyman an excellent opportunity to increase his profits. Cows should be dry between lactations 4 to 6 weeks. Feed a cow all the alfalfa hay and corn silage she will eat. This can mean 30 to 40 pounds of silage and 10 to 20 pounds of hay daily. Sterility in dairy animals is just as costly as contagious diseases.

NOVEMBER 1, 1928:

The prior Wednesday evening, papers were signed by B. A. Mau, representing J. W. Patterson, of Atlanta, Georgia, and the officers of the La Crosse County Guernsey Breeders, Inc. They are taking over the O. G. Clark cattle sale barn with its 203 cattle stanchions. With the purchase of this sale barn coupled with the pavilion sales barn the new capacity is for 303 head of cattle. This purchase is a logical step in the evolution of the county breed association and gives to La Crosse County Guernsey Breeders Inc. a barn unequaled in size by those owned by any other county association in the United States. The county association was organized 21 years prior to the purchase and they have held county sales for 15 successful years.

These Guernseymen are so familiar a part of everyday life in West Salem that we seldom think of what their organized effort has meant to every breeder of dairy cattle in La Crosse County, and an even wider area. Their sales, held without fail over a long period of years have attracted buyers from all over the United States and some foreign countries. This together with other advertising, exhibits at livestock shows; work in testing, service in state associations and innumerable like activities have served to make this area known as a source of dairy cattle. The buyers who came to West Salem in this past year alone have left hundreds of thousands of dollars and made cattle breeding and cattle buying and selling one of our most important businesses.

FROM THE WEST SALEM NEWSPAPER IN 1928:

The sixteenth annual sale of the La Crosse County Guernsey Breeders featured 354 purebred and grade Guernsey cattle passing through the Pavilion sale ring between one and eleven o'clock. The 265 grades were an unusually large offering. The 89 purebreds averaged $142.14 in price. The grades averaged between $125 and $130 after calves were eliminated in the calculation. The Chicago Guernsey Farm of Hinsdale, Illinois, purchased 13 purebred Guernsey cows and purchased the three top purebred cows at $320, $320, and $300 respectively. This farm sells certified milk in the Chicago area. Abe Green of Bridgewater, Massachusetts, bought the top selling grade, an 8 year old with a C.T.A. record of 460 pounds of fat for the last four years. J. B. Branson of Lincoln, Nebraska, purchased 18 head and Lewis N. Hoere of Monroe, Michigan, bought 24 including 3 purebreds.

A WEST SALEM NEWSPAPER AD IN 1928 BY QUACKENBUSH AND SON:

WHAT ABOUT A MILKING MACHINE?

What is a milking machine for? Is it not to save time, cut cost of labor, do a better and cleaner job of milking, more sanitary in every way than by hand milking? Nearly all certified dairies use milking machines. Certified milk producing requires everything sanitary about the barn; and the milker is one of the most important of all, as it should be kept clean to produce the cleanest of milk." Washing is one of the things to consider in choosing a milker. The New Automatic with nine pieces in each unit takes only three minutes to wash. A complete outfit for 30 cows, including motor, pump, vacuum tank, gauges, and two single units can be had for less than $300.

FROM THE WEST SALEM NEWSPAPER:

Skim milk had a black eye in 1928. It could be used as feed and a natural dewormer for hogs, but much was thrown away as useless. The Dairy Department of the University of Wisconsin College of Agriculture urged dairy farmers to have their milk condensed or dried for bakeries, candy, and animal feed. In 1927, 118 million pounds of milk were dried, an increase of 27 million pounds from the year before. The United States government had recently perfected a concentrated ripened skim milk that kept well, was high in food value and could be used for animal feed. One of the most important products that can be made from skim milk is casein for which there are many uses such as waterproof paint, plastics for fountain pens, artificial celluloid, massage cream and medicines. Whey remains after casein has been removed and is used for feeding infants and coating medical pills. Skim milk is also used for making soft cheeses.

DECEMBER 27, 1928:

> Two shipments of Guernsey cattle ten days apart left West Salem to Balfour Guthre Co. of Brentwood, California. A total of 188 head were purchased under the guidance of H. W. Griswold.

MAY 3, 1928:

> Fred Schomberg was attacked by a 1700 pound Guernsey bull owned by Carl Moos that had a "neighborhood" reputation for gentleness. Mr. Schomberg had secured the bull at the Moos farm and was leading him by staff to his own place a half mile distant. A few rods from the Pleasant Valley School the animal became restive, jerking on the staff and then suddenly turned and drove his head forward so that the staff was torn out of its leaders hands and the man knocked down against the roadside bank. In the dark the bull lunged into the bank and narrowly missed the prostrate man. A wire fence was near and Mr. Schomberg rolled under the wires with torn clothes and managed to escape although the bull repeatedly lunged against the wires. A call for help brought Carl Moos, George Garbers, and Herman Albers. Carl had a lantern and after some maneuvering managed to grab the staff and subdue the animal. "The bull will be dehorned."

In the same issue of the newspaper was the mention that perhaps a quarter mile from the bull incident a young Herb Lee was dragged by a pony owned by C. D. Griswold. Another farmer, Ervin Nuttleman, escaped his bull by climbing a tree. This was only a mile from where Mr. Schomberg was attacked.

1930s:

In the newspaper report from the 1930's near the foot of Mindoro Hill, Henry Grochowske was carried more than fifteen times around his hayfield caught in the curve of the hay rake teeth. The tongue of his rake broke and threw him unto the ground ahead of the rake teeth. The mules ran away breaking a score of fence posts and did not stop until they were tired out. He was cut and bruised from head to feet but miraculously escaped serious injury. He went to town for medical treatment and milked his cows that evening. He became extremely sore and later was confined to bed for several days.

Farm accidents are more prevalent than are generally recognized. Neighbors of mine have lost an arm in a corn picker and another, a leg in the power take off of the manure spreader connected to the tractor. At least two close friends in the community were killed: one was killed by being backed over by a farm implement and another by a car while driving a tractor.

These tragic accidents happened in one small rural community and do not include all the incidents within that community. Multiply this by all rural communities. The statistics if fully available would be numbing. Farming has always been a very dangerous occupation. Risks are not just from the weather and economics. The rewards are not commensurate.

MARCH 24, 1932:

> 600 people from La Crosse County attended the silver jubilee or 25th anniversary of the La Crosse County Guernsey Breeders' Association. H. W. Griswold was Master of Ceremonies. A. J. Glover, editor of Hoard's Dairyman, was the featured speaker. Editor Glover saw no virtue in price fixing because production cannot be controlled. Who will tell 7 million farmers what to produce? Rather than having a federal officer prying into his business, it would be better to combine hard work, conservative and progressive views shared by all dairy farmers. Gavin McKerrow, prominent in Guernsey circles, talked about selling Guernsey milk in Milwaukee and Chicago playing up the milk's golden color and richness. McKerrow recalled that H. D. Griswold and A.

J. Phillips by their writings and lectures made West Salem and its Guernsey cattle known to the state and nation.

MARCH 8, 1934:

THE **GUERNSEY JUBILEE** attracted 1500 to 2000 people to West Salem. Wisconsin Governor A. G. Schmedeman and his wife along with the Dean of Wisconsin College of Agriculture, Chris L. Christensen, arrived on the Northwestern train to be greeted at the home of state senator Harry Griswold. They enjoyed a dinner at the B. A. Mau home at 6 p. m. Dean Christensen spoke at a meeting attended by 200 at 7:30 p. m. His remarks noted that the price of butter very closely followed the purchasing power of city people. He recommended extensive culling of dairy animals and the removal of surplus dairy products from the market to feed the needy. The Governor's remarks included the endorsements of Senator Griswold and Assemblyman Mau. He then paid tribute to the Wisconsin founders of the Guernsey breed including the Hoards, Hill, A. J. Phillips, and Henry Griswold among others.

APRIL 8, 1934:

The Union State Bank of West Salem was told that they were approved after a bank examination to insure their deposits by the FDIC. Assessments were made to have insurance coverage up to July 1 for $2500 in full. After that date the coverage changes to $10,000. This was called a national mutual protection organization with federal government supervision. It will end all bank holidays and give confidence for everyone with future bank transactions.

Raymond Knutson and H. W. Griswold advertised a cow and heifer sale to be held December 12, 1934. The sale of 138 head averaged $50 with a top of $85. This was the first sale in the pavilion in over two years because of the depression. J. C. Eakman of Great Falls, Montana, purchased 27 head, including the top price for a 4-year old registered Guernsey consigned by Earl Jewett. Ralph Tratt also paid the top price of $85 for a 4-year old registered Guernsey consigned by Harry Grover of Galesville.

AUGUST 19, 1937:

Vilas Young of West Salem advertised for 100 fresh, close up, and backward springer Guernsey cows for a Connecticut buyer.

FEBRUARY 1958:

Vilas Young retired as director after 41 years and secretary- treasurer for 32 years. He was always working with the Guernsey cattle sales with up to nine in a year at the West Salem Sales Pavilion.

JULY 21, 1967:

> The 8th annual GREAT NORTHERN CLASSIC was held in the West Salem Sales Pavilion in 1967. This type of sale replaced the many mixed registered and grade Guernsey sales of the past as dairy cattle, especially the Guernsey breed, was diminished in popularity. The 45 head of young animals sold were selected by a committee going to individual farms to select a top quality animal and limiting the number to attract a buyer interested in production and type. The 45 head averaged $540 with the top price being $1275.

We have seen the interactions between a small Wisconsin community and the breed of Guernsey dairy animals in the early to mid twentieth century. These shared experiences brought attention throughout the United States. On the wall of my home next to the desk is a large framed poster advertising the Wisconsin Guernsey Picnic of June 21, 1928, showcasing J.C. Penney as the prominent guest speaker. From the West Salem newspaper dated September 27, 1934 it was noted that this prominent Guernsey dignitary visited the Griswold, Young, Lee, and Adolph Nuttleman Guernsey farms of West Salem the prior Tuesday. Mr. Penney created a cheese empire that became part of an anti-trust probe; Foremost Dairies USA is located in Baraboo, Wisconsin. His contribution to the dairy industry is largely unknown and unappreciated.

Chapter Fifteen:

James Cash Penney

Our fourth Guernsey pioneer, James Cash Penney was an agriculturist and philanthropist as well as a retail entrepreneur. Governor Zimmerman of Wisconsin at the 1928 Wisconsin Guernsey picnic chided that Wisconsin farmers had problems unsolvable by millionaires with a watch charm for a farm. Did he know about Penney's hard fought rise from near poverty? He obviously did not comprehend Penney's total commitment to farming and helping others less fortunate than himself.

In 1917, J. C. Penney gave up the Presidency and day-to-day operation of his flourishing company to devote more of his time to farming. He ran a 705 acre farm raising purebred Guernsey cattle in New York State from 1922 to 1953. He also operated a second farm in that state as well as eight or nine others in partnership in Missouri.

Ralph W. Gwinn was counsel for the J. C. Penney Company, and along with Penney incorporated the J. C. Penney – Gwinn Corporation in Florida in 1925 for the purpose of creating farm enterprises and philanthropy. The corporation purchased 120,000 acres of Florida land for $400,000 that same year. A sixty acre community with twenty-two new apartment buildings was created for retired ministers, lay church workers, missionaries, YMCA and YWCA secretaries, and their families. Farm land was used to entice farmers of "sterling character" to ultimately own a small farm based on the most up-to-date farming practices as taught to them by specialists hired by Penney. Bad weather and depressed farm prices undermined its success. In 1929, the J. C. Penney – Gwinn Corporation organized Foremost Dairy Products, Inc., which became the largest dairy products company in the south earning the nickname "longest milk route in the world."

J. C. Penney's formative years laid the foundation for these amazing accomplishments of the man best remembered today as a retail pioneer. He was born in 1875, the seventh of twelve children of a third generation Baptist minister and his wife in a farm home two and a half miles from Hamilton, Missouri. The population of Hamilton at that time was approximately 1200. J. C. Penney's parents set a high value on education, thus purchased a home in Hamilton in November of 1880, so their children could attend high school. Penny's father held the heretical view that pastors should be paid for their work. This eloquent speaker served his community with distinction and ran for Congress and other political offices. Penney's father was the greatest influence in his life, instilling in him to always abide by the concepts of the Golden Rule.

The family farm was a necessity for survival. As was the custom in many families in those days, the 8-year old son was told by his father that he would henceforth be required to earn money to buy his own clothes. The young lad's first venture was in raising hogs starting with the purchase of a pig for $2.50. He successfully marketed hogs until the age of 10, at which time his father demanded he sell his hogs even before they were marketable. The neighbors could not stand the smell! Later James Cash Penney Jr. remarked that it had been a necessary lesson in learning to co-operate with other people. He tried selling watermelons outside the grounds at the county fair but his father sent him home in shame. Fair merchants were required to be licensed, which young Penney was not. From this he learned not to take unfair advantage of others. His father made him quit a part-time grocery delivery position when he discovered that the grocer was mixing inferior coffee beans with superior ones and selling the mix as superior beans. Penney Sr. knew the value of money, but he also knew that one must treat another as he himself would want to be treated. Later J. C. Penney Jr. wrote: "The lesson soaked in. Father knew the importance of money, but he knew and practiced the Rule that is the most solid asset of civilized man."

Penney worked on his father's farm for two years after high school graduation. At the beginning of 1895 his father asked John M. Hale if he would teach his son the dry goods business. Thus Penney began working for Hale on February 4, 1895. Unfortunately, J. C. Penney Sr. died less than two months later on March 22, 1895. Penney's salary of $2.27 *per month* was the lowest of all the clerks in Hale's dry goods store. He was made fun of and other sales people interrupted his efforts and took sales away from him. Although discouraged, his inner self worth developed as a child along with his determination and tireless ambition propelled him to be one of Hale's top salesmen. By June of 1897, Penney's family physician noted his exhaustion, and fearing for his health, recommended he leave humid Missouri for the dry healthy climate of the West. At the age of 21 Penney recognized the inevitability of having to establish his own identity in the world away from his respected family.

Penney moved to Colorado and immediately obtained work at Joslin's Dry Goods store. Later he opened a butcher shop that needed the business of a nearby hotel to survive. In order to secure the business he had to give the chef a bottle of whiskey every week, which he did, but his moral opposition to alcohol weighed heavily on his conscience. He stopped, lost the hotel account, and went out of business. Although discouraged about working in a dry goods store, he began working at the Golden Rule chain store in Longmont, Colorado, because he felt it was God's will. It was in Longmont where he met Berta Alva Hess, a five foot three inch beauty with whom he fell deeply in love. Berta, who suffered from severe asthma attacks, had a tragic, childless first marriage which Penney had witnessed. His offer of marriage was responded to with the love and loyalty of someone given a new life. Penney's sterling character, self confidence, and independence overcame the hostility and distrust divorcees were treated with during that era. Penney did everything to protect her and she vowed to follow him anywhere.

On August 24, 1899, theirs was one of ten weddings performed during Cheyenne, Wyoming's Frontier Days. Their first son, Roswell, was born January 24, 1901.

Penney longed to own his own store, but inventory requirements discouraged him. Johnson and Callahan, the founders of the Golden Rule chain and the owners of the Golden Rule store in Longmont, Colorado, decided to open a new store and wanted Penney to be the manager and one-third partner. Inspired by their confidence in him, Penney said: "It fired my very soul with a desire and an ambition to be somebody." There were over two dozen Golden Rule merchants with volume purchasing power for quality merchandise. They were well trained in retail dry goods sales and the one reasonable price philosophy which guaranteed rapid turnover and success.

The three partners purchased a store on a dirty side street in Kemmerer, Wyoming for $2000. Frank Pfeiffer, the cashier of the First National Bank of Kemmerer, predicted the failure of Penney's store and refused to give him a loan because the cash only policy of the Golden Rule store did not fit the monthly wage payments of the area railroad and mining employees. Penney's partners offered him the loan at eight per cent, but Penney was able to get a $1500 loan from his home town bank in Hamilton, Missouri, at six per cent to go with his $500 of savings. Partnership papers were signed January 25, 1902, with a capitalization of $6000.

The 25 foot by 45 foot stark wooden and stone frame building of the new Golden Rule store was half a block south of a triangular park in the middle of the business district. It opened April 14, 1902, with the manager and co-owner Penney, Berta and baby Roswell living in the attic. Shoe boxes were used for chairs and packing cases for tables. Water was drawn from a well with ropes used to pull the water buckets up to the living quarters. Whenever Berta waited on customers, Roswell slept under the counter.

Kemmerer had a population of 900 by 1902. Sheep ranchers and farmers were prosperous. Railroad conductor and engineer wages were $125 to $135 per month. Coal miner wages ranged from $35 to $75 per month. Day wages were $1.50 to $2.00 per day. These pay rates exceeded those of the eastern United States.

Penney opened the store at 7 a.m. and stayed open until no one was on the streets late in the evening. At a time when Levi overalls sold for fifty-eight cents apiece, the opening day sales were $466.59 including $81.09 in shoes. From the day his Golden Rule store opened on April 14, 1902, through the end of the year, total sales were $28,898.11 with $8514.36 in profits divided among the three partners. The original inventory of $5500 was turned over almost four times. The store was stocked with work clothes, shoes, sheepskin-lined outerwear, Sunday suits, materials, notions, and staple goods needed for everyday life. Penney was just 26 years old, twice the age of the state of Wyoming.

Penney eliminated haggling on sales price and set the price low enough to earn a fair return without allowing the customer to carry a balance on his books. By sharing profits with his employees and not selling for all the market could bear, Penney created a successful formula that allowed him to have twenty-two stores within the next seven years.

Penney made it his business to memorize the names of his customers and where they lived, the better to help them fill their dry goods needs. He and Berta would borrow a horse and buggy to visit as many customers as they could. Even those only able to visit his store once or twice a year were favored with his specific knowledge of their names, needs and desires. Many times Penney would provide size and other particulars for a family member not present or for someone he had not seen in years. Penney's sincere interest in his customers made them feel important. Indeed, next to his family, his customers were the most important people in the world.

In February, 1903, he journeyed to Kansas City joining the Golden Rule buying syndicate on their spring buying trip. This opened up the benefit of Callahan's and others' experienced judgment and ideas and got his feet wet with supplier representatives. Berta gave birth to Johnson Callahan Penney on December 27, 1903, named in honor of Penney's two partners.

The population of Kemmerer jumped to 2000 by 1904. Profits were as follows:

1903	$ 9,850.83
1904	$11,258.24
1905	$13,844.42
1906	$15,128.33

This is almost a fifty-four per cent increase three years after 1903. James Cash Penney continued his long hours and thrifty ways, saving string and wrapping paper as well as money after the store moved to a more lucrative location in 1904. The size increased to 140 feet by 25 feet with merchandise even hanging from the ceiling. He and Berta moved to the frame cottage on Pine Avenue they had purchased in 1900. Berta built an enclosed back porch and finished the tiny loft in her spare time. These were the happiest years together for Jim and Berta.

In 1909 Penney, Berta, and sons moved to Salt Lake City to be closer to large banks and a distribution center with railroad connections to other states. The Penneys were settled in by their tenth wedding anniversary in August. Operating from his home at 371 Seventh Avenue, Penney spent most of his time on buying trips and checking out store locations. The rolling green farm community of Hamilton, Missouri was his favorite place for respite with Berta and their two sons accompanying him there as well as on buying trips to New York. Rapid expansion throughout 1910 increased the complexity of logistics and financing, Berta and "Jim" Penney and their two sons prepared to take a Christmas trip to the Holy Land and to Europe. Jim and Berta considered the trip to be a belated honeymoon.

Berta decided to have her tonsils removed before the trip, hopefully to moderate her chronic asthma symptoms. Her husband was checking out store sites in the Pacific Northwest, unaware that she was not waiting for his return to have them removed. After the surgery, Berta walked home during a December rainstorm. Within a week she had lobar pneumonia, and by the fifteenth of December she became very weak from an extremely high fever. A telegram was sent to Penney who rushed home. He was at her side when she died at 11:25 a. m. on December 26, 1910.

Energetic Berta who had "no time for aches and pains" left her loved ones in grief and shock. James Cash Penney, Jr., was totally devastated and entered a state of severe depression. He felt "mocked by life" and was extremely bitter. His faith in God and belief in "progress" were badly shaken. His mother and sister Letha moved to Salt Lake City to care for his two sons when he was away. Penney spent more time buying in New York City. At night he took long walks along the streets of The Bowery. His perceived weakness in the face of adversity haunted him, and he was tempted to use alcohol to ease his pain and loneliness. In a Bowery mission he listened to a businessman preach how he had gone from the gutter to redemption. Penney finally realized that his successful enterprise would continue without Berta and with or without himself. The organization had a momentum of its own with everyone wanting an interest in one or more stores.

The partnership type of expansion and large number of stores unnerved bankers in Salt Lake City and New York City. The Associate Partnerships were considered too cumbersome for nationwide expansion. With forty-eight stores in seven states in 1913, his associates helped conceive and incorporate The J. C. Penney Company. In 1914 Penney persuaded his board of directors to relocate the company headquarters to New York City. Sales increased from 2.6 million dollars in 1913 to 28.7 million dollars in 1919. In 1919 there were 197 stores in twenty-five states, and by the fall of 1929 there were 1400 stores in the forty-eight contiguous states.

On July 19, 1919, J. C. Penney married Mary Hortense Kimball of Salt Lake City. Mary was thirty-nine at the time of their marriage, four years younger than her husband. Mary was a graduate of Bryn Mawr College in 1899 and had studied French and music in Paris and Dresden. During World War I she worked at the Y.M.C.A. with the American Expeditionary Force. On September 28, 1920, their son Kimball was born. On February 15, 1923, Mary passed away. Abdominal pains a week prior to her death became violent, followed by internal bleeding. She became unconscious and passed away thirty minutes later. The official cause of death was "acute indigestion." Although saddened by the loss of Mary, whom he adored, the spiritual lessons learned after Berta's untimely death twelve years earlier allowed him to cope and recover. Mary's interest in philanthropy inspired Penney to devote much of the rest of his life to that endeavor.

The fact that in mid-life J. C. Penney devoted more of his time to agricultural pursuits including his horses, Angus and Guernsey cattle will come as a surprise to those who think of him as a department store mogul. More than that, he was primarily an agriculturist and devoted a majority of his years to agricultural pursuits. In December of 1921, he purchased Emmadine dairy farm of Hopewell Junction, Dutchess County, New York, where he began using and studying Guernsey cattle. The limestone based soil was excellent for dairy farming. The first herd sire purchased by J. C. Penney was

Langwater Foremost for the then record price of $20,000. This great bull lived up to more than his name. Langwater Foremost, born in April of 1915, sired sixty-eight registered daughters and eighty-seven registered sons that became known for their remarkable examples of type and milk inheritance through line breeding. Penney used his name to form the slogan "Foremost in Name and Breeding Fame." By 1927, Emmadine Farms Foremost Guernsey cattle were nationally famous. At the 1928 National Dairy Show, Foremost Guernsey cattle placed very well. Registered Guernsey cattle breeding became Penney's special interest. In 1951 Langwater Foremost was voted the fourth most influential bull in the Guernsey breed.

On August 26, 1926, James Cash Penney married Caroline Bertha Autenrieth in Paris, France, where she was working for the American Methodist Episcopal Bishop. Penney first met his petite, grey-blue eyed future wife in New York a couple years prior to their marriage. Twenty years his junior, her energetic personality clearly matched Penney's. She was his wife for the remaining forty-five years of his life and the mother of his only two daughters, Mary Frances, born May 28, 1927, and named after his mother, and Carol Marie born in April of 1930.

On October 23, 1929, the J. C. Penney Company went public, six days before the stock market crash and the beginning of the great depression. Sales dropped by nineteen million dollars. J. C. Penney had not taken a salary for the past twenty years. His net worth was entirely in his company stock and used as collateral for philanthropies and a failed Florida bank he had purchased. It became "an unnecessary catastrophe" in Penney's words as his 385,200 shares plummeted from $110 in October, 1929, to as little as thirteen dollars per share in 1932. His attempt to refinance in June of 1932 was rejected. Penney was broke. He began taking a salary in 1932 and continued to do so until sometime in 1935. His associates were well aware of his plight as well as his generosity. More than a thousand of them rallied to him donating portions of their salaries and stock shares that helped him eventually to recover financially.

Wilk Hyer, Mary Hess (the widow of Arthur Lee Hess, Berta's younger brother), and Herbert Penney each loaned him $52,000 without collateral which he used to buy the company's stock that was flooding the market. By 1940, he had accumulated 51,193 shares of stock. The holdings in company stock and Foremost Dairies, Inc. provided Penney with an increasingly comfortable lifestyle, but he never regained the fortune he had in the 1920s.

In 1929 Foremost Dairy Products, Inc. was organized and owned by J. C. Penney – Gwinn Corporation to control production and marketing of dairy products in the south. The five million dollar subsidiary was considered the largest dairy company in the south. Foremost Dairies became the third largest dairy company in the world by 1951. Today the Foremost USA name continues in the dairy industry. Foremost Farms USA, headquartered in Baraboo, Wisconsin, owns the Foremost trademark which originated from Penney's famed registered Guernsey bull.

The company's rapid growth domestically and internationally caused the Federal Trade Commission in 1962 to say that Foremost's "dominant presence" could affect competition, hence the company was ordered to release ownership of its nine most recent acquisitions. Also, Foremost sold all of its milk and ice cream plants east of the Mississippi River. In 1967 Foremost Dairies, Inc., Robbins, Inc., and McKesson merged. In 1984 Wisconsin Dairies Co-operative of Baraboo acquired the whey operations, research library, patents, and rights to the Foremost name in the United States and Canada from Foremost-McKesson. In January, 1995 the member-owners of Wisconsin Dairies Co-operative and Golden Guernsey Dairy Co-operative merged into Foremost Farms USA. On Friday, April 1, 2009, Foremost Farms USA ended its long-running milk bottling business by selling its Waukesha and Ashwaubenon plants to Dean Foods. Dean acquired the processing plants along with 282 employees and the Golden Guernsey and Morning Glory brands.

In 2010, Foremost Farms was the eighth largest dairy co-operative with 2,100 members and 5.6 billion pounds of milk representing nearly three per cent of the nation's milk supply. Revenues in 2010 were $1.4 billion. Foremost Farms USA now focuses entirely on wholesale markets for cheese, butter, dairy product ingredients, and bulk fluid milk. Foremost Farms has nine cheese plants, five dairy ingredient plants and a butter plant.

In the late 1930s J. C. Penney began buying the original home farm in Hamilton, Missouri along with surrounding acreage. Much more cautious with money, he devoted himself personally to Christian organizations. The company's evolution and Penney's life reflected the vast changes in America between 1875 and 1935. The transformation from a self-supporting rural, agricultural economy to a consumer-oriented urban and industrial economy occurred during the lifetime of many people. Penney was a risk taker often described by his associates as the smartest man they ever met. Study, observation, investigation, and analysis were the foundation of his success. Many enterprises disappeared during the times of recessions and depressions. Each new store was a gamble on the new manager and his business acumen. Penney eagerly discarded old ideas for new ones and chose men whom he regarded as capable or more so than he. In so doing, the J. C. Penney Company's system of efficient mass distribution contributed to raising the nation's standard of living.

According to Professor A. G. Ragsdale of the University of Missouri, "Mr. Penney could drive as hard a bargain as anyone and give an equivalent amount or more away. He pushed junior associates hard and himself harder. Penney is a great businessman and a true humanitarian."

The J. C. Penney Company had its own product testing laboratory. Private label goods were manufactured to strict specifications set by the company and checked for wear, fading, shrinkage, flammability and other parameters in the company laboratory. Samuel Walton, creator of Wal-Mart, attended the University of Missouri and trained with the J. C. Penney Company. Today Wal-Mart sets the standard for purchasing large volumes from manufacturers at the cheapest price based on particular specifications including bar codes.

There is nothing today that can match the laboratory testing by Penney for quality and durability. Policies successful in Kemmerer, Wyoming in 1902 provided the same good values in 1940. There were no charge accounts and no deliveries. Expensive buildings and fixtures were avoided. Many stores were rented space in Masonic Lodge Buildings. Penney advertisements stated that their stores were for "people who live simply, but well." The J. C. Penney slogan proclaimed "To serve the average American family with the merchandise it wants…Every dollar buying the full measure of real value."

• • •

J. C. Penney had many melancholy days especially around Christmas with December 26th being the anniversary of Berta's untimely death. His thoughts would gravitate to what might have been. Berta's death shocked him deeply. Penney cried on returning to Kemmerer in 1925 looking at his store and across the street to his old home. Late at night he would struggle with his grief.

The day the store originally opened in Kemmerer Berta got on her hands and knees to scrub the store floor. She courageously provided the necessary hard physical labor and moral support to her husband and their growing family at the very beginning when it mattered most. Hamlin Garland, West Salem, Wisconsin's Pulitzer Prize winning author, wrote a book about his mother that could just as easily be used to describe Berta Penney. In the first paragraph of *A Pioneer Mother* Garland wrote in 1922:

> She was neither witty, nor learned in books, nor wise in the ways of the world, but I contend that her life was noble. There was something in her unconscious heroism which transcends wisdom and the deeds of those who dwell in the rose-golden light of romance. Now that her life is rounded into the silence whence it came, its significance appears.

In another section he continued:

She was up in the morning before the light cooking for us all, and she seldom went to bed before my father. She was not always well and yet the work had to be done....There are always three meals to get and the dishes to wash, and each day is like another so far as duties are concerned. Sunday brings little rest for housewives even in winter.

... All her toilsome, monotonous days rushed through my mind with a roar, like a file of gray birds in the night – how little – how tragically small her joys, and how black her sorrows, her toil, her tedium.

Although Penney only had a high school education he was the recipient of seventeen honorary degrees and many other honors, awards, and citations. He received the honorary 33rd degree in Freemasonry on October 16, 1945, and he received the Horatio Alger award in 1953. In 1955 *Life* magazine covered his 80th birthday party. Five hundred business leaders in the July 17, 1967, issue of *U. S. News & World Report* named Penney as one of the "three greatest living American businessmen."

In 1928 Penney began his long association with 4-H by purchasing a 4-H grand champion steer. In 1930 one of his stores housed 46 calves for a calf club show he organized. Penney's dairy and farming activities enhanced good will and interest among the area farmers. The free publicity as well as Penney's participation at state fairs put the company's name in the national news. In 1969 J. C. Penney went to the White House where he and Mrs. Nixon accepted Honorary Co-Chairmanship of the National 4-H Club Foundation Advisory Council. Penney received the Partner-in-4-H Award at the 1969 Leader Conference. Mr. and Mrs. Penney received the Friend of 4-H Award in Missouri in 1970 for donating cattle and land to the University of Missouri. Up until his death in 1971 Mr. Penney, his family and his company gave substantially in time and money to 4-H, its leader forums, and to the capital expansion and refurbishing of the National 4-H Youth Conference Center in Chevy Chase, Maryland. Their main hall was dedicated to Penney in 1977. A large mural by the artist Dean Fausett portrays Penney, his many interests and dedication to 4-H. Sadly Mr. Penney did not live to see the building completed. In the years following his death, the J. C. Penney Company has continued its partnership with 4-H through many charitable giving programs.

After fracturing his hip on December 26, 1970, he was hospitalized and while there suffered a fatal heart attack on February 12, 1971. Fifteen hundred people attended his funeral at St. James Episcopal Church in Manhattan. Thousands of letters and telegrams of condolence were received. In his memory, his wife Caroline said, "He loved life and he thought young."

J. C. Penney's six principles for living epitomized his success:

1. Preparation
2. Hard Work
3. Honesty
4. Having confidence in others
5. Appeal to the life giving spirit of others
6. The practical application of the Golden Rule. Whatsoever you ask me to do for you, do even so to them.

James Cash Penney surpassed his father's faith in him. He predicted: "Jim will make it. I like the way he has started out."

Chapter Sixteen:

Reminiscing in Hamilton

J. C. Penney lived his first twenty one years in Hamilton, Missouri. Today Hamilton is a town of under 2000 people, and it lies just off of highway 36. The exit seems like other major highway exits in America today, complete with the ubiquitous gas station-convenience store on one corner. However, cruising down the broad and tidy main drag a few blocks is like going back to the quietude of small town America of the 1950s.

Dean Hales is the curator of the J.C. Penney Museum which occupies half of the handsome brick building shared with the public library. The librarian called him at his store in Cameron, a dozen miles away, and he graciously volunteered to come to share the Penney legacy and give us a tour of the points of interest in town. While waiting for Mr. Hales, my wife Kathy and I visited the local antique store where the woman in charge was only too willing to share her views about Hamilton's most famous son and his equally famous *pink* Cadillac. She said the town was unhappy that Hamilton's J.C. Penney store was closed shortly after he passed away in 1971. The company said the store was unprofitable. It is now a hardware store totally devoid of any reference to Penney or the fact that Mr. Penney sometimes would personally display livestock in his store in support of rural youth activities.

The Memorial Library – Museum building is roughly divided in half, with the library situated on the left side and the museum on the right. Dean Hales, creator, curator, and heart and soul of the museum, requested donations for its creation and received over $300,000 from throughout the United States. Mr. Hales and Mr. Penney's nephew Bob Penney created the museum in its present format. Upon entering, one is immediately confronted with a life-sized statue of a dapper J.C. Penney standing behind a counter, almost as if he were alive and waiting to be of assistance.

Inside the J. C. Penney Museum in Hamilton, Missouri

The many glass cases contain countless photos, documents, and artifacts spanning the entire Penney legacy. The walls are also lined with pictures and documents, as well as plaques of his oft-given speeches. Dean Hales had retrieved artifacts from a Kentucky church where Penney's grandfather preached. He also combed Penney's private office in New York for many of the items that are now on display, including the large but modest oak desk owned and used by Penney in New York. His nephew Bob actually inherited the desk and presented it to the Hamilton Museum at the time of the museum's dedication. None of Penney's children came back to Hamilton.

Of the many hundreds of items on display, three gave me a lasting impression of J.C. Penney. The first item consists of two video tapes produced by an elder J. C. Penney describing the lessons he learned in life, with scenes reenacted with his granddaughter and others. Second is a picture of the beautiful, ornate mansion owned by Mr. Penney in Florida where Herbert Hoover spent many a night as guest, including right after being elected President in 1928. Penney and Hoover were extremely close friends, and Mr. Penney stayed in the Lincoln bedroom several times during the Hoover presidency. The third is the description of Mr. Penney's funeral service by Norman Vincent Peale, author of the book *The Power of Positive Thinking*.

Dean Hales is a self-proclaimed NASCAR fanatic having traveled throughout the United States attending auto races. On the back side of his business card is a photograph of the 1947 Cadillac convertible J. C. Penney and his wife owned and drove around New York City. This car is shown parked outside the J. C .Penney Memorial Library – Museum. Sometimes the Cadillac is displayed in a tiny all-glass showroom that sits by itself on the edge of town just off the four lane highway. We did see the Cadillac stored in Mr. Hales' sparkling clean home garage. It is definitely white and not pink as the antique store woman vividly recalled!

The 1950's small town camaraderie is alive and well in Hamilton. That everyone knows and respects Dean Hales was obvious – many youths and older people waved and stopped for a chat as we continued our tour. We passed by the Penney high school and the brand new grade school. The school is located on the former county fair grounds where J. C. Penney Sr. sent his young son home for illicitly selling watermelons. According to Mr. Hales, the Penney family actually moved into Hamilton when J. C. Penney was twelve years old. The home he lived in, as well as the simple white farm home Penney was born in, is still standing. The farm home was moved to Hamilton in recent years and is open for tours at random times. Locals say it contains mostly period pieces unrelated to Mr. Penney and it more than likely will not reach its potential as a tourist attraction. Mr. Hales knew the Penney family all his life. The Hales' family grocery store was across the street from Penney's store. He lamented that it is a shame today few people in Hamilton have much interest in Mr. Penney's legacy.

Harold Henry knew J. C. Penney better than anyone left in Hamilton today. In fact, he owns and lives on the Penney farm. Our directions to the farm: from the library go to the only light in town, actually a flashing yellow light, and turn left onto old highway 36. Mr. Henry, along with everyone in town we talked to, warned us to be very careful because old highway 36 was in bad shape. Expecting the worst we travelled slowly and carefully exactly two miles to the farm. Parking on the gravel by the garage we found Mr. Henry outside greeting and urging us to move the car onto the grass under the shade tree. The 100° heat was worse than the road!

Mr. Henry remembers seeing Penney and three others riding through Hamilton on Palomino horses during the early 1940s. He especially recalled the plainsman's cowboy hat that Penney wore, and he said that Mr. Penney did enjoy riding those beautiful horses with fancy saddles. Mr. Henry was eleven years old when he first met the 71 year old J. C. Penney in 1946.

The J. C. Penney store was the town's favorite hangout especially in the summer when Mr. Penney spent a month in Hamilton. A plaque in the Museum designates it officially to be the 500th store Penney opened. In the

1930s and 1940s Penney's prize-winning livestock were occasionally exhibited in the store. In 1946 the local store manager and Harold's Boy Scout leader, Carlas Demarest, asked Harold Henry if he was interested in stoking the store furnace and putting toys together. Harold found no problem with that, and at age eleven he even worked behind the counter waiting on customers. Harold especially recalls that when a customer needed change from a purchase, a rope was pulled and "the jug thing" shot up a wire to the cashier.

In 1949 Harold's dad began working for Mr. Penney and the same year the fourteen year old Harold began working on the Penney farm. The first thing Harold learned to do was to load manure onto a spreader with a pitchfork. Each load needed two one hundred twenty pound bags of real rock phosphate spread over the top of the manure, and no load was ever allowed to be spread in the fields without the rock phosphate. The spreader was usually pulled by horses, then later on by a tractor. The rock phosphate was delivered by railroad cars into Hamilton. Harold was part of the crew of four or five who unloaded the box cars and brought the sacks out to the farm. The sacks were cumbersome and heavy. They did not even have a two-wheel dolly for stacking the sacks. Harold hated taking these heavy sacks and spreading the contents evenly on top of the manure. When Junior James (son of Orin James, J. C. Penney's partner on the home farm) and Harold were not hauling manure they were baling hay. All summer they baled and hauled heavy square bales.

On Saturdays when in Hamilton, J. C. Penney would pick up Junior James and Harold Henry at the farm. They would use a team of horses then later a tractor to pick up brush and sticks. Penney was very sensitive to attractiveness and he had "a thing" about everything being clean and orderly. He always carried a bucket or sack around the farm, which never failed to come back full of metal and debris, ready for the next empty bucket. He was known to take a broom to demonstrate to his store partners the proper way to get the floor cleaner. A full-time carpenter worked on the farm with sometimes as many as four or five additional workers. Mr. Henry says the buildings are showing their age and none are practical for today's usage.

J. C. Penney was a hard and harsh man to work for. Just as he set high standards for his own life, he expected and demanded a lot from his workers. Nevertheless, Mr. Henry said Penney was a fair man. When Harold was fifteen years old he came home late one evening from work at the Penney farm. He found his mother crying almost uncontrollably. Mr. Penney had stopped by and told her that her son would really amount to something! This coming from this famous man was overwhelming. As we shall see, Mr. Penney was an excellent judge of character and he was always a leader. Seventy plus years ago he built the first soil terraces in the county. He believed in having well-limed fields, and fifty years later they are still adequately limed.

J. C. Penney added acreage to the family farm until he owned almost two sections. During the 1940s, railroad cars came through the farm to pick up coal from a coal mine located on his land. The abstract which Mr. Henry has on his land title states that Penney received ten cents a ton for every ton excavated. The mine even had a little store for the workers. The wood on the farm was available to the miners and was used instead of coal to provide power and heat for the mine. The mine eventually became water logged, and as technology was not advanced enough at the time to correct the problem, the mine was permanently closed.

The original home farm was for horses. Penney was known for having the best studs and jacks in the nation. He sold mules and horses to the military for the war effort in World War I. Penney's first horse barn was destroyed by fire, so adjacent to the sales barn he erected a new one 240 feet long with individual stalls.

In 1948 or 1949 Penney built a sale barn on his farm with a distinctive front-stepped brick façade which was used for his spring Angus sales. Very slowly Orin James would bring out the sale bulls for the scrutiny of avid buyers. The longer he stalled the higher the price received! After the spring sale the barn would be used for storing hay, all of which had to be emptied out for bleacher seats to be reinstalled in time for the Angus sale always held the first Tuesday in March. J. C. Penney always believed that if you bred average cows to the best bull in the world you would create the world's very best animals. He has not been proven wrong. In 1940 he paid $30,000 for "Wonder Bull," and according to Mr. Henry everyone had to have a son of this Angus bull. Cars parked five deep and seldom did the sons go for under $10,000. "Wonder Bull" is buried on the farmstead and has his own tombstone.

Penney also always believed in having a partner in everything he did. He felt that more responsibility would be taken by all sides of the endeavor if partners were included in the undertaking. Penney never hired anyone unless he first had lunch with him: an aspirant who salted his food without first tasting it was never hired! A farm family near Chillicothe raising hogs and cattle on 3200 acres partnered with him. The children of the family are still operating the farm today. According to Harold Henry, J. C. Penney was the tightest man you would ever meet and he wasn't named "Cash" for nothing! Harold Appley ran Penney's Guernsey farm locally, ten miles north of Gallatin, Missouri. Appley and Penney went to a Guernsey sale in Oklahoma. Penney had begun to develop a paunch that concerned him. At breakfast he saw a penny scale and decided to weigh himself. He was about to drop the penny in the slot, but stopped. He turned to Appley and said that he would wait until they got home to weigh himself on Appley's bathroom scale.

The name J. C. Penney became synonymous with durability and practicality in clothing. He rigorously tested the clothing products he sold for toughness and resistance to abrasion and rejected those that did not meet his stringent requirements. Mr. Henry said that when Penney was in charge, clothes were produced that farmers could afford and wear confidently. Sometimes the good old days really were the good old days!

• • •

Harold's brother Charlie and his wife Joyce from Kansas City joined us in conversation that afternoon. Charlie taught vocational education at a college in Kansas City for thirty-eight years and has been retired fifteen years. Both Joyce and Charlie have choice memories of J. C. Penney. From their upstairs bedroom Joyce and her sister Elouise would see Penney coming up the road in his old green Plymouth coupe. He would never drive on the road, but on the bank of the road where their dad always planted flowers. Elouise said, "Dad will be mad tonight!" Their dad could say nothing as he lived in a house owned by Mr. Penney and worked for him. Although Penney had a place to stay in Hamilton and spent most of his time there, it was thought that he took the route out to the Orin James residence so he wouldn't have to buy his own dinner in town. Elouise worked at the Penney store and served as secretary for J. C. Penney when he was in Hamilton, and often took dictation for his letters. Joyce said Penney had the oldest overcoat she had ever seen. It was flared at the bottom and always clean, but he never exchanged it for another coat. She can still see him sitting on the fence at the Angus sales in that rustic old coat. Joyce said he could have always had a nice coat befitting his wealth and stature, but that was not his way.

Charlie remembers at about age twelve going trick or treating on Halloween at Mr. James' father-in-law's house. J. C. Penney was there. Before they could leave, Penney asked the youngsters, "Why do we celebrate Halloween?" They did not know. Charlie remembers the explanation having to do with Indians and their tribal rituals. Charlie Henry said you could not be around J. C. Penney without learning something.

Harold Henry and J. C. Penney could get "downright personal with each other." Harold claims to have known J. C. Penney a heck of a lot better than business people did. As a kid he did not hold him in awe as other people might. His favorite gambit was to tease Penney about Harry Truman. J. C. Penney would become red in the face, get all wound up and proceed to straighten out Harold. Harold couldn't help but to burst out laughing and soon Mr. Penney was laughing just as hard. Penney always had a sober countenance, but Harold could get him to laugh. One time later when both Truman and Penney were nearing the age of 90, Harold saw Truman on TV proclaiming that he was planning to live to be100. A day or two later he ran into Penney in town and told him that he had seen Penney's "old buddy" on TV. Penney barked, "Who's that?" He told him it was Harry Truman and about his goal. Penney growled, "I fully intend to myself!" He was not about to let Truman outdo him.

Even though J. C. Penney had met Harry S. Truman, he hated him with an absolute passion and believed with all his heart that Truman was a terrible person. He could not understand how a failed haberdasher could become President of the United States of America. Of course, he said a successful businessman would best be equipped to be President. However, not only was there no money to be made in the position, no businessman would mess with the job in the first place. How this reconciles with Penney's friendship with President Hoover is best left to the imagination.

Truman was a protégé of Tom Pendergast, who according to Mr. Henry "was hooked up with the mob," ran all the elections in Kansas City, and got whatever he wanted. The young Harry worked for him, including playing the piano and whatever else Pendergast told him to do. This was before Truman became President. The Pendergast machine was very powerful in Missouri for a long time, according to Harold Henry.

Such was the state of affairs in rural America in the aftermath of World War II that Truman was much detested. Only later with the excellent biography by David McCullough did the great leader from Independence, Missouri gain appreciation. Truman read the Christian Bible several times as a youth, was monogamous and devout. Since he fought and led in the trenches in World War I, he could appreciate the horrors of modern warfare as could no other President. This high school graduate was given the reins of the Presidency without being properly informed of the state of affairs by his predecessor, yet still performed with distinction. At the Hamilton Missouri Centennial celebration in 1955, Harry S. Truman honored the community with his presence and oration. Harold Henry thinks that Harry Truman was as good a President as any of them.

J. C. Penney and his family paid for half the Penney High School named in his honor. According to Bob Penney, his uncle instructed each member of the family what his or her share of the contributions would be. Since he was the sole provider of economic opportunities for most of his relatives, his word was law. None of the money would be forthcoming if it was not at least matched by the citizens of the community, which it was. The school is still there but has seen several additions over the years. J. C. Penney gave to many causes, but only if his donations were at least matched. He felt that if the citizens did not care enough for the project, then why should he. He was a partner in everything he did. According to Harold Henry, for several years Penney gave the commencement address which never varied at the school named after him.

Two deceased high school classmates of J. C. Penney had polar opinions of him. One admired him completely while the other totally detested him. Harold figures that much of the negative feeling toward Penney stemmed from pure jealously. He also asserts that J. C. Penney lived by the Golden Rule *usually*, but as he grew older he was much more determined to follow the Golden Rule *at all times*. Many rumors and stories from this small town circulate, but the underlying belief about Mr. Penney is that he was a good provider and a deeply caring man who was utterly devastated by the loss of each of his first two wives.

One time while Mr. Penney was working north of Hamilton near Gallatin he went to eat at McDonald's Tea Room, a fancy place that no longer exists. Ms. McDonald, proprietor, insisted she could not seat him because he was not wearing a jacket and tie. Mr. Penney gave up and left. When someone enlightened Ms. McDonald as to whom she had just turned away, she was horrified. She ran out to the parking lot begging him to return but he said that was okay, and left. He surprised her by showing up that evening, we assume properly attired! They became lifelong friends. As usual in a small town with slanted memories, it was told that Mr. Penney was denied service because he wore no suit coat, never came back, and Ms. McDonald regretted it forever.

Every week while in New York City, the avid reader Penney would read from cover to cover the Hamilton, Missouri, newspaper. In 1966 he read that Harold Henry had purchased his home farm. He wrote Mr. Henry a very nice letter saying that he preferred Mr. Henry owning that farm to anyone else. Unfortunately, at a later time this letter along with other memorabilia in his briefcase was stolen from Mr. Henry's car in Kansas City.

The farm initially had been purchased and paid for in full in 1962 by former dairy farmers from Illinois. However, just four years of poor management led to total bankruptcy and foreclosure in 1966. Harold Henry then bought the farm and paid a reasonable $330 per acre, but he had to borrow every penny. He thought if he had a weekly sale in the sale barn on the farm he could pay off the farm in ten years. He began his weekly cattle sales in 1966, but by 1972 he came upon hard times and had to sell his Red Angus herd. He had to do this twice. Throughout this tough time he followed the advice given him: Sell the cattle – keep the land. You can always replace cattle, but never the land. The value of the land went to $1100 per acre after he purchased it, but fell to $300 to $400 per acre in the 1980s.

Ten years after purchase of the farm he had enough to pay for it, but instead bought more land. Although Mr. Henry studied pre-law, he became an auctioneer. He sold mostly Black and Red Angus throughout thirty-eight states and Canada. As with most ambitious people, he wishes he had spent more time with his family. Both his and his wife Nancy's first spouses are deceased. They had been married eleven years in 2009 and between them had 37 grand and great grand children when we visited, with more on the way.

Henry says he does not care about money. His great joy is his family. He likes what he does and still dabbles in livestock. He would like to find a sound Foremost Guernsey bull or calf to carry forward the memory of J. C. Penney. In the three years prior to 2009 he had purchased two bulls tracing back to the Foremost bull from the University of Missouri. Henry is still experimenting with crossing the Guernsey with other breeds including red and white Holsteins. He says Guernsey milk no longer has the cream line or taste it once had.

Harold Henry leaves us with one thought as he approaches his seventy-fifth year. "Life has been so good to me. I'm the luckiest man in the world."

Chapter Seventeen:

The Foremost Legacy

In 1922 J. C. Penney purchased Emmadine Farms of Hopewell Junction, New York to develop his dream Guernsey dairy herd. Aware that dairy herds in Scotland and England stayed within a single family for generations while in the United States they averaged only ten years, seldom going over a quarter century, he decided one's lifetime was too short to develop a great dairy herd. With this in mind in 1936 he renamed Emmadine Farms and incorporated as Foremost Guernsey Association. The corporation was created to perpetuate the herd on a permanent basis. Sufficient funds were made available so that it would never have to be disbursed. The Foremost Guernsey Association Charter expired in 1996 with the provision that the remainder assets after the settlement of liabilities were to be transferred to the University of Missouri. However, J. C. Penney expressed a desire to see the Foremost Guernsey herd as part of the University during his lifetime rather than wait until 1996. Upon mutual agreement of all the entities involved, the transfer was moved to 1952.

This transfer was instigated when J. C. Penney was 76 years old and completed when he was 77. Most people at that age have fulfilled their productive accomplishments and are looking to leave, if they can, a lasting legacy that will enhance the world. The endeavors Mr. Penney made to make the world a better place by his own hand were not to be forgotten nor stopped by old age or his eventual passing. Nor was the beautiful, productive herd of Guernsey cattle he created with the help of his Creator to be taken from the face of the earth or sullied in any way. This world-renowned Guernsey herd was to be improved upon and maintained in perpetuity by the people he respected and trusted in the college of Dairy Science at the University of Missouri.

A letter from J. C. Penney dated January 31, 1952, with the letterhead "FOREMOST GUERNSEY ASSOCIATION", 330 West 34th Street, New York, New York, is as follows:

> Foremost Guernsey Association Inc. offers to the Board of Curators, University of Missouri, subject to approval by the New York State Supreme Court, for the use of its College of Agriculture, all assets of the corporation. These include one of the finest Guernsey herds in America, consisting of 200 head of cattle of varying ages; certain stocks and bonds; the proceeds from the sale of the farm at Hopewell Junction, New York, and miscellaneous assets, all to become the absolute property of the University of Missouri. The complete inventory of January 1, 1953, is attached, which of course will be subject to changes as the operations continue.
>
> It is my wish that this herd of Guernsey cattle be maintained by the college of Agriculture, Department of Dairy Husbandry, on a farm to be provided by the University of Missouri, for which assets of the Foremost Guernsey Association, Inc. may be used for providing land, buildings, and improvements, and that the income from the remaining capital assets and from the farm and herd operations be used as deemed best by the University in the further development of the herd and farm and for such research, teaching, demonstration, and

additional activities as may be considered appropriate by the University and related to the general objectives.

Missouri is my native state and I am proud of the work of its College of Agriculture. It is my sincere belief that the assets of this Corporation, as shown in the attached unaudited balance sheet, and including most especially the highly developed herd of Guernsey cattle, may make its research and teaching program more effective in the years ahead. The chairman of your department of Dairy husbandry has served on our Board of Directors since 1939 and is familiar with the ideals and goals I had in mind in establishing this herd and the possibilities for its future. It is my desire that the 'FOREMOST GUERNSEYS' now well and favorably known throughout America, be continued, believing it will be a great asset and continue to be an outstanding name in Guernsey history. The University may use my name in any manner it thinks best in connection with this gift.

I am tremendously interested in the improvement of agricultural practices and research and believe the University of Missouri may with the aid of this gift be in position to continue and further develop its leadership in the field.

We are taking steps to liquidate Foremost Guernseys, Inc., including the sale of the farm and propose to turn over to the Curators of the University of Missouri the Guernsey herd and all other assets as rapidly as possible and as the University may be in position to receive them. I am asking Professor A. O. Ragsdale to present this proposal through Dean J. H. Longwell and President Frederick A. Middlebush for your consideration and action."

Signed: J. C. Penney, President, FOREMOST GUERNSEY ASSOCIATION, INC.

A press release from The University of Missouri Office of Public Information dated June 5, 1952, contained the following:

J. C. Penney, a former Missouri farm boy, has given a world-famous dairy herd and other assets valued at nearly three-quarters of a million dollars to the University of Missouri to support research and teaching, particularly in the College of Agriculture, it was announced today by University president Frederick A. Middlebush.

President Middlebush said that Mr. Penney, a native of Hamilton, and now head of a nation wide chain of retail stores bearing his name, has given to the University of Missouri all the property, endowment, and assets of the Foremost Guernsey Association, Inc., of New York, an association which Mr. Penney founded and which was recently dissolved by the New York courts, upon Mr. Penney's request, to permit transfer of title to the University.

Included in the assets is the famous Foremost Guernsey herd of some 250 head of cattle, known throughout the agricultural world as one of finest purebred herds in existence. This herd will be brought to Missouri and kept intact by the University's College of Agriculture. The herd alone is conservatively valued at $200,000. President Middlebush said the name 'Foremost Guernsey' will be continued to designate the herd.

The farm land, buildings, and equipment at Hopewell Junction, New York, where the herd has been developed, also becomes the property of the University along with cash, stocks, and bonds included in the Foremost association's assets. In the terms of his gift, Mr. Penney specifies that the property in New York may be sold and the proceeds used to purchase, improve, and equip a farm near Columbia suitable for the maintenance of the herd in accordance with the purposes of the University.

In the letter making the gift to the University, Mr. Penney wrote: "I am tremendously interested in the improvement of agricultural practices and research, and believe the University of Missouri may with the aid of this gift be in a position to continue and further develop its leadership in this field."

"Missouri is my native state," Mr. Penney said, "and I am proud of its College of Agriculture."

Mr. Penney is internationally recognized as an astute business executive, and his success in business is one of the great epics of American initiative and enterprise, yet he has maintained an active interest in agriculture and has devoted much of his time and energy to the development of better farm practices and to activities designed for better farm living.

He has sponsored agricultural research in cooperation with the College of Agriculture and is well informed on the University's entire teaching and research policy.

Mr. Penney is considered unique among America's millionaire farm owners in that he insists that each of its farms operate on a strictly business basis, pay its own way and show a profit, but at the same time make constant improvement and institute modern methods of better farming. His holdings include seven farms in Missouri, the largest of which includes his birthplace near Hamilton in its 2000 acres. Others are located near Gallatin, Trenton, Chula, and Breckenridge.

In establishing and developing Foremost Guernseys, Mr. Penney has conferred frequently with the Department of Dairy Husbandry of the University, and particularly with its chairman, Prof. Arthur C. Ragsdale. Prof. Ragsdale was a member of the Board of Directors of the Foremost Guernsey Association and it was partly through this connection that Mr. Penney kept informed on the over-all research programs of the University.

Mr. Penney says in his letter: "The chairman of your Department of Dairy Husbandry has been on our board since 1939 and is familiar with the ideals and goals I had in mind in establishing this herd, and with the possibilities for its future."

In making the gift, Mr. Penney said it was his wish that the Guernsey herd be maintained by the Department of Dairy Husbandry on a University farm. He suggested the assets of the Association might be used if necessary to provide land, buildings, and improvements, and further suggested "that income from the remaining capital assets be used as deemed best by the University in further development and improvement of the herd and farm for such research, teaching, demonstrations, and additional activities as may be considered appropriate by the University and related to the general objectives."

Dr. John H. Longwell, director of the University's Division of Agricultural Sciences and dean of the College of Agriculture, today joined President Middlebush in expressing gratitude for the fine tribute Mr. Penney pays to the University, and for the confidence he has shown in the University's educational and research program.

"The College of Agriculture is particularly appreciative of the gift of this fine herd, one of the top dairy herds in the United States," Dean Longwell said.

Dean Longwell explained that the herd will afford excellent material for dairy husbandry students particularly, and for further research for dairy cattle breeding. He also announced that Lawrence R. Rainey of St. Albans, Mo., one of the most widely recognized Guernsey breeders of the Middle West, has been appointed superintendent to manage the Foremost Guernsey herd and farm, and that Mr. Rainey assumes his duties this summer.

Dean Longwell said that the present plans of the University include establishment of a "J. C. Penney Foremost Guernsey Foundation," which would set up an advisory board to help guide the Foremost Guernsey program toward the objectives which both Mr. Penney and the University have in view.

He said the tentative plan calls for the board of the new foundation to include members of the staff of the University and representative Guernsey breeders of Missouri interested in further development of the fine breeding herd. He added that the College of Agriculture hopes the value of the Foremost herd may be enhanced for years to come by maintaining it as a unit.

"Mr. Penney's action in providing for the future security of this herd is a good illustration of his keen foresight," Dean Longwell said, "for he has not only developed an outstanding breeding program, but has made provision for perpetuation of the herd as a unit."

Many fine herds of cattle have been developed in this country," the dean continued, "but too often these herds are dispersed by the owner or by his estate, and much of the value of the entire breeding program is thereby lost."

Writing several years ago of his interest in agriculture, Mr. Penney said: "I had not been in mercantile business long before I realized the prosperity for the farmer meant prosperity for us. As I analyzed statistics and observed the fluctuations of rural well-being, as reflected in sales reports, I became convinced that the greatest need of the farmer everywhere was better cattle."

"When I began the study of purebred cattle," he continued, "I was astonished and considerably distressed to learn that every great herd which had been built up in the United States had been dispersed upon the death of the owner to settle his estate. I also discovered that the average life of a breeding unit in America was less than ten years, and that few had been in existence as long as a quarter of a century. Since I knew that the span of my lifetime would be too short a period to work out the plan I had in mind, and being desirous that posterity should profit from my work, I evolved the unique plan of endowing a herd of cattle."

It was thus that the Emmadine Farm was established at Hopewell Junction, New York, later to be incorporated in 1936 as the Foremost Guernsey Association. At the time of the incorporation Mr. Penney stated publicly it was his intention that the Foremost Association was to run until 1996, a period of sixty years, as a corporation and then the herd and other property were to be transferred to the University of Missouri for use by its College of Agriculture. Recently Mr. Penney decided that he wants to see the University of Missouri take over the Guernsey herd now, rather than have the transfer take place after his death.

A condensed balance sheet for the Foremost Guernsey Association as of January 1, 1952, lists current assets, including accounts receivable, inventories, stocks, annuities, cash, and fixed assets, including land and buildings, totaling $760,535.24; deferred charges to operation and unexpired insurance, $3,820.09; for a total of $764,355.33 in assets. Current liabilities are shown as $40,033.17, leaving a net worth of $724,322.16 that the University will receive.

Prof. Ragsdale said that the history of the Foremost Guernsey herd and its accomplishments is a full story within itself, a project in which he is very proud to have had a small role for some years. He said Mr. Penney's idea of setting up an endowment for a breeding herd is another example of the shrewd business sense which has marked the merchant's success.

The corporation was founded for the purpose "of instituting, conducting, and carrying out scientific, agricultural or biological experiments, research, study and investigations concerning animal life; improving, developing and experimenting with and studying the fertility of the soil and its effect upon crops for the feeding of animals, and the effect of such feeding upon breeding, production, and elimination of disease; and particularly experimenting with and studying dairy cattle in connection with the foregoing objectives and purposes; and the publishing or otherwise disseminating information related to these purposes."

At that time, agricultural and dairy husbandry leaders throughout the nation lauded Mr. Penney's actions as one of the foremost steps in the history of American cattle breeding. Writing in the January 15, 1937, issue of the Guernsey Breeders' Journal, Karl B. Moser, secretary of the American Guernsey

Cattle Club, said: "Mr. Penney, in founding this organization, has builded a living monument to a cause and not to himself. He has chosen to keep mobile his great interest in American agriculture after he has gone, rather than have it fixed in granite, bronze, or marble statue which time will look upon with a query as to its meaning. His monument shall live in the warm bloodstream of man's greatest source of life's sustenance, the dairy cow."

The press release of June 5, 1952, continued to discuss the bequest in more detail including the original farm, foundation animals, and the outstanding milk production records for the time as well as the longevity of the Guernsey animals, especially Mixter Faithful who produced sixteen calves while living to be over twenty-two years of age.

What this press release established above all else was the extraordinary gift the College of Agriculture of the University of Missouri was receiving from James Cash Penney and the University's acknowledgement of its commitment to continue to develop and improve the Foremost Guernsey herd in perpetuity. Implicit in the document was the desire to continue research in all areas of biological and agronomic dairy farming using this great herd and the re-established Foremost Farm in Columbia, Missouri, and disseminating the knowledge to further enhance dairy farming throughout the nation if not the world.

There was nothing that indicated that should anything change in the dairy industry, the College of Agriculture of the University of Missouri might at its discretion violate the understanding between them and Mr. Penney's legacy. There was a plan to create the "J. C. Penney Foremost Guernsey Foundation" to help guide the wishes of Mr. Penney and the University. I could find nothing in the information gleaned at the University and elsewhere that this ever happened. The J. C. Penney legacy to the University of Missouri should be prominent in the dairy industry today considering the extraordinary gift in 1952, just by building on its foundation.

The College of Agriculture at the University of Missouri was established in 1870, with the first Agricultural Experiment Station established in 1888. Shortly after this, dairy husbandry and research began. Little documented scientific knowledge on dairying had been done prior to this time. In 1887 Professor J. W. Sanborn purchased four Jersey cows and a bull. On April 17, 1901, the Missouri legislature enacted a law creating the Department of Dairy Husbandry in the College of Agriculture. Of the $40,000 appropriated for the department, $30,000 was used to build a dairy building known today as Eckles Hall, named after Clarence Henry Eckles, the first head of the Department of Dairy Husbandry. He was selected for that position in June, 1901, and since then, breeding, calving, health, and production records have been kept at the College of Agriculture.

The first dairy bulletin from the Agriculture Extension was published in 1894, bulletin number 26 explaining the care of milk and making of butter on the farm. In the winter of 1895-1896 the first course of dairying was offered in proper methods for making butter and cheese. The course incorporated the Babcock Butterfat test established in 1890.

The Department of Dairy Husbandry became internationally known in the dairy industry in 1910 when one of its foundation Holstein cows Chief Josephine 64687, produced 26,861 pounds of milk and 740 pounds of butterfat in one year. This annual record was the second best in the world at that time. In 1911 "Old Jo" as the cow was known was exhibited on agricultural trains throughout America. She traveled 4,000 miles and was seen by an estimated 100,000 people. The prominence of "Old Jo" and her offspring in the University of Missouri herd prompted out-of-state students, including many graduate students, to enroll in the dairy program.

The University's dairy program contributed ground-breaking research in the early decades of the twentieth century. They proved there was little difference in milk production efficiency in dairy animals. The inherited capacity to consume large amounts of feed always indicated the good producer. Working with the USDA in 1906, an exhaustive study of milk pigments was done using chromatography methods developed by Professor Leroy S. Palmer. The significance of his research and methodology was used by many scientists including six Nobel Prize winners. In 1927, Charles W. Turner worked on the endocrinology of milk secretion including the development of the mammary gland in the embryo, puberty, pregnancy, lactation, and involution. A method for measuring the volume of blood flowing through the udder was devised. Professor Turner was able to prove the gross efficiency of the mammary gland was ninety percent. The energy required to transfer milk precursors from the blood into milk was less than ten percent of the energy involved. This and studies made of the endocrine glands and precursors of milk have been used by the medical profession and manufacturers of dairy equipment. As a pioneer in artificial insemination, the college provided the first college level course on the subject in 1941.

There were 710,000 dairy cows in Missouri according to the 1890 census with most farms and even urban dwellers having a milking cow for family needs. Dairy cow numbers peaked in in the state in 1933 with 1,068,000 dairy cows. Cow numbers remained at about a million head until 1954, decreasing to 800,000 in 1968 then to 225,000 in 1988. Bulk milk cooling and mechanization beginning in the 1950's along with a cost/price squeeze brought about the gradual descent in the prominence of dairying in the state. According to Hoard's Dairyman Missouri ranked 21st in the nation with 99,000 milk cows in 2010, a drop of 7.5% in cows from 2009 and an 11% drop from 2008, when it had 110,000 dairy cows. In 2010 the national herd average was over 21,000 pounds of milk per cow with Missouri ranking 44th at 14,596 pounds. Missouri produced one billion 445 million pounds of milk in 2010, a drop of 7.8% from 2009.

In April 2009 we requested the opportunity to visit the Dairy Science Department at the University of Missouri and their Foremost Guernsey herd. Prior to our visit, in an e-mail dated April 23, 2009, Professor Barry Steevens discussed aspects of the Foremost herd:

> The Foremost Guernsey Dairy herd is still at the University of Missouri however the herd is smaller. There are about 25 lactating Guernseys and an additional 27 head of young stock. The farm also has a herd of 200 head of registered Holsteins. We use the Guernsey herd for teaching and outreach activities. We shifted to more Holsteins as most research requires Holsteins as they represent 96% of the dairy cattle in the US.
>
> When the Foremost Dairy was established by J. C. Penny it was designed more for teaching and did not have facilities for research. We have replaced or remodeled nearly all of the original facilities. Today we have a 160 cow free stall barn with "Calan" doors which allow for individual feed intake. These tools are necessary for conducting nutrition research.
>
> The Guernsey cattle are managed in a confinement system with the Holsteins. We have discussed setting up a pasture based grazing system at our Foremost Dairy in Columbia. Budget and available people to manage the second unit has held us back from implementing a grazing dairy.
>
> We pooled the two dairy herds back in 1979 because of budget restrictions.
>
> The University of Missouri does have a 90 cow grazing dairy at the Mt. Vernon Agricultural Experiment Station at Mt. Vernon, Missouri. Most cows at that station are Jersey X Holstein or straight Jersey.
>
> Your last question is interesting. There is no question the genetic base is limiting in the Guernsey breed. Back in 1980 Dr. Harry H. Herman, a leader in AI [artificial insemination], Guernsey breeder and leader with NAAB commented to me that if he could live a second life he would try to cross

breed the Guernsey with a red and white Holstein. He felt the genetic base of the Guernsey breed was too narrow.

We do have a sense of loyalty to the University of Missouri Foremost Guernseys as we continue to carry on with the blood line.

I suppose one could ask the question as to why the J. C. Penny stores now carry clothes made in other countries versus made in USA only.

I have several documents I would be glad to share. One is about the original transfer of the dairy herd to University of Missouri curators.

Sincerely,

Barry J. Steevens
State Extension Dairy Specialist

In June 2009 my wife Kathy and I did visit the University of Missouri in Columbia to discover firsthand what had been happening in the intervening years with J. C. Penney's Guernsey herd. Professor Barry Steevens, the State Specialist of the Animal Sciences Dairy Extension, warmly welcomed us and allowed us to peruse the archives of the University of Missouri Foremost legacy. We had a wide ranging discussion with him about trends in the dairy industry in general and specifically the Foremost Dairy Farm legacy.

We remembered the early 1970s when the price of corn and soybeans was then at an all time high, encouraging many dairy farmers to abandon the dairy business to cash in on the bounty. The price for corn and soybeans, as could be expected, eventually returned to historic patterns, but the dream that the higher prices would return kept farm land values very high. Farmers were land wealthy allowing them to borrow more than was prudent. Most farmers neither had a business plan nor paid attention to the concept of profits and losses. As times got tougher they blamed their situation on the failure of the banker to provide them with adequate funds. When the unprecedented high interest rates of the 1980s came along many were unprepared and suffered catastrophically.

We noted that in 2008, one year prior to our meeting, the price received per hundred pounds of milk was over twenty-one dollars, while in June 2009 it had fallen to between eleven and twelve dollars. The price of fluid milk had dropped more than fifty per cent in the previous fifteen months while the cost to the consumer for fluid milk had dropped only fifteen per cent. The cash spot price for cheddar cheese was about forty per cent lower while the retail cheese price had not changed. Marketers claimed a price squeeze when milk prices went up unexpectedly and now needed to recoup. Over time, however, the farm/retail price gap always continues to widen. Of course you have those such as William Niskanen of CATO saying that the price of milk is maintained by a government authorized "cartel." He wonders what President Obama thinks of this. The 65,000 dairy farmers as participants in this "cartel" must wonder what milk price gyrations would be like in a "free market."

Milk marketing orders have been in existence since the 1930s. At one time farmer milk prices increased the further away you were from Eau Claire, Wisconsin. The contour fields and crop rotations used to produce milk in Wisconsin were considered the low cost or "ground zero" point for determining United States milk production costs. So much for comparative advantage and economic efficiency; you need a fairness doctrine to distort free enterprise at whatever cost to the nation.

According to *The Economist* the National Milk Federation Producers culled milking cows by 101,040 to reduce milk supply during the month of July 2009. There were plans for a further culling going forward. The federal government has a Milk Income Loss Contract (MILC) program to issue payments to farmers in bad times. No one really understands the effects of all these manifestations. Every time there is a bad time, there are fewer dairy farmers the next time around.

The dollar's strong purchasing power against major currencies caused a drop in exports of powdered milk, the main dairy export. In May 2008 U. S. exports of milk powder were 102 million pounds. It reached a low of 28 million pounds in February 2009 but recovered to 40 million pounds by April. Twenty-one million pounds of butter were exported in May 2008 but only four million pounds in April 2009. Likewise cheese exports fell from 27 million pounds to 19 million pounds.

According to Professor Steevens, the conventional fixed housing and total mixed ration foundation of the typical American farm requires around sixteen dollars per hundred pounds to break even. There is no cure to the cost-price squeeze. Professor Steevens said it would be okay if the government got out of the pricing of milk if they also minded their own business when the price of milk became high.

As modern dairying advances there are many ground breaking new ideas that become part of conventional wisdom. One of them is called "Total Mixed Ration." The idea is to cut hay pre-bud stage to get as high a digestibility with as much protein and total digestible nutrients as possible and less fiber. This results in up to seven cuttings of hay in Missouri and five in Wisconsin. If it is cut so soon and short it cannot possibly be bailed. It is used for ensilage with hopefully each particle being no more than four inches in length. This is mixed together with corn silage and grain and fed in loose housing for ever larger herds in milking parlors. The problem is that often there is not enough fiber to make quality milk. If the legume particles become longer than four inches, the cow will nose down to the bottom of the trough to get the "good stuff." In 1987 a grant of $7000 was given by the American Guernsey Cattle Club to the University of Missouri to study "Hay vs. silage upon rumination and digestion."

Total mixed ration is a particular disadvantage for the Guernsey, a natural grazing animal. The Guernsey loses the quality of its milk and profit advantage when fed this manipulated diet. This abnormally high-digested feed is not conducive to a long productive life and the normally high quality milk with its beta carotene yellow color, high protein, butterfat and solids. This is why the Guernsey is no longer seen in very large commercial operations.

We were invited to go to the Foremost Farm the morning after visiting Professor Steevens. We met with John Denbigh, the farm manager, and several employees on a very muggy 100° day after milking. They were recuperating in the air conditioned office when we arrived and they treated us to some University of Missouri ice cream.

The sign posted at the entrance to the farmstead indicated that Foremost Farms is a research facility. According to Professor Steevens the bequest from J. C. Penney was created more as a show place and for education than for research. The animals are one-third pastured, fed one-third home-grown feed and the remainder being purchased feed. The feed is provided by a different department at the University.

A show place it definitely was not. Harold Henry specifically wanted us to see the bronze statue of J. C. Penney's favorite bull, Langwater Foremost. We found it near the office entryway on a cluttered shelf with various other memorabilia piled haphazardly, everything covered with dust and grime, hardly a fitting tribute to the man who generously endowed this University. Everything we noted was no more presentable than that on an average dairy farm. A half dozen employees or students were there for the roughly one hundred cow milking herd.

An essay entitled *A Legacy of Leadership, Integrity, and Foresight* edited by Peter Vogt dated March 1, 2001, by the Foremost Farms USA Charitable Foundation stated that the dairy research, teaching, and demonstration program at the University of Missouri still included thirty Foremost Guernseys, each of which could trace her lineage back to the bull Langwater Foremost. John Denbigh, the herdsman, said that the buying and selling of registered Guernsey cattle during the past few years had probably eliminated any of the animals related to Langwater Foremost.

If this is true, Penney's legacy which was to last for several generations, at minimum, has been forfeited, a sadly squandered opportunity for the Guernsey breed as a whole.

The first herdsman of the Foremost Guernsey herd in the College of Agriculture at the University of Missouri was Bryan Lail. During his tenure he kept the milking herd at one hundred cows with it being the fifth best producing herd in America. There were 268 registered Guernsey cattle received by the University of Missouri in 1953. Conservatively there must have been a minimum of 125 milking cows. When Mr. Lail retired there would have been a twenty per cent reduction in milking cows from when he started.

In the Foremost Guernsey herd, a foundation cow received by the University of Missouri was Foremost Quantity, who had a lifetime production of 137,889 pounds of milk and 6,294 pounds of butterfat in eight lactations. She was awarded the Liebers trophy for lifetime production in 1952 by the American Guernsey Cattle Club.

In July 1982, the number of milking registered Guernsey cows was 60. In July 1983 it was 38, and by July 1984 it was 34. In December 1988, total animals had shrunk to 72 head with a milking herd of 35 cows. Production per cow was 12,437 pounds of milk and 569 pounds of butterfat. This most assuredly was not a leadership position in productivity in the Guernsey breed.

According to the "History of the Dairy Science Department Special Report 382" published in December, 1988: "Due to budget limitations, the Holstein herd was moved to the Foremost Farm. The Holstein Farm was converted to a dry cow and heifer facility. This move has been to the detriment of the Foremost Guernsey herd from the standpoint of milk production and general appearance and is a situation the Dairy Science Department hopes to improve." The gift to the University of Missouri was adequate to purchase 600 acres of land west of Columbia, Missouri, and to erect all the buildings necessary to properly house and care for all the 268 head of registered Guernsey cattle in the J. C. Penney bequest with funds still available "to aid in the perpetuation of the herd." The Holstein herd took over the legacy of J.C. Penney as well as his goal and dream of maintaining one of the worlds' premier Guernsey herds in perpetuity.

In a letter to Professor Steevens from Harry A. Herman, Professor Emeritus of the University of Missouri, dated January 12, 1989, we see the full extent of the debilitation of the Foremost Guernsey herd at the University of Missouri. The letter concerned a proposed dairy facility for Foremost Farm:

> I am glad to have the opportunity to comment on the above facility without going into structural details.
>
> No where do I find any provisions for carrying out the objectives for which the Foremost Guernsey Herd was donated to the University of Missouri in 1952 by J. C. Penney.
>
> We need to be fully aware of the fact that the Foremost Guernsey herd and farm were given to the University Principally for perpetuation of the Foremost blood lines. The herd, farm and all buildings, resulted from the Penney gift. The herd of some 275 head was moved to the present facility in 1953.
>
> For Years, until 1979, the Guernsey herd was maintained separately and did fairly well with a continual turn-over of management, some of which was sadly lacking in ability, judgment and dedication. Since the two herds have been combined, the Guernsey herd has lost numbers, fared only fairly well in production, and the breeding program to effectively promote the Foremost bloodlines has been sadly neglected. The present herd is about one-third the size of the herd in 1953. The University of Missouri and the Dairy Science Department is the subject of wide spread criticism among not only Guernsey breeders, but other purebred breeders who know of the original gift ($745,000 net) and the failure to carry out its objectives. Mr. Penney did not specify the herd should not be used for research but our original understanding was the herd would be preserved as a unit and make a presentable appearance to the public.

Good herd management dictates separate herds. Holsteins are larger and the docile Guernsey cannot compete for shelter and at the feed bunk. The Guernsey herd at Foremost will not reach its production potential so long as the herds are mixed. This obvious mistake should be corrected.

Research is important. However, from the standpoint of student teaching, public approval (good dairymen - - taxpayers - - the farm press and others) the appearance of the dairy farm and its herds must be of first consideration. Our department has long been considered strong in research but it has also been 'damned to high heaven' for the poor appearance of the farm and the herd. Research can be conducted in many areas without detracting herd appearance. Where animals for research are subjected to regimes that greatly alter physical appearance facilities should be provided to house and keep such animals from the main herd.

On the subject of research would it not be possible to inaugurate some genetic studies involving cattle performance? Also research directed at salvaging the remaining best of the 'Foremost' genetic factors and enlarging upon them.

If anyone desires to read the original plan for the Foremost Guernsey Herd I have a bountiful file; we should not let the integrity and ability of the Department be continually questioned in this respect.

I supervised the dairy herd and farm from 1929 to 1953 and realize some of the problems.

These are the most pertinent points in Professor Herman's letter. Professor Herman's letter and advice obviously were ignored. The major excuses were that the original facilities as set up did not allow for separation of animals to conduct proper research and that most of the dairy animals in the United States were Holstein. However, it would not have been that expensive or cumbersome to separate the individual Guernsey animals for proper research. Any institution, especially a non-profit one, unwilling or unable to conduct its affairs to meet all moral and legal obligations, should never accept a bequest that contains conditions it is not fully prepared to fulfill under any and all circumstances. Every endeavor has obstacles that must be overcome to meet the obligations accepted, including those of the University of Missouri. Foresight, will, and a very little creative imagination would have sufficed to maintain the Foremost Guernsey herd in the leading position it was in 1952. It did not exist. It does not to this day, and it is now too late.

The Foremost bloodline was to be extended and improved upon in perpetuity to make one of the world's best Guernsey herds even better. The original 267 animals were not to be infringed upon, either by lowering the number of animals or by deviating from the quality of management that J. C. Penney demanded. This is the reason the man who always carried *The Golden Rule* book wherever he went gave his gift to the University of Missouri in the first place. He had given gifts to the University prior to the 1952 bequest and Professor A. C. Ragsdale, chair of the Dairy Husbandry Department at the University, was on the Board of Directors of Foremost Farms, Inc. Why would Mr. Penney not fully expect his wishes to be fulfilled?

The University of Missouri gave an honorary doctorate to J. C. Penney in 1953. This meant that the man himself was held in high esteem for his accomplishments, a degree not given merely in recognition of his gift. Imagine if such respect had carried forward to include his desire that the name FOREMOST GUERSNEY would continue to be an outstanding name in Guernsey history.

Further imagine the thought, research, and creativity enabling not only the perpetuation of the Penney gift, but also the entire Guernsey breed as a whole. The productive life of the Guernsey is the weakest point in the breed today, and very few commercial herds include Guernsey cattle. However, seven of the Foremost Guernsey foundation animals in 1952 had an average productive age at retirement of 17.6 years. This longevity is unheard of in today's dairy industry with its intense demand for productivity. The genetic foundation was there at the time of the gift. The University of Missouri could have worked not only to keep this genetic gift intact, but also to enhance the entire Guernsey breed amidst the innumerable scientific changes in feeding and management.

Even today the dairy milking herd, while being unsubsidized by the University, is able to use the surplus in the Foremost Guernsey fund in an unprofitable year to cover expenses, and then add back to it in a good year. Their mostly Holstein herd remains subsidized by the Guernsey fund. A few years back the American Guernsey Association held their annual meeting in Missouri. According to John Denbigh the fund – money intended to continue the legacy of the Foremost Guernsey herd – was tapped to help sponsor the event.

The 114,000 Guernsey animals registered in 1952, the year J. C. Penney gave Foremost Farms Inc. to the University of Missouri, seems astonishing when compared to the fewer than 5000 animals registered annually in recent years.

Chapter Eighteen:

Whatever Happened to the Guernsey?

Today there are only 40,000 registered Guernsey cattle throughout the entire world. In 1952 there were 114,000 Guernsey animals registered that year with the American Guernsey Cattle Club, now known as the American Guernsey Association. Since 1952 annual registrations have declined steadily, and in 1997 fell below the 7,000 registered in 1910. The numbers have never recovered. Guernsey registrations were 5,101 in 2008, with a drastic 15.4 per cent reduction in 2009 to 4,315, followed by a recovery to 4,844 in 2010, but once again a then a drop in 2011 to 4,635.

Registrations of Guernsey Cattle

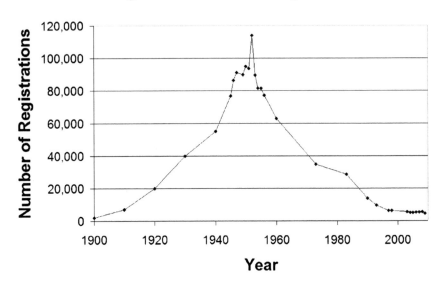

Registrations of Guernsey Cattle by Selected Year

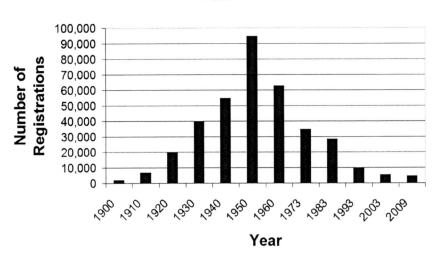

At the 120th annual meeting of the American Guernsey Association held in La Crosse, Wisconsin, June 23, 1997, it was recommended that the association "investigate the use of more criteria in the selection of brood cows and sires to involve more genetic diversity, longevity, and strength for the breed." Diversity, longevity, and strength are still crying issues in 2012, if not more so. The meeting recognized the devastation Johne's disease was having on the entire dairy industry. Johne's is an infectious disease wherein the hardy bacterium *Mycobacterium paratuberculosis* becomes embedded in the lower part of the small intestine preventing nutrient absorption. It is common in all ruminants, and in dairy animals is responsible for decreased milk production and death. Johne's disease was particularly hard on the susceptible Guernsey, but today is under control.

In 1952 the Holstein breed registered 190,000 head and reached peak of 492,000 registrations in 1984. Recent Holstein registrations were 339,908 in 2010 and 360,149 in 2011. The Jersey breed registered 60,000 animals in 1952 declining to 35,000 during the 1970's, but climbed back to over 60,000 in the 1980s. The Jersey breed continues its positive momentum in registrations with 90,366 in 2010, 96,174 in 2011, and exceeded 100,000 in 2012.

Another way of appreciating the fall in Guernsey registration is to compare it with that of the Brown Swiss dairy breed, probably considered a minority breed in registrations in 1952 with only 23,385. By 2005 Brown Swiss registrations had fallen by more than half to 10,076, which were still twice as many as the Guernsey had in the same year. The Brown Swiss registration continues to recover with 10,658 registered in 2010 and 11,172 in 2011.

The denouement of the Guernsey breed can be traced to a Penn State University milk pricing study during World War II sponsored by the Holstein breed that emphasized total pounds of milk without regard to the components of the milk. This caused a Federal Milk Marketing Order to be changed to pay for milk on volume only. The extra solids including more butterfat, protein, the beta-carotene golden color and excellent taste of Guernsey milk were ignored in the pricing mechanism.

1952 Major Breeds

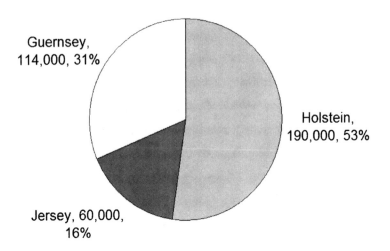

Guernsey, 114,000, 31%

Holstein, 190,000, 53%

Jersey, 60,000, 16%

2005 Major Breeds

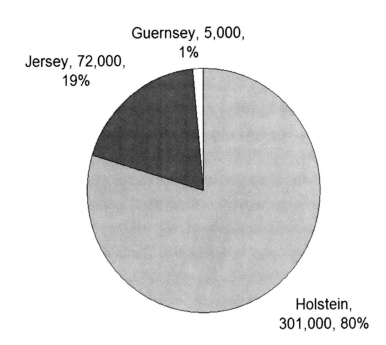

Guernsey, 5,000, 1%

Jersey, 72,000, 19%

Holstein, 301,000, 80%

With the emphasis on volume over the quality of the milk, Guernsey breeders began breeding for tall cows with extreme dairy character and the subsequent higher milk production. They also bred for animals that scored well with excellent show ring capabilities. But this focus has been accompanied by some devastating changes. The emphasis on stature without the accompanying strength is not natural for the Guernsey breed. The Guernsey lends itself well to a grazing and roughage environment that precludes this extreme emphasis on pounds of milk per cow. This high milk production has a negative effect on reproductive fertility, an effect that a more modest sized Guernsey would not experience. The natural ruggedness of the Guernsey has been smothered out in the United States.

According to the United States Department of Agriculture the Guernsey has the shortest productive life of the five major dairy breeds. The productive life of the Jersey, the smallest dairy breed, is 174 days longer, while that of the Holstein, the largest dairy breed, is 43 days longer.

Dutch Mill Telestar Fayette, born in July 1977, was purchased from Roy Jacobs of Sparta, Wisconsin, at the Iowa State Fair where Fayette was Grand Champion by First Midwest Breeders, now known as Genex. Doug Wilson, who was responsible for the purchase, stated that the Guernsey breed was at a low point even before Fayette was born.

Dutch Mill Telestar Fayette has produced more All-Americans than any other Guernsey on the USDA nexus. Fayette sired very large highly productive animals. His popularity was such that he is the only Guernsey bull to sell 100,000 units of semen in a single year, and his semen was still being sold almost 34 years after his birth. He had 9000 daughters under test. His daughter pregnancy rate was a minus three. One point is equal to four more open days, thus three points means twelve extra days to become pregnant compared to other registered Guernsey cows unrelated to him. Productive life from Fayette is a minus one and a half months. That means that his daughters and extended family will have that much less time in milk production compared to the average of the Guernsey breed. At the time of Fayette, science had not advanced to the point where studies could be made of fertility pregnancy rate, productive life comparisons, and other meaningful results. Today we are into genomic studies and testing. His huge popularity can only have multiplied the Guernsey downward trend. Two recent popular bulls have augmented this trend: Coulee Crest RO Silverado had a daughter pregnancy rate of minus 4.2, while his sire Jensgolden Proking Royal Oak had a daughter pregnancy rate of minus 3.7. This is far worse than Fayette at a critical time of Guernsey breed strength in the United States.

This table shows the decline in DPR (Daughter Pregnancy Rate) of US Guernseys:

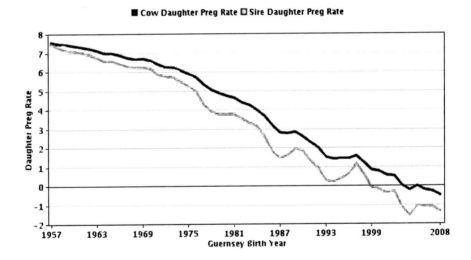

A 1942 article published in the *Guernsey Breeders' Journal* written by Professor George R. Barrett of the University of Wisconsin established through extensive research that the break even point for a dairy cow was four and a half years of age or two full lactations. Peak production for a Guernsey cow is not established until six years of age, and today it is a goal to get past that point. Recall the Foremost herd with their longevity. There were seven foundation cows with an average 17.6 year lifespan. In other words they were productive on average to that age. A goal of a lifetime with eleven daughters and 160,000 pounds of milk was advocated in 2007 article entitled *What Kind of Guernsey Cow For The Future?* by John O. Mozier, D.V.M. and Seth Johnson, Secretary of the American Guernsey Association. They emphasized the native registered Guernsey cattle on the Isle of Guernsey today that are rugged, smaller in stature with less dairy character which could benefit United States Guernsey herds and contribute to their competitiveness in a commercial dairy environment.

The Guernsey Young Sire program was at its peak in the 1970s with forty to fifty young bulls in the program. In 2008 twenty bulls were sampled and six approved, compared to a sampling of 1200 bulls in the Holstein breed and 150 to 175 in the Jersey breed. As the number of herds is reduced the danger of too much inbreeding out of necessity threatens to destroy the long term future of the Guernsey breed in the United States.

In a February 25, 2009, article entitled *The Current Position of the Guernsey Breed* published by The World Guernsey Cattle Federation stated that there is a possible leadership awareness that time is not on their side. Pooling global resources to control this problem is vital. A tight degree of genetic management with individual breeders pledging their cattle resources for the overall benefit of the breed could prevent further deterioration. Absolute co-operation and discipline is a must. Genomic evaluations have begun. With only 40,000 registered Guernsey cattle worldwide, it is necessary to focus more on heifers from younger bulls than was done in the past. Continuous use of older bulls limits the ability to produce enough genetic diversity.

Adding to this quandary, the small number of registered Guernseys dispersed throughout the world prohibits taking advantage of the significant amount of A2 milk and lack of A1 milk as compared to other major breeds. While experiments by the Food Standards group have not proven negative health aspects of A1 milk, it is interesting to note that the more numerous Jersey and Holstein breeds, as well as the dairy industry in New Zealand, are moving genetically to produce higher percentages of A2 milk. According to Deb Lakey, Wisconsin Guernsey Breeders' Association Secretary, the crossings of the registered Guernsey with other breeds, with subsequent offspring rebred to registered Guernsey bulls – a practice once accepted by the American Guernsey Association for registration – have less A2 milk than registered Guernsey cattle not participating in that program.

It must be noted that commercial dairy herds – those large herds without registered animals – have pretty much abandoned the Guernsey. The Guernsey has lost that important market due to its shortened lactation life and milk production compared to other breeds. Of the six United States major dairy breeds' association records for 2011, the Guernsey placed at the bottom with 16,216 pounds of actual milk production per cow. This was a drop from 16,713 pounds the year before. All the other breeds had a mature equivalent milk production of at least 18,137 pounds of milk, with the Holstein having the staggering average of 25,472 pounds of milk per cow. If there is no economic gain or even with just an anticipation of a loss in a commercial herd, the Guernsey breed is destined to encompass an ever smaller group of purebred true believers. We can only hope the people responsible for the future of the Guernsey breed will work unselfishly together and by some miracle bring about the rejuvenation of the breed.

• • •

In 2010 the very excellent dairy publication *Farmshine,* owned and edited by Dieter Krieg of Brownstown, Pennsylvania, featured three excellent, very small registered Guernsey herds – two near Millersburg, Ohio and the other near Sugarcreek, Ohio. The three dairy farms milk only between 32 and 40 cows with milk productivity per cow for the herds around 16,000 pounds. The owners of these herds emphasize the less feisty even temperament of the Guernsey, along with the extra beta-carotene making the milk more nutritious compared to that of other breeds. These owners also emphasize not pushing for productivity nor breeding for large animals. They use young sires from a variety of cow families to broaden the genetic base as well as to improve the quality of the animal. One of the owners claims that the Guernsey breed "is much better than thirty years ago, with better feet and legs, more strength and better udders." The farms range in size from 90 to 160 acres with cropping and pasture use reminiscent of the mid twentieth century. These dairy families are extremely happy with their registered Guernsey lifestyle. The three dairymen agree that the Guernsey is the right breed for them under today's price structure.

From June 16-21, 2010, the American Guernsey Association held its annual convention in the Amish county of Lancaster, Pennsylvania. A total of 575 people attended the convention including 176 aspiring young people who represent the future of the Guernsey breed. The adults raised over $9000 in the youth program auction which included $2100 for a Bonnie Mohr painting donated by Hoard's Dairyman. The convention sale which included semen, embryos and animals averaged $3793 per unit. This was a very commendable display of enthusiasm and togetherness by a group known for their outgoing friendliness, sincerity, and loyalty.

Despite the nation's financial anxieties, and in particular the financial situation of the American Guernsey Association, all of the convention leaders emphasized important milestones, progress, challenges, and the prospect for a bright future for the registered Guernsey. Bonnie Ayers, a successful Guernsey breeder from Mechanicsburg, Ohio, received the Distinguished Service Award and was the effective mature cheerleader for the future. She noted the enthusiastic convention spirit, especially among its young people. She said, "Don't forget the promise of the future." She noted the Guernsey breeds' exceptional heritage. The Guernsey Journal is 100 years old; and Hoard's Dairyman, the owner of one of the nation's most prominent registered Guernsey herds, is celebrating the 125th year of its publication. She encouraged all to become life members of the National Dairy Shrine in Fort Atkinson, Wisconsin, a truly great repository of dairy history and progress.

Seth Johnson, the very capable American Guernsey Association Secretary-Treasurer, also received the Distinguished Service Award for his dedicated service and loyalty to all of America's Guernsey breeders. While describing the financial situation of the American Guernsey Association as "miserable," he noted the strong desire of so many to see the breed succeed. "A strong and vibrant breed association is needed."

The American Guernsey Association moved to a smaller office in late 2010 and has put their condo up for sale. The condo offices were small and sorely in need of renovation. The newly rented facilities feature offices for the four employees. Historical records are kept in the basement. The rent is very favorable according to Ida Albert because they are housed with other dairy organizations interested in their survival. There is no longer any display befitting a national headquarters. The renewed Association vigor could act as a springboard to the revitalization of the Guernsey breed as seen in a few isolated instances. The aforementioned successful Ohio registered Guernsey herds are small in size and they do not rely on high energy feeding programs to maximize production. New vitality could be introduced in the Guernsey population in the United States by crossing with the rugged, grazing, cost-efficient registered Guernsey cattle from other countries, cattle not bred for show ring pizzazz and maximum productivity. Genomics at present is an expensive method for searching for positive traits, and in the long run this high tech method will only hasten to narrow the breeds' genetic diversity. The Guernsey does not do well housed together with dairy animals of other breeds. Does it not make good sense to return to the methods, principles and values that elevated the Guernsey to its former premier status?

• • •

In every chapter the ghosts of four sturdy Guernsey pioneers, all born in the nineteenth century, have been casting their shadow. Henry Daniel Griswold,

William Dempster Hoard, James Cash Penney, and Adoniram Judson Phillips had high standards and the work ethic of rural America of the era in which they lived. Their paths surely crossed in West Salem, Wisconsin, if not elsewhere. Griswold would have been 75 and still very active when Penney went to West Salem in 1928 for the Wisconsin State Guernsey Picnic. Phillips had died in 1917, but was a good friend of Griswold and encountered Hoard at the Monroe County fair, inspiring his ownership of Queen Vashti. A panel discussion by these four stalwarts of the American dream would be foreign to our spoiled life styles: their inspiration to own Guernsey dairy cattle, their creative and artistic talents, sacrifices, self denial, moral and ethical values, and above all their enthusiasm would violently rock the boat in the twenty-first century!

Their separate and combined wisdom can only be documented as far as we know it. Combined and alive it would set the standard and explanation for the survival and success of agriculture in the United States of America.

Sources

CHAPTER ONE

Whyte, Edna Gardner. Personal list of accomplishments

Wicher, Shirley B. Census of West Salem, Wisconsin. www.census.gov

CHAPTER TWO

A History of Ten Centuries: A brief history of the Guernsey breed of dairy cattle. The American Guernsey Cattle Club, 1950.

Caldwell, William H. *The Guernsey*. The American Guernsey Cattle Club, 1948.

Hill, Charles L. *The History of Wisconsin Guernseys*. Rural Life Publishing Company, Lake Mills, Wisconsin, 1948.

"Law of the United Kingdom." http://en.wikipedia.org/wiki/Law_of_the_United_Kingdom

Luff, Bill. "History of the Guernsey Breed." August, 2004. website of the World Guernsey Federation. wgcf@guernsey.net .

Luff, Bill. Interview at annual meeting of the American Guernsey Association in 2008.

Prentice, E. Parmalee. *The History of Channel Island Cattle Guernseys and Jerseys.* Mount Hope Farm of Williamstown, Massachusetts, 1941.

Woodford, Keith. *Devil in the Milk: Illness, Health and the Politics of A1 and A2 Milk.* Craig Potton, New Zealand, 2010.

Food Standards Australia New Zealand: http://www.foodstandards.gov.au/scienceandeducation/factsheets/factsheets/a1anda2milkaugust2015227.cfm

CHAPTER THREE

A History of Ten Centuries: A brief history of the Guernsey breed of dairy cattle. The American Guernsey Cattle Club, 1950.

Byrd, Richard Evelyn. "Exploring the Ice Age in Antarctica." National Geographic Society, October 1935.

Caldwell, Charles H. *The Guernsey.* The American Guernsey Cattle Club, 1941.

Hill, Charles L. *The History of Wisconsin Guernseys.* Rural Life Publishing Company, Lake Mills, Wisconsin, 1948.

CHAPTER FOUR

Guernsey Breeders Journal. March 15, 1952, June 15, 1952, and August 2009.

Norton, Edward, secretary-treasurer. *Volume One: The Annual Meetings from 1877 to 1893.* The American Guernsey Cattle Club.

Rice, V.A. of the University of Massachusetts. "Seventy-five Years in Breeding." The American Guernsey Breeders Journal, January 1, 1952.

Sparr, Sidney L. and Opperman, George W. *The Dairy Cow Today.* Hoard's Dairyman, 1995.

The American Guernsey Registry: Volume 1, 1884. Volume 28, 1913-1914. Volume 29, 1915. Volume 30, 1916.

"Depression of 1882–85."
http://en.wikipedia.org/wiki/Recession_of_1882-85

CHAPTER FIVE

Hill, Charles L. *The History of Wisconsin Guernseys.* Rural Life Publishing Company, Lake Mills, Wisconsin, 1948.

Hoard's Dairyman. November 2009.

Hoard's Dairyman. August 10, 2011.

Hoard's Dairyman online. www.hoards.com

Johnson, David, Ph.D. Assistant Director of Research, Cal/West Seeds. Personal interview, June 2009.

Larson, Steven A., Editor. "HD Story – A Mix of Old and New." *Hoard's Dairyman*, February 24, 2009.

Osman, Lorn H. *W. D. Hoard – A Man for His Time.* W. D. Hoard & Sons Co., 1985.

Rankin, George William. *The Life of William Dempster Hoard.* W. D. Hoard & Sons Co., 1925.

"Research for a Growing Wisconsin – Wisconsin's Alfalfa Story." College of Agriculture & Life Sciences, University of Wisconsin, January 1983.

"Seed Today." 4th quarter 2007 Volume 4 Number 2. Country Journal Publishing Decatur, Illinois.

CHAPTER SIX

Hill, Charles L. *The History of Wisconsin Guernseys*. Rural Life Publishing Company Lake Mills, Wisconsin, 1948.

Osman, Lorn H. *W. D. Hoard – A Man for his Time*. W. D. Hoard & Sons Co., 1985.

Phillips, A. J. *Queen Vashti*. La Crosse Engraving Company, 1907.

CHAPTER SEVEN

American Guernsey Registry and Breeders' Journal. January 1903.

Butterfield, Consul Willshire. *History of La Crosse County, Wisconsin*. Western Historical Society Company, Chicago, 1881.

Kindschy, Errol. *Leonard's Dream*. Inter-Collegiate Press Inc., Shawnee Mission Kansas, 1981.

Milwaukee Journal-Sentinel. December 24, 2006. http://jsonline.com/features/travel/29230814.html

Phillips, A. J. *Queen Vashti*. La Crosse Engraving Company, 1907.

CHAPTER EIGHT

Griswold, Donald. "Grandfather's Bad Trip across Minnesota." Sauk Centre Herald, July 1, 1971.

Griswold, Florence. Personal communication and written notes, 2008.

Griswold, Harry. Personal communication and written notes.

Griswold, William M. "What was the Extent of Henry Griswold's Services to his Community." Marian College thesis. November 1, 2006.

U. S. Government Printing Office. 76th Congress, 3rd Session, 1941.

CHAPTER NINE

Cargill online. www.cargill.com

Collisson, Charles F. "An Interview with Dr. Babcock." *De Lavel Monthly*, February 1923.

Wicher, Shirley B. Census of West Salem, Wisconsin. www.census.gov

CHAPTER TEN

University of Wisconsin-Madison. Agricultural Library Archives.

CHAPTER ELEVEN

La Crosse County Guernsey Breeders. Secretary-Treasurer Reports, including archives.

Bernasek, Anna. *The Economics of Integrity*. HarperCollins, 2010.

Guernsey Breeders' Journal, Purebred Publishing Inc., December, 2011.

Telephone conversation with Deb Lakey, Secretary of Wisconsin Guernsey Breeders' Association; January, 2012.

CHAPTER TWELVE

Freeland, Chrystia. "The Triumph of the Family Farm." *The Atlantic*, July/August, 2012, pages 50-53.

CHAPTER THIRTEEN

"A Founders History of the Tri-State Milk Co-operative." Protein Press, a publication of Tri-State Milk Co-operative. Fourth Quarter 1990, page 8.

Nuttleman, Edna. Personal interview and Norbert Nuttleman scrapbook. June, 2009.

Pralle, Bernard and Mary. Personal interview and private archives. 2008.

CHAPTER FOURTEEN

Kindschy, Errol. West Salem Historical Society President.

La Crosse Newspapers Incorporated. West Salem, Wisconsin. 1914 – 1918, 1928 – 1967.

CHAPTER FIFTEEN

Behr, Joan. Personal e-mail June 19 2012. joan.behr@foremostfarms.com

Curry, Mary Elizabeth. "Creating an American Institution." Garland Publishing Inc. New York January 1, 1993.

Garland, Hamlin. *A Pioneer Mother*. The Bookfellows of Chicago, 1922.

"Hamilton's Favorite Son." *Rural Missouri*. May 2008.

Harding, C. B. *The Guernsey Breed*. Hillsboro Press an Imprint of Providence House Publishers, 2000.

Hoard's Dairyman. April 25, 2009, page 282.

Karg, Pamela J. Foremost Farms USA Co-operative field editor. Baraboo, Wisconsin.

Krueger, David Delbert. "Annals of Wyoming." The Wyoming History Journal. Spring 2008.

Ragsdale, A.C. "The James Cash Penney Story." *Guernsey Breeders' Journal*, 1952.

Vogt, Peter. "The Foremost Name: A Legacy of Leadership, Integrity & Foresight." Foremost Farms Charitable Foundation, Inc., March 1, 2001.

CHAPTER SEVENTEEN

Hoard's Dairyman. "Cow Numbers Highest in Over a Decade." March 10, 2009, page 167.

Hoard's Dairyman. "National Herd Average Goes Over 21,000." March 10, 2011, page 161.

Ragsdale, A.C. "The James Cash Penney Story." *Guernsey Breeders' Journal*, 1952.

Herman, H. A., and Ricketts, Rex. "History of the Dairy Science Department." Special Report 382. College of Agriculture, University of Missouri-Columbia. December 1988.

Hoard's Dairyman. "Hoard's has Heard." July 2009, page 446.

Niskanen, William A. "How to Turn a Recession into a Depression." CATO Policy Report, March/April 2009.

The Economist. July 11, 2009, page 31. July 25, 2009, pages 63-64.

CHAPTER EIGHTEEN

Crosser, Blaine of Select Sires, Plain City, Ohio. Telephone conversation March 10, 2009.

Farmshine. Volume 31, No. 42. June 25, 2010.

Guernsey Breeders Journal. August 1997.

Harding, C. B. *The Guernsey Breed.* Hillsboro Press an Imprint of Providence House Publishers, 2000.

Hoard's Dairyman. August 10, 2012. Page 496.

Johnson, Leonard. Personal communication. LJohnson@brownswissusa.com

Mozier, John O., and Johnson, Seth. "What Kind of Guernsey Cow for the Future." http://www.guernsey.net/~wgcf/PageMill_Resources/GW07%20 45-51.pdf

Mykrantz, Susan. "Guernseys Good as Gold for these Dairymen." *Farmshine.* Volume 31, Number 40, June 11, 2010, pg 30.

Penney, J. C. *Foremost Guernseys 1920-1942.* Rudolf Orthwine Corporation. New York, 1942.

Telephone conversation with Deb Lakey, Secretary of Wisconsin Guernsey Breeders' Association. January, 2012.

Wilson, Douglas of Genex Cooperative, Inc., of Shawno, Wisconsin. Telephone conversation on March 11, 2009. Genex was First Midwest Breeders' when Douglas Wilson negotiated the purchase of Dutch Mill Telestar Fayette from Roy Jacobs at the Iowa State Fair.

Index

CPSIA information can be obtained at www.ICGtesting.com
Printed in the USA
BVOW05s1842111114

374660BV00001B/31/P